Working Memory a

MW01252904

The rapid growth in the numbers of older people worldwide has led to an equally rapid growth in research on the changes across age in cognitive function, including the processes of moment-to-moment cognition known as working memory. This book brings together international research leaders who address major questions about how age affects working memory:

- Why is working memory function much better preserved in some people than in others?
- In all healthy adults, which aspects of working memory are retained in later years and which aspects start declining in early adulthood?
- Can cognitive training help slow cognitive decline with age?
- How are changes in brain structures, connectivity and activation patterns related to important changes in working memory function?

Impairments of cognition, and particularly of working memory, can be major barriers to independent living. The chapters of this book dispel some popular myths about cognitive ageing, while presenting the state of the science on how and why working memory functions as it does throughout the adult lifespan.

Working Memory and Ageing is the first volume to provide an overview of the burgeoning literature on changes in working memory function across healthy and pathological ageing, and it will be of great interest to advanced undergraduates, postgraduates and researchers in psychology and related subject areas concerned with the effects of human ageing, including several areas of medicine.

Robert H. Logie is Professor of Human Cognitive Neuroscience, and Research Director for the School of Philosophy, Psychology and Language Sciences at the University of Edinburgh, UK. He is also Group Leader for Human Cognitive Ageing within the cross-council-funded Centre for Cognitive Ageing and Cognitive Epidemiology. His research and teaching interests lie in the cognition of human memory in the healthy, ageing and damaged brain, focused on experimental behavioural studies of working memory. He has published over 170 peer reviewed papers, 50 book chapters and 12 books.

Robin G. Morris is Professor of Neuropsychology at King's College London, UK, and Consultant Clinical Neuropsychologist at King's College Hospital, where he is Head of the Clinical Neuropsychology Department. He is also Head of Neuropsychology in the King's Health Partners Neurosciences Academic Group. His main interests are in the neuropsychology of memory and also of executive functioning, and he has conducted research on a range of patients with neuropsychological disorders, including those with focal brain damage, schizophrenia, cerebrovascular disease and Alzheimer's disease. He has published over 220 peer reviewed papers and 40 book chapters, and recently received the British Psychological Society Barbara Wilson Neuropsychology Award.

Current issues in memory
Series editor: Robert H. Logie
Professor of Human Cognitive Neuroscience, University of Edinburgh, UK

Current Issues in Memory is a series of edited books that reflect the state of the art in areas of current and emerging interest in the psychological study of memory. Each of the volumes in the series is tightly focused on a particular topic and is designed to be a concise collection containing chapters contributed by international experts.

The editors of individual volumes are leading figures in their area and provide an introductory overview. Example topics include: binding in working memory, prospective memory, autobiographical memory, visual memory, implicit memory, amnesia, retrieval and memory development.

Other titles in this series:

The Visual World in Memory
Edited by James R. Brockmole

Forgetting
Edited by Sergio Della Sala

Current Issues in Applied Memory Research
Edited by Graham M. Davies and Daniel B. Wright

Spatial Working Memory
Edited by André Vandierendonck and Arnaud Szmalec

Working Memory and Ageing

Edited by Robert H. Logie and
Robin G. Morris

Psychology Press
Taylor & Francis Group
LONDON AND NEW YORK

First published 2015
by Psychology Press
27 Church Road, Hove, East Sussex BN3 2FA

and by Psychology Press
711 Third Avenue, New York, NY 10017

*Psychology Press is an imprint of the Taylor & Francis Group,
an informa business*

© 2015 Psychology Press

British Library Cataloguing in Publication Data
A catalogue record for this book is available from the British Library

Library of Congress Cataloging in Publication Data
Working memory and ageing / edited by Robert H. Logie and Robin G.
Morris.
pages cm
Includes bibliographical references and index.
ISBN 978-1-84872-117-3 (hardback) -- ISBN 978-1-84872-126-5
(softcover) -- ISBN 978-1-315-87984-0 (ebk) 1. Memory--Age factors. 2.
Short-term memory. 3. Cognition--Age factors. 4. Aging--Psychological
aspects. I. Logie, Robert H. II. Morris, Robin, 1958-
BF378.A33W67 2014
155.67'1312--dc23

ISBN: 978-1-84872-117-3 (hbk)
ISBN: 978-1-84872-126-5 (pbk)
ISBN: 978-1-31587-984-0 (ebk)

Typeset in Times
by Saxon Graphics Ltd, Derby

Printed and bound in the United States of America by Publishers Graphics,
LLC on sustainably sourced paper.

Contents

Illustrations

Tables

Figures

Contributors

Rebecca A. Charlton, Department of Psychology, Goldsmiths University of London, UK

Mark J. Horne, Department of Psychology and Centre for Cognitive Ageing and Cognitive Epidemiology, University of Edinburgh, UK

Angela Kilb, Department of Psychology, Plymouth State University, USA

Ulman Lindenberger, Max Planck Institute for Human Development, Berlin, Germany

Robert H. Logie, Department of Psychology and Centre for Cognitive Ageing and Cognitive Epidemiology, University of Edinburgh, UK

Robin G. Morris, Department of Psychology, King's College Institute of Psychiatry, University of London, UK

Irene E. Nagel, Freie Universität Berlin, Department of Educational Science and Psychology, Berlin, Germany; and Max Planck Institute for Human Development, Berlin, Germany

Moshe Naveh-Benjamin, Memory and Cognitive Ageing Laboratory, University of Missouri, USA

Lars Nyberg, Department of Integrative Medical Biology, Department of Radiation Sciences, Umeå Center for Functional Brain Imaging, Umeå University, Sweden

Lewis D. Pettit, Department of Psychology and Centre for Cognitive Ageing and Cognitive Epidemiology, University of Edinburgh, UK

Timothy A. Salthouse, Department of Psychology, University of Virginia, USA

Anna Stigsdotter Neely, Department of Psychology, Umeå University, Sweden

Introduction

Working memory and the ageing brain

Robert H. Logie and Robin G. Morris

Rapid growth in the number of older people worldwide has led to an equally rapid growth in research on the changes across age in cognitive functions. Core among these functions are those associated with the processes of moment to moment cognition known as working memory; the ability to keep track of our thoughts, our actions and changes in our environment, that pervades our every waking moment, and is crucial for effective independent living. Whereas there is widespread agreement that age-related changes in working memory function are important to study, there are ongoing debates as to the precise characteristics of working memory with differing approaches that drive different programmes of research. In particular, some approaches to cognitive ageing focus on why some people show faster cognitive decline with age than others (e.g., Salthouse, Chapter 1). Other approaches focus on whether there are different working memory functions that are differentially affected by age in all healthy adults (Logie, Horne and Pettit, Chapter 2), and whether age-related changes in long-term memory affect working memory in similar ways (Kilb and Naveh-Benjamin, Chapter 3). Multiple research groups are exploring the possibility that cognitive training might help to slow age-related cognitive decline (Neely and Nyberg, Chapter 4), whereas advances in brain imaging techniques are allowing major advances in understanding of how age-related changes in brain connectivity and structure (Charlton and Morris, Chapter 5) and in patterns of brain activation (Nagel and Lindenberger) are associated with age-related changes in cognitive abilities. The chapters in this book are written by leading international researchers on cognitive ageing who offer authoritative reviews and commentary on these major areas of debate, highlighting where there are popular myths, where there have been genuine advances in knowledge and where equivocation remains.

Salthouse takes a tour in Chapter 1 through more than twenty-five years of research on cognitive ageing that has emphasised the analysis of individual differences as a tool for exploring the relations between ageing and working memory. He argues that although increased age is clearly associated with lower performance on a wide range of cognitive tasks, many of which are assumed to assess working memory, important questions remain regarding what performance in the latter set of tasks represents in terms of actual human capacities. He also explores the degree to which the working memory construct is distinct from other constructs such as fluid intelligence, and suggests that working memory may reflect a subset of the abilities that together contribute to the broader construct of intelligence. He concludes that it is not yet clear whether working memory offers a construct that drives age-related changes in cognition, and much remains to be investigated regarding the relationship between the construct of working memory, using multiple measures and other constructs including fluid intelligence.

The theme that working memory might comprise a set of cognitive abilities is taken up in Chapter 2 by Logie, Horne and Pettit. They start with the assumption that working memory consists of a range of different cognitive functions, each with its own capacity limits and characteristics. These authors review evidence demonstrating that these functions differ in their sensitivity to increasing age in all healthy adults, with performance on visual short-term storage tasks showing steep decline throughout the adult lifespan, measures of temporary storage in the context of processing showing a less steep decline across age, but again starting in early adulthood, and performance on verbal short-term storage tasks showing no decline until late old age. They go on to describe evidence for the use of different strategies being used by older and younger people when performing the same task. For example, a task designed to measure visual short-term memory might indeed be measuring what is intended in younger adults, but could be measuring the use of verbal strategies to perform a visual short-term memory task in older adults. This challenges the assumption of measurement invariance when using the same tests to measure and compare cognitive ability across people of different ages. The chapter considers in detail the specific issue of whether older people are more vulnerable than younger people to the cognitive cost of performing two tasks as the same time. Evidence is described demonstrating that there is no age-related dual task cost when the tasks are chosen to engage different functions in working memory, and neither task requires a speeded response. These studies show that there can be little or no dual task cost for healthy adults of any age if account is taken of the single task abilities of each individual. The authors conclude that working memory is not constrained by general limited capacity attention, but instead comprises multiple components that can operate in parallel, and whereas age may affect the operation of individual components, healthy older people appear to retain the ability to engage those components in concert to support task performance.

In Chapter 3, Kilb and Naveh-Benjamin contrast the robust findings of age-related dual task costs with tasks such as free recall that rely on long-term memory, with the mixture of the presence or absence of dual task costs when combining tasks associated with working memory. They start with the general assumption that working memory is constrained by the capacity of a general attentional system, and that performing two tasks concurrently involves dividing this attentional capacity between the tasks. They note in particular that memory tasks such as those requiring free recall are more vulnerable if a secondary task load, such as response time, is present during encoding. The retrieval phase appears much less vulnerable. In contrast, response times on the secondary task tend to slow during the retrieval phase of a concurrent memory task. These effects are particularly salient in older healthy people, and the conclusion is that age might affect the ability to divide attention between the tasks. A possible account for the differences at encoding and retrieval are that older participants focus on the accuracy of recall so as to avoid giving the impression to the experimenter that they have a poor memory, but this is at the expense of response time. This trade-off between accuracy and speed in older people has been shown in a number of previous studies, some of which are also mentioned in chapters 1 and 2 of this volume. The chapter then goes on to review evidence suggesting that when working memory tasks are combined, a number of studies have demonstrated a lack of a dual task cost and a lack of a differential effect of dual task demands on older compared with younger people. This points to the suggestion that these aspects of working memory function may be much less vulnerable to the impact of healthy ageing than are other aspects of cognition such as encoding and retrieval from long-term memory or speed of processing.

The highly controversial and contemporary topic of cognitive training and working memory capacity is addressed in Chapter 4 by Neely and Nyberg. This area of research has seen widespread public as well as scientific debate because the prospect of improving working memory and staving off the decline in cognition with age, or offering an effective cognitive intervention for attentional disorders, has very wide appeal. As a result, this is an area that has seen an impact of commercial pressures in marketing some of the training techniques without necessarily having solid evidence to support the claims associated with the products. Neely and Nyberg review a wide range of studies with very different age groups, and conclude that there is strong evidence for a beneficial effect of training on performance of tasks that are similar to those that were trained. The clearest evidence for these benefits comes from use of training tasks that get progressively harder as people improve with practice. These results are consistent with a long history of research showing that performance improves with this form of adaptive practice on the tasks that are being practised. The finding that there is a benefit in performance of similar tasks also fits with the idea that the skills that are being practised during training can be applied to other tasks that rely on those same skills. Where there is much more controversy is whether there are more general benefits of cognitive training such as a general increase in working memory capacity and better performance in tasks that are thought to require different cognitive abilities from those that have been trained. Where these general benefits are reported, it is possible that training results in automaticity of some cognitive skills, thereby releasing some existing working memory capacity and giving the impression that the overall capacity has increased. Alternatively, there might be an improvement in control of the focus of attention on tasks, leading to improved performance. However, as Neely and Nyberg demonstrate, there are few studies that provide evidence for this kind of 'far transfer' from training, and of those studies that have reported such evidence several have proved difficult to replicate, or fail to show maintenance of the benefits weeks or months after the training has ceased. This area of research has tended to lack a theoretical basis and to lack well defined and robust training and testing paradigms that are adopted across different research groups. If both of these limitations are addressed, the authors remain optimistic that some forms of cognitive training could be beneficial in combating age-related cognitive decline.

Cognitive changes with age occur along with reductions in the integrity of brain connectivity and brain structures. In Chapter 5, Charlton and Morris note that brain pathologies are increasingly likely to develop with increasing age, and these are accompanied by a rise in the number of risk factors such as hypertension and diabetes. Even in people who might be considered as progressing through 'healthy ageing', vascular damage in the brain affects the small vessels supplying blood to the white matter axons that are required for efficient neuronal transmission. The authors then review a wide range of studies providing evidence that changes in working memory performance with increasing age are associated with neurovascular white matter damage and the potential risk factors that make this damage more likely. Further, the authors argue that where a decline is observed in a specific working memory function, then this can often be attributed to a reduction in the integrity of brain white matter. The age-related contrasts are addressed in both cross sectional and longitudinal studies. In addition, the authors provide a critical analysis of the advantages and limitations of different measures of white matter using magnetic resonance imaging (MRI), notably diffusion tensor imaging, and magnetisation transfer. A major conclusion is that since working memory relies on a wide network of connections in the brain, then relatively small reductions in the efficiency of white matter connectivity can have disproportionate effects. Clearly major issues remain to be explored such as the relationship between those aspects of working memory that do or do not show declines in working memory (see chapters 1, 2 and 3), and the changes with age in the integrity of the networks in the brain that are most likely to be involved in performance of different working memory functions.

In Chapter 6, Nagel and Lindenberger consider the evidence from functional imaging studies for the relationship between age-related decline in working memory and age-related differences in patterns of blood-oxygen level dependent (BOLD) brain activation associated with performing working memory tasks in fMRI. They view working memory as a core cognitive function that is vulnerable to decline in normal ageing, but differentially so across different individuals. The consistent finding across studies is that adult age differences and changes in working memory performance are associated with differences in activation of a fronto-parietal network that is widely thought to be important for performing working memory tasks. The authors argue that it is important to consider individual differences in working memory that occur throughout the lifespan, not least because differences in the way in which working memory and other aspects of cognition are deployed when confronted by a cognitive task within the scanner will result in differences in the pattern of BOLD response, even if identical tasks are used for all participants. These individual differences may well be even greater as people age, an argument consistent with the evidence discussed in chaper 2 that older adults might adopt different strategies than younger people when performing the same task. However, as Nagel and Lindenberger note, individual differences are only rarely considered in imaging studies on working memory ageing, and this can create difficulties in obtaining consistency of results across as well as within studies. The authors argue that observed age differences are often confounded with levels of performance, without considering the possibility that older adults might engage additional cognitive functions to compensate for a decline in their underlying ability. They argue that high working memory proficiency in old age appears to be linked with activation patterns found in younger people rather than with the idea that performance is supported by additional activation to compensate for effects of age. They conclude that longitudinal studies and the use of a range of research techniques that combine information on working memory performance, BOLD activation, brain structure, neurotransmitter systems and genetics offer the most promising route to novel insights into the neurobiological mechanisms that support high levels of working memory functioning of some older individuals.

For some, research on age-related changes in working memory is about why some individuals decline with age more rapidly than others; for others the research is more about the general principles of how ageing affects working memory in all healthy individuals even if the effects are greater for some individuals than others. This contrast in approaches reflects a more general contrast in the study of working memory between a focus on what drives differences between individuals in working memory capacity, and a focus on understanding the cognitive architecture of working memory in all healthy adults. Often this contrast is interpreted as a fundamental difference in theoretical assumptions rather than a fundamental difference in the kind of research questions being addressed. Both general approaches are likely to be important for genuine and substantial future advances in understanding working memory function across the lifespan. We hope it is clear from the chapters presented here that many major advances in research techniques and understanding have already been achieved, even if major areas of uncertainty and debate remain.

1 Individual differences in working memory and aging

Timothy A. Salthouse

This chapter reviews research conducted in my laboratory over the past 25 years in which aspects of working memory (WM) have been examined in adults of different ages. My thinking has been strongly influenced by Welford's discussions of the role of WM in age differences in cognitive functioning in his 1958 book *Ageing and Human Skill*. Although I don't believe he used the term working memory, his description in the following passage of a fundamental age-related limitation clearly resembles contemporary ideas about the relation between aging and working memory:

> It is conceived that data are somehow held in a form of short-term storage while other data are being gathered. Obviously, unless data can be so held, the amount of information that can be simultaneously applied to any problem is very small indeed. It would appear that in old people the amount that can be stored tends to diminish, and that what is stored is more liable than it is in younger people to interference and disruption from other activity going on at the same time. Such a decline in short-term retention would be capable of accounting for a very wide range of observed age changes in learning and problem solving …
>
> (p. 285)

As implied by the quotation above, WM has been of interest primarily because of its relation to other aspects of cognition; in fact, WM can be defined as memory in the service of cognition. Because a wide range of cognitive tasks have been reported to have negative age relations, WM has been postulated to be a critical limiting factor, or a processing resource, that could be contributing to adult age differences in many different cognitive tasks. This view was articulated by Salthouse and Skovronek (1992) in their statement that:

> [I]ncreased age seems to be associated with progressively greater difficulties when information must be simultaneously stored and either transformed or abstracted. This decreased ability to keep the intermediate products of earlier processing available, while also transforming or abstracting information, necessarily impairs the identification of abstract relations among sets of

elements ... Because the solution of many cognitive tasks requires abstraction of higher order relations, people with smaller working-memory capacities, such as older adults, are likely to be less successful than those with larger capacities, such as young adults.

(p. 119–120)

Indirect evidence for a role of WM in age differences in cognition is available in numerous studies in which larger age differences favoring young adults have been found when conditions in the tasks could be assumed to make greater demands on working memory. Examples of this phenomenon in my research are findings that the age differences in performance were larger with: more complex (i.e. alternating or second-order relations compared to simple sequential relations) series completion problems (Salthouse & Prill, 1987), larger angular discrepancy between cubes in a cube comparison task (Salthouse & Skovronek, 1992) more operations in spatial integration tasks (Salthouse, 1987, 1988; Salthouse & Mitchell, 1989), geometric analogy tasks (Salthouse, 1988), paper folding tasks (Salthouse, 1988, 1992a; Salthouse et al. 1989b), integrative reasoning tasks (Salthouse, 1992a; Salthouse et al. 1989b) and cube assembly tasks (Salthouse, 1992a).

A more detailed investigation of the phenomenon of larger age differences at greater levels of task complexity with integrative reasoning and paper folding tasks was conducted by Salthouse et al. (1989b). The specific goal in that project was to investigate whether this "complexity effect" at least in part reflected a failure to preserve earlier information during the performance of the task. The procedure consisted of comparing decision accuracy when all relevant information was available in a single display with accuracy when the relevant information was distributed across multiple displays, and therefore information integration was presumably required. The critical finding was that the slopes of the functions relating decision accuracy to number of premises or number of folds were very similar when only a single premise or fold was relevant to the decision as when the relevant information was distributed across multiple displays, and that this was equally true at all ages. Because no integration is required when the relevant information is presented in a single display, poorer performance with additional premises or folds can be presumed to reflect inability to preserve earlier information during the presentation and processing of later information. These results are therefore consistent with the interpretation that most of the age differences in these tasks are attributable to a failure to retain information from early premises or folds during the presentation of subsequent premises or folds, and that they are unlikely to be due to a limitation associated with integrating information.

A related finding was reported by Salthouse, Mitchell and Palmon (1989a) with a spatial integration task. In this case, no age differences were evident in the accuracy of merely recognizing information, but young adults were more accurate than older adults when the trials involved several displays but all of the relevant information was contained in a single display. As in the other study, these results imply that the age-related difficulty was in maintaining information during the performance of the task. In both situations the inability to preserve relevant information during the processing of other information is consistent with a failure of working memory.

Assessment of WM

Different conceptualizations of WM have guided how it has been measured, and many of the measurement methods have been incorporated in studies comparing adults of different ages. As elaborated below, the assessments can be categorized as either within-context methods, including measurement of redundant information requests and accuracy of recognizing probes of earlier information, or out-of-context methods, including measures evaluating updating of continuously changing information or measures involving simultaneous storage and processing.

Within-context measures

In an article published in 1990, within-context assessments of working memory were described as follows:

> Within-context assessments of working memory consist of information about memory functioning derived during the performance of ongoing cognitive tasks. That is, these evaluations are not obtained from tasks deliberately designed to assess specific attributes of memory capacity, but instead are inferred from observations collected while research participants are performing other cognitive tasks.
>
> (Salthouse, 1990, p.104)

Redundant information requests

Several examples of within-context assessments of working memory in tasks involving sequential presentation of relevant information were described by Welford (1958). For example, in different experiments subjects were asked to locate a target cell in a matrix, to determine the correspondence between elements in an electrical circuit, or to determine the relative positions of horses in a horse race. In each case, older adults were reported to make more uninformative or redundant information inquiries than young adults.

Salthouse and Skovronek (1992) investigated within-context assessments of working memory with a cube comparison task in which the subject was to decide if two displays portraying 3-D cubes could represent the same object. In some conditions the subjects were required to make explicit requests (via commands on a computer) to view the contents of specific cube faces, and the number of times the same cube face was re-examined was recorded. These repeated cube face examinations were assumed to occur because the subject was unable to maintain relevant information while it was being processed, and hence a larger number of repeated information requests might be symptomatic of a smaller, or less effective, working memory. As expected, older adults made more redundant (i.e. repeated) requests for information in the cube comparison task than young adults, and they also made more redundant information requests in a successive version of the Raven's Progressive Matrices task. That is, in contrast to the traditional format in which all information is simultaneously available, in the successive version the participant selected specific cells in the matrix to be examined sequentially. Repetition of a previously examined cell was designated a redundant information request. A particularly interesting result in this study was that the number of redundant requests in the Raven's Matrices task and in the cube comparisons task were significantly correlated in both young adults (r = .41) and older adults (r = .34), which suggests that the tendency to make redundant information requests is a meaningful individual difference dimension not restricted to a specific cognitive task.

The sequential version of the Raven's task was also administered in a later study (Salthouse, 1993), and once again older adults were found to make more redundant cell examinations than young adults. Two complex span WM tasks were also administered to the subjects in this study and, surprisingly, the number of redundant information requests was only weakly related to the WM measures (i.e. r = −.12 for young adults and r = −.09 for older adults). These results raise the possibility that a greater number of information requests may reflect lack of confidence or excess cautiousness as much as, or more than, a failure to preserve prior information. However, this inference should be considered tentative because no information about the reliability of the measures was available, and therefore it is possible that the weak correlations might simply have been a consequence of low reliability.

Probes

If WM reflects the ability to preserve information during ongoing processing, individuals with high levels of WM might be expected to have better recognition of earlier presented information in the task than individuals with lower levels of WM. Salthouse and Mitchell (1989) applied this logic in a spatial integration task in which sequentially presented line segments were to be synthesized into a composite figure and compared with a target pattern. In addition to complete comparison figures, probes of the line segments from a prior frame were occasionally presented to test for recognition of the earlier information. Somewhat surprisingly, no significant age differences were found in the accuracy of recognizing probes. Salthouse and Skovronek (1992) also did not find significant age differences in probe recognition of prior cube faces in a sequential version of the cube comparison task.

However, young adults were more accurate in probe recognition than older adults in other studies. For example, Salthouse (1992b) found that older adults were less accurate than young adults when recognizing probes of prior premises during the performance of an integrative reasoning task. And in two separate studies involving a sequential version of the Raven's matrix reasoning task, Salthouse (1993) found older adults to be less accurate than young adults in recognizing contents of prior cells. Furthermore, the correlations of probe recognition accuracy with age in the two studies were −.50 and −.70, and the correlations with Raven's accuracy were .67 and .60, and thus the results are consistent with the possibility that age differences in preserving relevant information contributed to the age differences in task performance.

The preceding review reveals that results comparing adults of different ages on within-context assessments of WM have been somewhat inconsistent. Among the possible reasons for the inconsistencies are potentially low reliability of the measures, or uncontrolled variations in task strategy. Despite the inconsistencies, more research investigating within-context WM measures is nevertheless desirable because these types of measures are likely to be informative about the mechanisms involved in the relations between WM and cognitive functioning, and the impact of age on these mechanisms.

Out of context WM assessment

Tasks deliberately designed to evaluate properties of WM rather than other aspects of cognitive functioning can be considered as out-of-context WM assessments. Two major categories of out-of-context assessments have been employed: measures of the accuracy of updating the status of continuously changing information; and measures of the accuracy of remembering information while processing the same or other information in various complex span tasks.

Updating

Updating tasks require the subject to maintain the status of several continuously changing variables. Welford (1958) described early versions of what is now known as the *n*-back task, and one of the first published studies using this task was an age-comparative study by Kirchner (1958). A version of the *n*-back was used in a study by Salthouse, Atkinson and Berish (2003) and, as in Kirchner's study, significant age differences were found, favoring younger adults.

Tasks requiring updating of numbers with arithmetic operations, and of spatial positions with arrows indicating location transformations, have been examined in several studies in my laboratory (e.g. Salthouse, Babcock & Shaw, 1991; Salthouse, 1992c; Salthouse, 1995). In every case, older adults were found to be less accurate than young adults. Significant negative age correlations were also reported in a spatial updating task used in Salthouse, Atkinson and Berish (2003) and Salthouse, Pink and Tucker-Drob (2008), and in a color counters numeric updating task in Salthouse, Pink and Tucker-Drob (2008).

Yntema and Trask (1963) may have been the first to use a keeping track task involving sequential presentation of exemplars from categories with occasional probes of the most recent exemplar from a target category. A version of this task was used in a study by Salthouse, Atkinson and Berish (2003) and, as with most WM tasks, significant age differences were found, favoring younger adults.

Talland (e.g. 1968) described tasks in which the participant was to recall the non-repeated item in a list last, or an adaptation of the running memory task introduced by Pollack, Johnson and Knaff (1959) in which the requirement was to recall the last *n* items in a list of unpredictable length. Talland reported age differences in both types of tasks, and the running memory finding was replicated by Siedlecki, Salthouse and Berish (2005) in a task in which the participant was instructed to recall the last three words in the list. Running memory tasks in which the participant was to recall the last four letters or dot positions were also administered in Salthouse, Pink and Tucker-Drob (2008), and in both tasks there were significant negative correlations between age and performance accuracy.

Simultaneous storage and processing

Case, Kurland and Goldberg (1982), and Daneman and Carpenter (1980) developed complex span WM tasks with both storage and processing requirements, in that the subject was to remember some information while processing the same or other information. Several versions of complex span tasks have been developed in my laboratory, including computation span (Salthouse & Prill, 1987; Salthouse & Mitchell, 1989; Salthouse et al., 1989), reading span and listening span (Salthouse & Babcock, 1991), and line span (Babcock & Salthouse, 1990; Salthouse & Skovronek, 1992). One or more of these tasks have been included in numerous studies, and age differences favoring young adults have consistently been found. Other variants of complex span tasks developed by Engle and colleagues (e.g. Conway et al., 2005) were used in Salthouse, Pink and Tucker-Drob (2008) and, again, moderately large age differences were found.

Although research from my laboratory represents only a small proportion of the research concerned with age differences in WM, it is clear from the results reviewed above that increased age is often associated with lower levels of performance in tasks postulated to measure WM. Many of the studies in my laboratory involved moderately large samples of adults across a wide age range, and therefore the age trends with these data may provide good estimates of the relations between age and WM. Figure 1.1 portrays the age relations with six WM tasks in samples of 724 adults (for the operation span and symmetry span tasks), 1,460 adults (for the computation span and reading span tasks), and 1,563 adults (for the running memory tasks). It can be seen that for every measure the age trends were nearly linear between 25 and 85 years of age.

WM relations

The information in the preceding sections indicates that most measures postulated to assess WM have been found to have significant age relations, and thus it is reasonable to conclude that there are age differences in WM as the construct is assessed by these tasks. However, because a large number of cognitive variables have been found to have significant age differences, it is possible that the measures may not represent anything special. Information relevant to this point is illustrated in Figure 1.2, which portrays age trends in measures of reasoning, memory and speed in the same format as Figure 1.1. Note that the age trends with these measures were all quite linear and, if anything, were more strongly negative than those for the WM measures in Figure 1.1. A key question with respect to aging

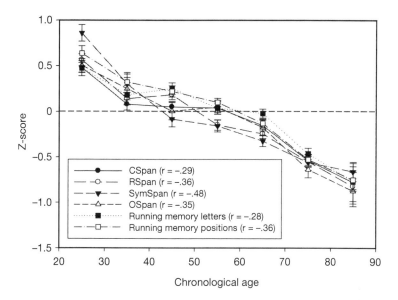

Figure 1.1 Means and standard errors of z-scores representing performance in six working memory tasks as a function of age

Source: Data from various Salthouse studies.

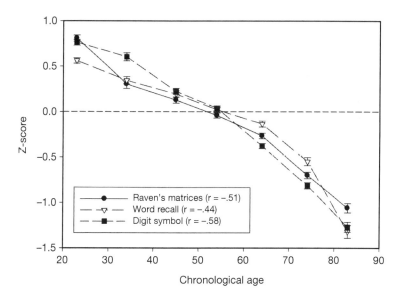

Figure 1.2 Means and standard errors of z-scores representing performance in tests of reasoning (Raven's Matrices), memory (Word Recall), and speed (Digit Symbol) as a function of decade

Source: Data from various Salthouse studies.

and WM, therefore, is not whether WM measures are related to age, because that certainly seems to be the case, but rather the nature of the relations of WM measures with measures of other types of cognition.

Internal relations

Internal relations can be conceptualized as relations among hypothesized components within the same task, or among measures from similar tasks. As an example, Salthouse and Babcock (1991) proposed that processing efficiency, storage capacity, and coordination effectiveness are the primary components of complex span tasks, and they obtained measures of each hypothesized component from adults across a wide age range. Path analysis models suggested that a large proportion of the age differences in WM were mediated through components postulated to reflect processing efficiency and coordination effectiveness. Reanalyses of these data were conducted by Salthouse (1994) to identify the proportional contributions of the different components to individual differences in WM. The results revealed that the combination of the three components accounted for 60% of the variance in complex span measures of WM, with 50% accounted for by the processing efficiency component alone. Furthermore, the largest contribution to the age-related variance in complex span WM measures was variability in processing efficiency.

Motivated in part by this discovery of strong relations between processing efficiency and WM, a number of studies were conducted to investigate the reduction in cross-sectional age-related variance in WM after controlling the variance in various measures of speed (e.g. Salthouse, 1991, 1992b, 1993; Salthouse & Babcock, 1991; Salthouse & Meinz, 1995). In every case the results revealed a moderate to large attenuation of the age-related variance in WM, and the following interpretation of these results was proposed:

> One possible interpretation of the relation between speed and working memory is that working memory has a dynamic quality, perhaps somewhat analogous to someone trying to juggle several objects simultaneously. That is, just as the number of items that can be successfully juggled depends on the rate at which they can be caught and tossed, so might the limits on the number of distinct ideas that can be kept active (or mentally juggled) in working memory be set by the rate at which information can be processed. From this perspective, therefore, working memory might be interpreted as the set of items currently active in consciousness, and age differences in working memory might be hypothesized to originate because increased age is associated with a reduction either in the ability to activate new information or in the ability to maintain the activation of old information.
>
> (Salthouse, 1992b, p. 422)

A key aspect of this conceptualization of WM is that aspects of processing efficiency or effectiveness are at least as important as aspects of information storage, particularly with respect to age differences in WM.

Although complex span tasks are distinguished from simple span tasks by a requirement for simultaneous processing in addition to storage of information, most studies in which complex span tasks have been used have only considered storage measures in their analyses, and have either ignored the processing component, or have treated it as an exclusionary criterion by discarding data from participants with low levels of processing accuracy. However, it may only be meaningful to neglect one component if there is little variation across people in the measures of that component, or if the measures of that component have a weak relation to the relevant construct. Research from my laboratory and from other laboratories suggests that neither of these conditions is likely to be true (e.g. Babcock & Salthouse, 1990; Duff & Logie, 2001; Salthouse & Babcock, 1991; Waters & Caplan, 1996). For example, Salthouse, Pink and Tucker-Drob (2008) found substantial individual difference variance, and significant age differences, on measures of both storage and processing in complex span tasks. Moreover, an unpublished study (Salthouse & Tucker-Drob, 2008) found significant relations between the storage and processing measures. Three models of possible organizations among the storage and processing measures from different complex span tasks (i.e. operation span, symmetry span, and reading span) considered in that study are portrayed in Figure 1.3. The model in the top panel represents the possibility that all of the measures reflect a single modality-independent WM construct. The model in the bottom left panel postulates that the measures are best organized in terms of the modality-specific WM tasks from which they were derived, and the model in the bottom right panel postulates the existence of separate constructs corresponding to storage and processing components. The models were examined with data from the two studies in Salthouse, Pink and Tucker-Drob (2008).

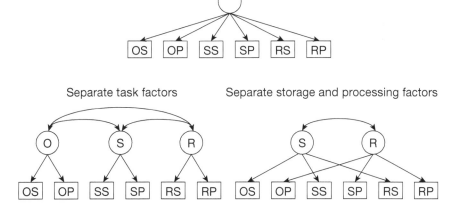

Figure 1.3 Three alternative models of the organization of storage and processing measures in complex span WM tasks

Key: OS = operation span storage, OP = operation span processing, SS = symmetry span storage, SP = symmetry span processing, RS = reading span storage, RP = reading span processing

The best-fitting model in both studies had separate, but moderately correlated ($r = .73$ and $.47$ in the two studies), storage and processing constructs. Similar results were reported by Unsworth et al. (2009) in a study involving 138 young adults. That is, in the Unsworth et al. study a model based on separate task constructs did not fit the data very well, but a model with separate processing and storage constructs had a good fit, with an estimated correlation of .61 between the processing accuracy and storage constructs. These results have at least two important implications. First, they suggest that it can be misleading to ignore the processing measures in analyses of complex span performance because people differ in their levels of processing accuracy, and individual differences in processing accuracy are related to individual differences in the storage measures. And second, at least with these types of complex span WM tasks, it appears that the individual differences are more consistent with a general, modality-independent WM factor rather than with several separate modality-specific factors.

Another issue relevant to internal WM relations concerns the magnitude of correlations of WM measures with each other because moderate correlations would be expected if the various measures represent a single coherent construct. Initial information relevant to this question based on small samples of 20 young and 20 old adults who each performed several WM tasks was reported in Salthouse (1988). The WM tasks consisted of: repeating a digit sequence in reverse order (backwards digit span), repeating digits after subtracting two from each digit (subtract 2 span), identifying the missing digit when the sequence was repeated in random order (missing digit span), and remembering digits while simultaneously performing arithmetic operations (computation span). Large age differences favoring young adults were found in all except the missing digit span task. Most importantly in the current context was the finding that the measures were moderately correlated with one another, and to a similar extent in the two age groups. Similar results with a somewhat different combination of WM tasks were reported by Waters and Caplan (2003).

Subsequent studies in my lab have revealed correlations between measures from computation span and listening or reading span tasks ranging from .40 to .79 (e.g. Salthouse, 1991, 1992c, 1993; Salthouse & Babcock, 1991; Salthouse, Babcock & Shaw, 1991; Salthouse & Kersten, 1993; Salthouse & Meinz, 1995), and similar values have been reported in studies by other researchers (e.g. deFrias, Dixon & Strauss, 2009; McCabe et al., 2010). Correlations between measures from other complex span tasks ranging from .52 between operation span and symmetry span to .71 between operation span and reading span were reported by Salthouse and Pink (2008).

One issue relevant to age differences in WM measures is whether the structure is similar at different ages. Studies by Park et al. (2002) and Hale et al. (2011) found similar patterns of interrelations of WM measures at different ages. Johnson, Logie and Brockmole (2010) also found a strong common WM factor at all ages, although there was also evidence of age differences in the residual variances in some measures. No formal comparisons were conducted on the data from Study 2 in Salthouse, Pink and Tucker-Drob (2008), but inspection of the standardized coefficients among the WM measures in Table 1.1 reveals that the pattern was similar in three different age groups, with very strong relations of the WM construct with a Gf construct in each group, suggesting qualitatively similar WM constructs at each age.

It is clear from the results summarized in Table 1.1 that there are moderate correlations among different measures postulated to assess WM. Although these results are consistent with the assumption that the measures represent a common construct or dimension of individual differences, that information is only relevant to the convergent validity of a construct, and information about discriminant validity is also needed to establish that the construct is distinct. That is, in addition to determining that the measures presumed to represent the same construct are moderately correlated with one another, it is also important to determine if they have weaker correlations with measures assumed to represent different constructs because otherwise the constructs may not be truly distinct, and they could reflect the same underlying dimension of individual differences.

External relations

External relations refer to relations of WM measures with other cognitive abilities, either in the role of a mediator of the cross-sectional age-cognition relations, or in other types of correlational analyses. Early studies in which WM was examined as a mediator of the age differences in other cognitive tasks were reviewed by Salthouse (1990). Many of the studies published at that time had a number of limitations, such as the use of a single variable as a mediator, which includes

Table 1.1 Standardized coefficients for Gf and WM relations with a hierarchical WM model in three age groups

			Age group		
			18–39	*40–59*	*60–98*
Study 1, N = 708					
WM	→	Storage	.70	.93	.73
	→	Processing	1.02	.92	.79
Storage	→	OSpan storage	.56	.54	.66
	→	SymSpan storage	.80	.64	.75
Processing	→	OSpan processing	.43	.44	.62
	→	SymSpan processing	.51	.57	.57
WM	← →	Gf	.90	.94	1.03
Fit statistics					
	CFI		.95	.95	.97
	RMSEA		.08	.08	.06

Source: Data from Salthouse, Pink and Tucker-Drob (2008)

task-specific influences and measurement error in addition to the construct of interest, and consideration of only one mediator at a time, which means that the mediator absorbs all of the variance that it shares with other potential mediators in addition to any unique variance it might have. Furthermore, the sample sizes in most of the early studies were often rather small, which resulted in low power and imprecise estimates of the relations. Finally, few of the studies considered alternative models of the relations among the measures to evaluate the plausibility of different patterns of influence (cf. Salthouse, 2011a). Despite these limitations, a sizable reduction in the cross-sectional relation of age to the measure of cognitive performance when the variation in the WM measure was controlled was found in every study conducted in my lab (e.g. Salthouse et al., 1989; Salthouse, 1991; Salthouse, 1992b; Salthouse & Kersten 1993).

The focus in more recent studies in my laboratory has been on identifying the cognitive abilities involved in WM tasks, and investigating whether the WM-ability relations were similar at different ages. The analytical approach has been termed contextual analysis because the target variables, in this case measures assumed to assess WM, are analyzed in the context of other cognitive abilities.

A schematic illustration of the contextual analysis approach is portrayed in Figure 1.4. The bottom portion of the figure illustrates that the target variables in this type of analysis can be single variables, first-order latent constructs, or second-order latent constructs. Although not included in the figure, each of four abilities was represented by three to six measures from separate cognitive tests, and thus the assessment of the constructs was not only relatively broad, but had minimal measurement error. The portion of the model in which the cognitive abilities and age are simultaneous predictors of the target variable is essentially equivalent to multiple regression, and therefore the coefficients for these paths indicate the unique influences of each predictor when influences of other predictors are controlled. Advantages of contextual analyses over other types of analyses are better representation of the cognitive abilities by relying on latent constructs instead of single variables, and information about the unique influences of each predictor because the predictors are considered simultaneously rather than separately.

Results of contextual analyses on a variety of different WM measures, including *n*-back, backwards digit span, complex span, and updating, were reported in Salthouse (2005), Salthouse, Atkinson and Berish (2003) and Salthouse, Pink and Tucker-Drob (2008). As in many reports by other researchers (e.g. Ackerman, Beier & Boyle, 2005; Colom et al., 2005), the analyses revealed strong relations of individual WM measures with a reasoning or fluid ability (Gf) construct.

Contextual analysis results with the Salthouse, Pink and Tucker-Drob (2008) data are reported in Table 1.2. The results with individual variables were reported in the original article, but those with latent constructs representing storage and processing, and with a hierarchical WM construct, have not been published before. Two results of the contextual analyses summarized in Table 1.2 are particularly noteworthy. First, none of the unique age relations was significant when considering influences on the reference cognitive abilities. These findings suggest

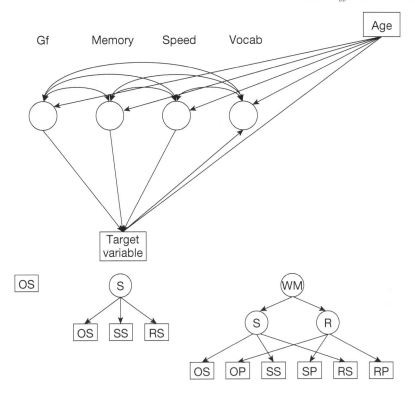

Figure 1.4 Schematic illustration of contextual analysis model (see main text for details)

that all of the age-related influences on the WM variables or constructs were shared with age-related influences on other cognitive abilities. In other words, these results imply that if people were equated on the levels of these cognitive abilities, little or no cross-sectional age differences would be expected on the WM measures.

The second noteworthy finding in Table 1.2 is that the Gf relations were stronger with processing constructs than with storage constructs, and when both types of measures were included in a hierarchical model of WM. An implication of these results is that the relations of complex span measures to Gf may be underestimated when only storage measures are used to assess WM.

It is clear from the results just discussed, and from similar results in many studies from other laboratories, that the WM and Gf constructs are strongly related to one another. An important question therefore concerns the nature of that relation. In particular, is WM the critical constituent of Gf, and possibly of age differences in many different cognitive tasks, or is WM merely another aspect of a broader Gf construct? Because it is not easy to distinguish these possibilities on the basis of behavioral observations at a single point in time, positions on this issue have primarily been based on theoretical arguments rather than empirical data.

Table 1.2 Contextual analysis results with the model in Figure 1.4 applied to data from Table 1.1

	Age		Cognitive Ability			
	Total	*Unique*	*Gf*	*Mem*	*Speed*	*Voc*
Study 1, N = 708						
Single variables						
Operation span storage	−.33*	.03	.40*	.07	.20*	.03
Operation span processing	−.23*	−.08	.37*	.11	−.04	.19*
Symmetry span storage	−.50*	−.10	.71*	−.05	.01	−.13*
Symmetry span processing	−.21*	.01	.69*	−.08	−.15	.06
Latent constructs						
Storage	−.49*	−.09	.77*	−.03	.10	−.12
Processing	−.26*	−.07	.98*	−.02	−.26*	.16
Hierarchical WM	−.59*	−.09	.97*	−.02	−.02	−.04
Study 2, N = 213						
Single variables						
Operation span storage	−.32*	−.01	.57*	.14	−.07	−.06
Operation span processing	−.18*	.20	.74*	.02	−.06	−.14
Symmetry span storage	−.60*	−.11	.65*	−.04	.14	−.27*
Symmetry span processing	−.18*	−.03	.57*	.13	−.25	.05
Reading span storage	−.22*	−.12	.40*	.05	−.03	.21
Reading span processing	−.05	−.22	−.05	.25	−.10	.45*
Keeping track	−.15*	.08	.55*	.15	−.20	−.09
Running memory letters	−.17*	.24	.78*	−.03	.02	−.12
Running memory positions	−.35*	.15	.81*	.04	.03	−.19
Latent constructs						
Storage	−.50*	−.09	.69*	.03	.01	−.12
Processing	−.28*	.16	.82*	.22	−.17	.01
Hierarchical WM	−.56*	−.01	1.10*	.15	−.17	−.10
Updating	−.41*	.27	1.09*	.06	.03	−.16

Source: Data from Salthouse, Pink and Tucker-Drob (2008)

Note
* p<.01. The signs have been reversed for the processing measures based on errors such that higher scores with all variables represent better performance.

Although not definitive, one type of empirical information relevant to this issue can be derived from comparisons of the unique prediction of WM and Gf on other cognitive measures. The logic of this asymmetric prediction procedure is schematically represented in Figure 1.5. Panel A indicates that the WM and Gf constructs have been found to be correlated with each other, and Panel B indicates that each construct has been found to be correlated with other cognitive variables, represented as the target variable in the figure. The most interesting information concerns the three proportions of variance in a target variable that can be identified when two constructs are used as simultaneous predictors, as illustrated in Panel C.

The rationale underlying the procedure is as follows. If the WM and Gf constructs represent essentially the same dimension of individual differences, then most of the variance in the target variable should be shared across the two predictors, with little that is unique to either predictor. Another possible outcome is that the constructs might each have some unique prediction, perhaps with proportions in the same ratio as the simple correlations of the constructs with the target variable because level of reliability might impose similar constraints on the total and unique influences. What might be the most interesting outcome would be if one construct dominates the prediction of the target variable, with much greater unique influences than those associated with the other construct.

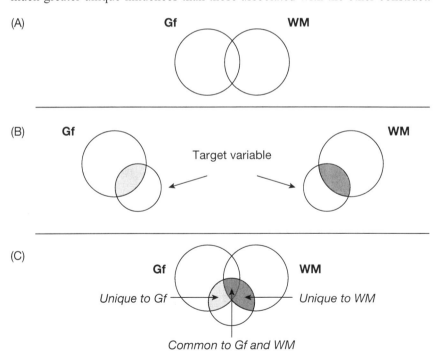

Figure 1.5 Schematic illustration of the logic underlying the asymmetric prediction procedure to identify unique influences of Gf and WM

That is, an asymmetric pattern such as this would be informative in indicating which construct had the greater overlap with, and possibly was more central to, the target variable.

The asymmetric prediction method was recently applied by Salthouse (2011b), with scores on the connections variant of the trail-making test serving as the target variable. The major finding was an asymmetric pattern, with no unique prediction of WM on the connections variables when variance in the Gf construct was controlled, but significant unique prediction of Gf when the variance in the WM construct was controlled.

In order to explore the generalizability of this asymmetric pattern, different combinations of variables from Study 2 in Salthouse, Pink and Tucker-Drob (2008) were examined. Four variables were hypothesized to reflect Gf, but they involved different types of stimulus material and processing operations than the variables used to define the Gf construct. Five updating measures were examined, two involving verbal information (keeping track and running memory letters), and three involving visual-spatial information (color counters, matrix monitoring, and running memory positions).

Because simultaneous prediction results could vary according to the particular manner in which the Gf and WM constructs were operationalized, the analyses were repeated with different operationalizations of the constructs. One analysis was conducted with the most comprehensive assessment of the constructs, consisting of six Gf measures (i.e. Raven's, Shipley, letter sets, spatial relations, paper folding, and form boards), and six WM measures (i.e. both storage and processing measures from three complex span tasks). The second analysis was conducted with a narrower Gf construct based on only Raven's, Shipley, and letter sets tests, and a narrower WM construct based on only storage measures from the three complex span tasks.

Results of these asymmetric prediction analyses are presented in Table 1.3. Inspection of the entries in the table reveals that the results were very similar with the broad and narrow assessments of the Gf and WM constructs, which suggests that the results of simultaneous prediction analyses are not specific to a particular method of operationalizing the relevant constructs. The most important finding was that for most of the target variables the only significant unique influences were with the Gf construct. This might have been expected for the new Gf variables, but it was surprising to find that this was also true for many of the variables selected to represent the updating aspect of WM (with the exception of the color counters and running memory letters tasks). Because the pattern of results was very similar across narrow and broad operationalizations of each construct, it is not the case that Gf is simply a more amorphous, or less coherent, construct than WM. Instead these results suggest that Gf may represent a superordinate or broader dimension of individual differences than WM, and that it encompasses the WM construct as well as a variety of other types of controlled processing.

Table 1.3 Simultaneous prediction of new Gf variables from Gf and WM constructs based on the model in panel C of Figure 1.5

Target Variable	Gf		WM	
Model	Total	Unique	Total	Unique
Analysis synthesis				
Broad Gf and WM	.68*	.73*	.48*	−.06
Narrow Gf and WM	.69*	.75*	.42*	−.09
Mystery codes				
Broad Gf and WM	.79*	.74*	.63*	.07
Narrow Gf and WM	.77*	.67*	.60*	.13
Logical steps				
Broad Gf and WM	.78*	.83*	.57*	−.06
Narrow Gf and WM	.81*	.89*	.50*	−.12
Concept formation				
Broad Gf and WM	.48*	.46*	.37*	.03
Narrow Gf and WM	.47*	.42*	.35*	.07
Keeping track				
Broad Gf and WM	.49*	.54*	.34*	−.06
Narrow Gf and WM	.46*	.43*	.32*	.03
Color counters				
Broad Gf and WM	.62*	.34*	.61*	.36*
Narrow Gf and WM	.64*	.44*	.58*	.28*
Matrix monitoring				
Broad Gf and WM	.60*	.77*	.34*	−.22
Narrow Gf and WM	.59*	.71*	.30*	−.18
Running memory letters				
Broad Gf and WM	.54*	.27	.54*	.35*
Narrow Gf and WM	.57*	.39*	.52*	.25
Running memory positions				
Broad Gf and WM	.67*	.70*	.50*	−.03
Narrow Gf and WM	.67*	.67*	.46*	−.00

Note

* $p<.01$. Values in the "total" columns are simple correlations and values in the "unique" columns are β coefficients obtained in a regression equation with both Gf and WM as simultaneous predictors. Variables used in the Broad Gf and Wm assessments included those in the narrow assessments plus spatial relations, form boards, and paper folding in Gf, and processing measures from operation span, symmetry span, and reading span. Variables used in the narrow Gf and WM assessments were Raven's, Shipley abstraction, and letter sets for Gf and storage measures from operation span, symmetry span, and reading span.

Conclusion

Strong relations of age have been found with many measures hypothesized to reflect WM, and the WM measures have frequently been found to have moderate to strong correlations with a variety of cognitive measures. This combination of results is consistent with the proposal that decline in WM functioning contributes to age-related cognitive differences. However, the conclusion must still be considered tentative because of questions about the construct validity of WM, and particularly if and how the WM construct is distinct from other constructs such as fluid ability (Gf). Rather than merely assuming that WM is the core of cognition, or the driving force underlying age-related differences in cognitive functioning, the nature of the relations of WM to other constructs needs to be systematically investigated in adults of different ages.

Because results are most convincing when they are obtained with strong methods, several suggestions can be offered to improve future research on relations of aging and WM from an individual differences perspective. First, it is desirable to rely on multivariate assessment of all relevant constructs, and to conduct analyses on latent constructs rather than single observed variables to minimize measurement error (and maximize reliability) and obtain a broader representation of the constructs. It is widely acknowledged that no single measure is a pure reflection of a theoretical construct or process, but it may be possible to converge on a good approximation of the construct by aggregating across multiple measures. This is a different approach to the "process purity" problem than reliance on methods designed to isolate the critical process, but results obtained with a broader construct based on variance shared across different cognitive measures may be more generalizable than those based on a single measure.

Second, moderately large samples, involving hundreds of participants, should be employed because many of the individual difference analyses are based on correlations, and the confidence interval around a correlation coefficient depends on sample size. Third, the research questions should be investigated with theoretically relevant models and analyses, and not exclusively with simple correlations. And finally, future research should examine possible moderators of WM relations. Much of the currently available research suggests that WM has similar meaning and relations with other aspects of cognitive functioning at all ages, but much more information about the potential moderating effects of age on WM-cognition relations is needed before the role of WM in age-related differences in cognition can be considered to be understood.

References

Ackerman, P. L., Beier, M. E. & Boyle, M. O. (2005). Working memory and intelligence: The same or different constructs? *Psychological Bulletin, 131*, 30–60.

Babcock, R. L. & Salthouse, T. A. (1990). Effects of increased processing demands on age differences in working memory. *Psychology and Aging, 5*, 421–428.

Case, R., Kurland, D. M. & Goldberg, J. (1982). Operational efficiency and the growth of short-term memory span. *Journal of Experimental Child Psychology, 33*, 386–404.

Colom, R., Abad, F. J., Rebollo, I. & Shih, P. C. (2005). Memory span and general intelligence: A latent-variable approach. *Intelligence, 33*, 623–642.

Conway, A. R. A., Kane, M. J., Bunting, M. F., Hambrick, D. Z., Wilhelm, O. & Engle, R. W. (2005). Working memory span tasks: A methodological review and user's guide. *Psychonomic Bulletin & Review, 12*, 769–786.

Daneman, M. & Carpenter, P. A. (1980). Individual differences in working memory and reading. *Journal of Verbal Learning and Verbal Behavior, 19*, 450–466.

de Frias, C. M., Dixon, R. A. & Strauss, E. (2009). Characterizing executive functioning in older special populations: From cognitively elite to cognitively impaired. *Neuropsychology, 23*, 778–791.

Duff, S. C. & Logie, R. H. (2001). Processing and storage in working memory span. *The Quarterly Journal of Experimental Psychology, 54A*, 31–48.

Hale, S., Rose, N. S., Myerson, J., Strube, M. J., Sommers, M., Tye-Murray, N. & Spehar, B. (2011). The structure of working memory abilities across the adult life span. *Psychology and Aging, 26*, 92–110.

Johnson, W., Logie, R. H., Brockmole, J. R. (2010). Working memory tasks differ in factor structure across age cohorts: Implications for differentiation. *Intelligence, 38*, 513–528.

Kirchner, W. K. (1958). Age differences in short-term retention of rapidly changing information. *Journal of Experimental Psychology, 55*, 352–358.

McCabe, D. P., Roediger, H. L., McDaniel, M. A., Balota, D. A. & Hambrick, D. Z. (2010). The relationship between working memory capacity and executive functioning: Evidence for a common executive attention construct. *Neuropsychology, 24*, 222–243.

Park, D. C., Lautenschlager, G., Hedden, T., Davidson, N. S., Smith, A. D. & Smith, P. K. (2002). Models of visuospatial and verbal memory across the adult life span. *Psychology & Aging, 17*, 299–320.

Pollack, I., Johnson, L. B. & Knaff, P. R. (1959). Running memory span. *Journal of Experimental Psychology, 57*, 137–146.

Salthouse, T. A. (1987). Adult age differences in integrative spatial ability. *Psychology and Aging, 2*, 254–260.

Salthouse, T. A. (1988). The role of processing resources in cognitive aging. In M. L. Howe & C. J. Brainerd (Eds.). *Cognitive Development in Adulthood.* New York: Springer-Verlag.

Salthouse, T. A. (1990). Working memory as a processing resource in cognitive aging. *Developmental Review, 10*, 101–124.

Salthouse, T. A. (1991). Mediation of adult age differences in cognition by reductions in working memory and speed of processing. *Psychological Science, 2*, 179–183.

Salthouse, T. A. (1992a). Why do adult age differences increase with task complexity? *Developmental Psychology, 28*, 905–918.

Salthouse, T. A. (1992b). Working memory mediation of adult age differences in integrative reasoning. *Memory & Cognition, 20*, 413–423.

Salthouse, T. A. (1992c). Influence of processing speed on adult age differences in working memory. *Acta Psychologica, 79*, 155–170.

Salthouse, T. A. (1993). Influence of working memory on adult age differences in matrix reasoning. *British Journal of Psychology, 84*, 171–199.

Salthouse, T. A. (1994). The aging of working memory. *Neuropsychology, 8*, 535–543.

Salthouse, T. A. (1995). Influence of processing speed on adult age differences in learning. *Swiss Journal of Psychology, 54*, 102–112.

Salthouse, T. A. (2005). Relations between cognitive abilities and measures of executive functioning. *Neuropsychology, 19*, 532–545.

Salthouse, T. A. (2011a). Neuroanatomical substrates of age-related cognitive decline. *Psychological Bulletin, 137*, 753–784.

Salthouse, T. A. (2011b). What cognitive abilities are involved in trail-making performance? *Intelligence, 39*, 222–232.

Salthouse, T. A. & Babcock, R. L. (1991). Decomposing adult age differences in working memory. *Developmental Psychology, 27*, 763–776.

Salthouse, T. A. & Kersten, A. W. (1993). Decomposing adult age differences in symbol arithmetic. *Memory & Cognition, 21*, 699–710.

Salthouse, T. A. & Meinz, E. J. (1995). Aging, inhibition, working memory, and speed. *Journal of Gerontology: Psychological Sciences, 50B*, P297–P306.

Salthouse, T. A. & Mitchell, D. R. D. (1989). Structural and operational capacities in integrative spatial ability. *Psychology and Aging, 4*, 18–25.

Salthouse, T. A. & Pink, J. E. (2008). Why is working memory related to fluid intelligence? *Psychonomic Bulletin & Review, 15*, 364–371.

Salthouse, T. A. & Prill, K. A. (1987). Inferences about age impairments in inferential reasoning. *Psychology and Aging, 2*, 43–51.

Salthouse, T. A. & Skovronek, E. (1992). Within-context assessment of age differences in working memory. *Journal of Gerontology: Psychological Sciences, 47*, 110–120.

Salthouse, T. A. & Tucker-Drob, E. (2008). *Aging, cognitive abilities, and working memory*. Unpublished manuscript.

Salthouse, T. A., Atkinson, T. M. & Berish, D. E. (2003). Executive functioning as a potential mediator of age-related cognitive decline in normal adults. *Journal of Experimental Psychology: General, 132*, 566–594.

Salthouse, T. A., Babcock, R. L. & Shaw, R. J. (1991). Effects of adult age on structural and operational capacities in working memory. *Psychology and Aging, 6*, 118–127.

Salthouse, T. A., Mitchell, D. R. D. & Palmon, R. (1989). Memory and age differences in spatial manipulation ability. *Psychology and Aging, 4*, 480–486.

Salthouse, T. A., Pink, J. E. & Tucker-Drob, E. M. (2008). Contextual analysis of fluid intelligence. *Intelligence, 36*, 464–486.

Salthouse, T. A., Mitchell, D. R. D., Skovronek, E. & Babcock, R. L. (1989b). Effects of adult age and working memory on reasoning and spatial abilities. *Journal of Experimental Psychology: Learning, Memory, and Cognition, 15*, 507–516.

Siedlecki, K. L., Salthouse, T. A. & Berish, D. E. (2005). Is there anything special about the aging of source memory? *Psychology and Aging, 20*, 19–32.

Talland, G. A. (1968). Age and the span of immediate recall. In G. A. Talland (Ed.), *Human Aging and Behavior* (pp. 93–129). NY: Academic Press.

Unsworth, N., Redick, T. S., Heitz, R. P., Broadway, J. M. & Engle, R. W. (2009). Complex working memory span tasks and higher-order cognition: A latent-variable analysis of the relationship between processing and storage. *Memory, 17*, 635–654.

Waters, G. S. & Caplan, D. (1996). The measurement of verbal working memory capacity and its relation to reading comprehension. *Quarterly Journal of Experimental Psychology, 49A*, 51–79.

Waters, G. S. & Caplan, D. (2003). The reliability and stability of verbal working memory measures. *Behavior Research Methods, Instruments, & Computers, 35*, 550–564.

Welford, A. T. (1958). *Ageing and Human Skill*. New York: Oxford University Press.

Yntema, D. B. & Trask, F. P. (1963). Recall as a search process. *Journal of Verbal Learning and Verbal Behavior, 2*, 65–74.

2   When cognitive performance does not decline across the lifespan

Robert H. Logie, Mark J. Horne and Lewis D. Pettit

Rejecting the dull hypothesis

Studies of changes in cognitive ability across the adult lifespan have established that a wide range of abilities decline as people get older. Older people typically perform more poorly on cognitive tasks than younger adults, even when the groups are matched on education and there is no evidence of neuropathology in the older group. The fact that age-related cognitive decline is such a ubiquitous finding in the research literature led Perfect and Maylor (2000) to suggest that additional reports of poorer performance in older than in younger adults might make a very limited contribution to our understanding of *how* and *why* cognition changes with age. They suggested that the classic psychological experimental paradigm, where the aim is to determine whether an experimental manipulation or a comparison between different groups of participants allows us to reject the null hypothesis, is of limited value in the field of cognitive ageing. They further suggested that predicting poorer cognitive performance by older people might be seen as rather less interesting than having a rationale to predict that older people would perform as well as or even better than younger people on specific cognitive tasks. They referred to the latter as 'rejecting the dull hyothesis'. That is, if we select any cognitive task, then the hypothesis that older people will perform more poorly than younger people is hardly groundbreaking, but showing the kinds of cognition that are insensitive as well as those that are sensitive to increasing age and why they are unaffected or are affected might yield more substantial insight.

This view of cognitive ageing research was supported by Salthouse (1996, 1998, 2000; see also Chapter 1 in this volume) who argued that monolithic interpretations of cognitive ageing are much too simplistic, and that an exploration of the relative degree of independence in age-related differences in different cognitive abilities would lead to more fruitful research. Therefore, research should be directed towards exploring whether there are differing age-related trajectories across different cognitive domains, what mediating lifestyle or congenital factors might be related to differences between people in their rates of age-related cognitive decline, and whether there are differential profiles of cognitive abilities in older compared with younger adults.

It is also possible that older people will perform the same tasks using different strategies from those used by younger people, and so the same task might not be measuring the same cognitive abilities in the different groups. Therefore, older people might maintain levels of performance on a task by using stategies that draw on cognitive functions that are relatively insensitive to the effects of increasing age (see Nagel and Lindenberger, Chapter 6 in this volume). Alternatively, older people might show poorer performance on a task because they are using strategies that are not optimal for the task, rather than reflecting a decline in the ability that the task was designed to measure.

Taking this approach to the study of cognitive ageing relies on three major assumptions that should be tested against empirical evidence. The first assumption is that cognitive decline in ageing is not simply a product of the overall slowing with age observed in both physical and mental functioning. This would require evidence for the influence of other factors, not related to speed of mental operations and of motor responses that affect different individuals in different ways at different ages. The second assumption is that cognition is not a unitary concept, but comprises a range of different cognitive abilities that differ in their sensitivity to increasing age. This would require a plot of the age-related trajectories of performance on tasks that can be demonstrated to be assessing different cognitive abilities. The third assumption is that people of different ages adopt different strategies for performing the same tasks. This would require evidence that there is a qualitative change in, for example, the nature of errors generated by different groups, and not just a difference in the overall scores achieved.

There is a wide range of evidence demonstrating the influence on age-related cognitive decline of differences between individuals. In one well-known longitudinal study Wilson et al. (2002) looked at the change in cognitive ability of 694 older (mean age = 75.9, sd = 6.9 when first tested) healthy members of religious groups over a six-year period. Longitudinal decline in story retention, word retention, word generation, word knowledge, digit span, perceptual speed and visuospatial ability was found to be more rapid in those who were older at the start of the study. Initially, this could be taken as support for the 'dull hypothesis', with the additional suggestion that general cognitive decline might accelerate with age. However, it was also found that there were wide individual differences in performance across all ages. Performance at initial testing was not a strong predictor of rate of subsequent decline, and there were different rates of decline across different measures of cognitive ability as well as across individual participants. The authors concluded that age affects different people and different cognitive functions in different ways rather than resulting in some form of global decline.

In a very substantial series of studies, Deary and colleagues (e.g. Deary, Batty & Gale, 2008; Gow et al., 2008; Deary et al., 2012; see review in Deary, Whalley & Starr, 2009) showed that childhood mental ability measured at age 11 is associated with an individual's level of cognitive ability as well as their general state of health and whether individuals were still alive at the age of 79, as well as over the following 13 years. This was based on follow-up (from 2000 and continuing) of the Scottish Mental Surveys of 1932 and 1947 in which all 11 year olds in Scotland were tested for their general mental ability. These results have shown clearly that ageing is associated with very different changes in ability across different people. Moreover, differences between individuals in childhood can and do affect cognitive performance throughout the lifespan, with many individuals retaining their high levels of childhood mental ability in later life.

The longitudinal study of individuals from the Scottish Mental Surveys and a wide range of other birth cohorts has reinforced the conclusion that individuals are affected by age in different ways, and the focus of those studies is now on identifying what might be the major factors that can account for those differences. However, it is often the case in large-scale studies of individual differences in mental ability, whether longitudinal or cross-sectional, that there is reliance on a global measure of cognitive ability such as IQ, derived from the common variance among a collection of cognitive tests. There tends to be less consideration of the effects of age on different cognitive functions, based on the assumption that the observed common variance across a battery of tests is sufficient. Typically, the residual variance from individual tests is treated as noise in the data set. Unfortunately, this approach misses the possibility that there are multiple different cognitive functions that collectively contribute to overall mental ability. On the same principles it would be possible to derive a single overall measure of biological health based on common variance across individual tests of heart, liver, kidney, respiratory, digestive, endocrine, immune and central nervous system function. This kind of overall measure might be useful for indicating general system integrity and overall health. But this, too, might be seen as 'testing a dull hypothesis' that older people tend to be less healthy than younger people. Such a measure would not be very informative about how each of those systems individually contributes to the overall health of an individual across their lifespan, nor would it aid diagnosis of specific pathologies or inform the choice of clinical interventions. So, if we accept that different cognitive functions have been identified, why would we assume that a derived measure based on the common variance across a battery of different tests would be sufficiently informative about how each of those functions individually contributes to overall cognitive health, or how those functions are each affected by healthy ageing or by specific neuropathologies? In this chapter, we will focus on a set of such separable cognitive functions that are collectively referred to as working memory.

Working memory: The collective

As will be clear across the other chapters in this book, there is general agreement among the research community that working memory refers to moment-to-moment cognitive processing and temporary information storage. However, there are very different theoretical perspectives about the nature of working memory and how it supports ongoing cognition. Our own perspective is that working memory is not a single, limited capacity system, but comprises a set of different cognitive functions each with their own capacity and characteristics, which act in concert and in different combinations to support everyday tasks (e.g. Baddeley et al., 1986; Baddeley, 2007; Baddeley & Logie, 1999; Logie, 1995; Logie et al., 2011; Logie & Niven, 2012; Logie & van der Meulen, 2009). Specific functions have been identified for temporary phonological storage and subvocal rehearsal thought to support immediate memory for short verbal sequences. Other functions have been identified for temporary storage of visual appearance of single stimuli or stimulus arrays, and of sequences of movements to targets or pathways. Still other functions are thought to activate and retain current representations of stored knowledge on a temporary basis, for example as visual images (Borst, Niven & Logie, 2012; Logie, 1986; van der Meulen, Logie & Della Sala, 2009). Finally, several executive functions have been identified, respectively to support the performance of two or more concurrent tasks (Logie et al., 2004) and to inhibit irrelevant material, switch between tasks, and update the contents of immediate memory (e.g. Emerson & Miyake, 2003; Miyake et al., 2000). The focus in this kind of theoretical framework has been to explore how different domain-specific cognitive functions are used to carry out different kinds of cognitive tasks, and to account for differential rates of decline for different cognitive abilities as well as for selective impairment of specific cognitive functions following focal or diffuse brain damage.

Evidence for the differential rates of decline in different working memory abilities across the lifespan was reported by Logie and Maylor (2009). Working in collaboration with the British Broadcasting Corporation (BBC), Logie and Maylor (2009; see also Brockmole & Logie, 2013; Johnson, Logie & Brockmole, 2010; Maylor & Logie, 2010) collected data from an internet study of five tests, each of different aspects of working memory. These were: Digit Span for immediate typed serial recall of visually presented digit sequences; Working Memory Span for semantic processing of sentence sequences and ordered recall of the final word of each sentence; immediate recall of Feature Binding in arrays of colour, shape and location combinations; immediate recall of visually presented square matrix patterns in the Visual Patterns Task; and identifying which hand holds a ball in a human figure shown in different spatial orientations in the Man and Ball Task. Figure 2.1 shows z-scores for the five tests from 111,188 participants age 8–80, standardised on the scores for the 20-year-old participants. Logie and Maylor (2009) analysed the data from 73,018 of the participants aged 18–79. Scores for four of the five tasks peaked in the early 20s; Digit Span performance peaked in the late 30s. The mean scores on the Visual Patterns and Feature Binding tasks started to show a decline in the early 20s and the decline continued across the adult lifespan. From Figure 2.1, it is clear that scores on the Visual Patterns and Visual Feature Binding tests for people in their late 40s were lower than those for 8–10-year-olds (see Brockmole and Logie, 2013). However, the performance on the Digit Span task was at the same level aged 60 as it was at age 20. The difference in decline between these widely used measures of different aspects of working memory suggests that different abilities are required to carry out each task. These results provide further support for the hypothesis that working memory comprises a collection of different cognitive functions that are differentially affected by age (see also Nagel & Lindenberger, Chapter 6 in this volume).

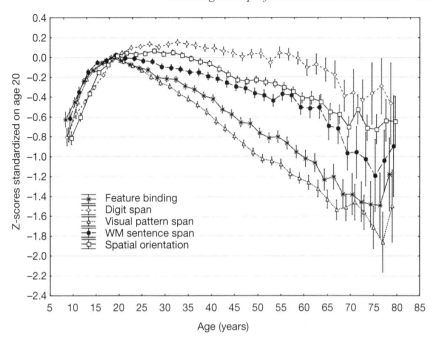

Figure 2.1 Z-scores standardised on 20-year-olds for five measures of different working memory functions

Source: Collected via the internet from 111,188 participants aged 8 to 80 years

A more detailed analysis was carried out by Johnson, Logie and Brockmole (2010) on scores for the five working memory tests from 95,199 of the 18–90-year-old participants from the BBC internet study. This incorporated additional data (included in Figure 2.1) from participants who completed the online tests after the Logie and Maylor (2009) analysis had been completed. Factor analysis showed that working memory task scores could be considered to be the result of a single ability, represented by common variance across tests for a single factor. Moreover, each task appeared to be measuring the same cognitive ability (i.e. measurement invariant) across groups that were close in age. However, this was not the case outside the age range 18–35 years. Crucially, when considering the tests one by one, they each appeared to be measuring different cognitive abilities in different age groups.

It is widely assumed that cognitive tests known to have robust psychometric properties are measurement invariant: that is, they measure the same abilities on the same scale when used with different individuals and with different groups. The simple analogy is the use of a ruler which measures length in exactly the same way whether measuring a bookshelf, a person, an elephant or the rudder of a ship. However, if the ruler is made of elastic, then the measurement of different objects would not be comparable. What Johnson, Logie and Brockmole (2010) found was that the proportion of test-specific variance (or residual variance) relative to the contribution to common variance from each test shifted when testing older compared with younger people. This is illustrated in Figure 2.2 which shows the residual variance across the five tests and across the full adult age range. It is clear from the figure that the balance of residual variance to common variance changes substantially across the different age groups, and that the nature of the change differs across the different tests. For example, a test of immediate serial ordered recall of digits and a test of verbal working memory span contributed more to common variance in younger people than it did for older people, for whom there was more test-specific variance. For the test of immediate recall of visual matrix patterns, and for the test of spatial orientation, the proportion of test-specific variance was larger in younger people than older people, with the latter group showing a greater contribution to common variance from these tests. In other words, older people appeared to be using a task-specific ability for remembering digit sequences, whereas younger people relied more on some general ability for this task. For visual pattern memory and spatial orientation, the results were the converse, with younger people seemingly using task-specific abilities for these

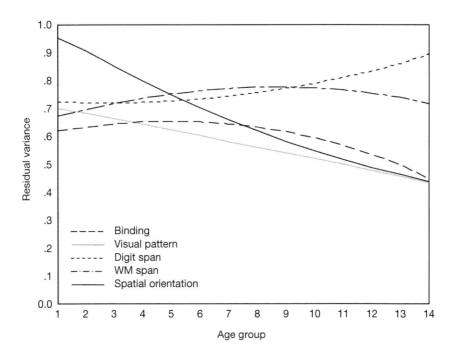

Figure 2.2 Residual variances from fitted regression lines for 95,199 participants across five working memory tests and 14 age groups

Source: Reprinted from Johnson, Logie & Brockmole (2010) with permission from Elsevier

Key: Age group 1 = 18–20 years; Age group 14 = 80–90 years. Other groups are in 5-year age bands, e.g. Group 2 = 21–26 years; Group 3 = 26–30 years and so on to Group 13 =75–79 years.

tasks, but older people relying on some form of more general ability. The results of the factor analysis suggested that there was only one general ability factor across the full age range. The test of measurement variance showed that older and younger people rely to differing extents on that general ability and this depends on which test they are being asked to perform. It is not the case that older people increasingly rely on a rapidly diminishing general ability for all tasks. For some tasks, notably short-term verbal memory, older people appear to rely more on task-specific abilities.

The evidence for measurement variance across age for tasks that are very similar to those that are widely used for assessing different cognitive abilities raises concerns about studies that use the same tests for younger and older participants and then attempt to compare overall cognitive performance between groups without considering qualitative differences in the performance patterns (e.g. types of errors). It is equally problematic for large-scale individual difference studies that use a fixed test battery across large groups to investigate age-related changes in performance and the influence of independent predictors. For example, older people might attempt to use verbal coding and processing for all tasks. This would be an efficient strategy for retaining digit sequences and for a verbal working memory task, but would result in poorer scores on a task that was originally designed to measure visual short-term memory ability. So, the poorer performance of an older person on a visual memory task might arise from them using a strategy that is not optimal for the task, rather than reflecting a poor visual memory capacity. To ensure that the test was indeed measuring short-term visual memory, there would have to be some form of diagnostic measure of performance that indicates how the test was being performed, for example whether errors are based on visual similarity among items. If there were instead evidence for phonologically based errors based on names attributed to the visually presented material (e.g. see Brown, Forbes & McConnell, 2006), this would suggest that the test is unlikely to be measuring visual short-term memory ability, but rather might be measuring the ability of the individual to use verbal labelling and verbal short-term memory to perform a test that was originally designed to test visual short-term memory. This lack of measurement invariance would not necessarily be evident from the psychometric properties of each test. For example, a test could generate highly reliable scores on different occasions but those scores could be generated by very different sets of cognitive abilities (for a more detailed discussion see Anderson, 1978; Logie et al., 2011; Logie et al., 1996).

Other studies have shown that manipulations within the same experiment do not necessarily have the same effect on younger and older participants. Sander, Werkle-Bergner and Lindenberger (2011) found that associative learning performance improved when participants of different ages were given an increase in encoding duration. However, older adults needed a significantly longer time than younger adults to show increased ability. One possible interpretation is that there is simply general slowing of cognitive function as people get older. However, it is also possible that older adults attempt to perform visual processing tasks using an alternative strategy, such as verbal recoding of visually presented stimuli, to successfully complete the task, and it takes additional time to implement such a strategy. This raises the question as to whether there might be an association between improved verbal memory ability across the lifespan and declines in visual memory ability in old age, if older people are more likely to use verbal strategies to perform a visual memory task. A further consequence of this would be a higher positive correlation between visual and verbal task performance in older adults if they are using their verbal abilities to undertake both tasks than there is in younger adults who use different abilities for each task. Alternatively, given the evidence that different working memory abilities decline at different rates across age, do measures of these different abilities show decreasing intercorrelations with increasing age?

Park et al. (2002) suggested that visuospatial and verbal working memory systems are distinct and based on domain-specific short-term memory subsystems, but are highly interrelated. Using a series of visual, verbal and executive short-term memory tasks, they did not find any behavioural evidence to suggest that cognitive resources become more general and less specific. They reported little evidence that cognitive abilities increasingly rely on a single general ability or that they become less domain-specific across the lifespan, a process known as dedifferentiation. Park et al. (2002) are explicit that their findings relate only to behavioural results, and are not indicative of any changes with age in networks in the brain that support working memory functions. They propose that behavioural data patterns in younger and older participants may look similar in terms of performance, but that this may not reflect underlying changes in the neural mechanisms being used. Indeed Li, Lindenberger and Sikstrom (2001) suggest that the mild cognitive deficits seen in normal ageing are due mainly to neurochemical shifts in still relatively intact neural circuits (see Nagel & Lindenberger, Chapter 6 in this volume and Charlton & Morris, Chapter 5 in this volume). They do not go on to discuss whether these shifts are caused by the processes of ageing, or are the products of changes in behaviour that occur as people get older. The possibility that performance in WM tasks in older people may be moderated by behavioural change is discussed later in this chapter.

In summary, from the cognitive behavioural literature there is a strong case for rejecting the dull hypothesis for some tasks. There are differences in the age-related decline in performance across different WM tasks, and not all cognitive abilities are poorer in older compared with younger individuals.

Dual-tasking and adult ageing

A further area of debate concerns the extent to which the ability to undertake two concurrent tasks, or dual-tasking, declines in healthy ageing. A typical experimental dual-task procedure involves participants undertaking a memory task, whilst concurrently performing a secondary task at the encoding, memory maintenance or retrieval stage. Different assumptions about the cognitive architecture of working memory generate rather different hypotheses regarding the age-related changes in dual task ability, and these hypotheses in turn generate different experimental designs to assess dual-task performance. Advocates of a single capacity or shared resources model of working memory (e.g. Barrouillet, Bernardin & Camos, 2004; Cowan, 2005) would suggest that dual-task ability would be moderated by the overall load on the individual. For example, performing two tasks concurrently would comprise a higher demand on attention than performing one task on its own, and therefore dual-task performance for two high-demand tasks should be poorer overall than performance of one of the tasks on its own, regardless of the type of each task. In contrast, the multiple component model of working memory (Baddeley, 2007; Baddeley & Logie, 1999; Logie, 1995; Logie et al., 2011) leads to the prediction that performing two tasks concurrently should be possible if the specified tasks involve the use of separate components of working memory. Dual-task costs in performance would result when the two tasks draw on the same component of working memory. We focus here on combinations of immediate serial ordered verbal recall and visuo-spatial processing and memory tasks.

One of the earliest studies to address dual-task ability and healthy ageing was set in the context of a study of the effects of neurodegenerative disease on dual-task ability. Baddeley et al. (1986; see also Baddeley et al., 1991) studied groups of younger and older healthy adults as control participants for comparison with a group of patients suffering from Alzheimer's disease. Here, we will focus only on the data from the 20 younger (20–31 years) and 28 older (57–72 years) healthy participants. All participants were first tested on their ability to repeat back random sequences of aurally presented digits, with their immediate verbal memory span taken as the longest sequence that could be recalled without error. The participants were then tested on their ability to use a stylus to follow a randomly moving target around a computer screen. Their visuo-motor tracking span was taken as the fastest speed at which the stylus was kept on the target for 40% to 60% of the time. Participants next were asked to repeat back aurally presented digit sequences set at the length of their individual verbal memory span, and at the same time to follow the moving target at their own individual maximum tracking speed. Results are illustrated in Figure 2.3. Older participants were not significantly more affected than the younger participants by the requirement to perform the two tasks concurrently compared with performing each task on its own. Moreover, the dual-task cost was around 15% to 20% relative to single task performance. This is despite the demands of the two tasks being set at the maximum ability level for each participant under single task conditions. If only a single, general purpose working memory resource was supporting performance on each of these two tasks, and each was being performed at the limits of each participant's ability, then performing both tasks together at these same levels of demand should have been virtually impossible without a very substantial overall drop in performance. Clearly this was not the case. It turned out that the Alzheimer's patients did show a very dramatic dual task cost of around 43%, much larger than that of either control group. So, the experimental design was not simply insensitive to the effects of dual task load. These results also pointed to the possibility that there is a separate function within healthy working memory that supports the performance

Digit recall accuracy (%)

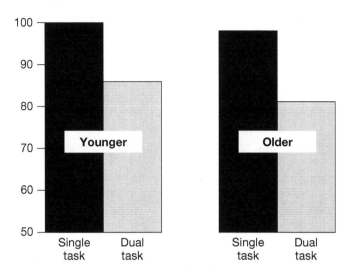

Figure 2.3 Dual task performance for digit recall as a percentage of single task (at span) performance in younger and older healthy participants.

Source: Data reproduced from Baddeley et al. (1986)

of two concurrent tasks that use different working memory components. This function appears to be damaged in Alzheimer's disease, even when taking account of impairments in the working memory functions for verbal short-term memory and for visuo-motor tracking under single task conditions.

In a study focused on healthy young participants, Cocchini et al. (2002) demonstrated a lack of a dual-task cost for healthy younger adults. Here again, the single task abilities of each individual were measured and task demands for each task were set at the span levels for each participant. In this case, serial ordered digit recall, recall of visual matrix patterns, and visuo-motor tracking were carried out as single tasks and in paired combinations. To avoid input and output conflicts, a preload procedure was used, with, for example, a span length digit sequence presented for subsequent retrieval. During a retention interval of 15 seconds, visual matrix patterns were presented for immediate recall. The complexity of the patterns was set at the previously measured span for each individual. After the retention interval the previously presented digit sequence was to be recalled. For other combinations, a preload of a matrix pattern was presented for subsequent recall with digit sequences presented for immediate recall during the interval. In other conditions, the memory tasks were combined with visuo-motor tracking or with repeating aloud an irrelevant word (articulatory suppression). When verbal memory and visual memory tasks were combined using the preload procedure, there was no impact on memory performance of either task compared with when each task was performed on its own. When each memory task was combined with articulatory suppression there was poorer performance on the verbal memory task, but not the visual memory task. When the memory tasks were combined with visuo-motor tracking, there was disruption of visual memory task performance, but not of verbal memory performance.

In a later study, Logie et al. (2004) again used the technique of initially measuring digit recall span and visuo-motor tracking span performed as single tasks by each participant, and then concurrent performance of both tasks. However, in the dual-task conditions, the demand of one of the tasks was fixed at each participant's own span while the demand of the other task was systematically decreased below span or increased above span. Results from a group of younger (20–34 years) and a group of older (63–80 years) participants for digit recall are shown in Figure 2.4. As shown in the left plot on the figure, when digit sequence length was increased with single task digit recall, then performance declined. As shown on the right plot, when digit sequence length was increased while performing visuo-motor tracking with tracking speed fixed at the maximum speed for each individual participant, then performance on digit recall again declined with increasing sequence length. However, as shown in the centre plot, when the digit sequence length was fixed at the span level for each participant, but the tracking speed was gradually increased, there was no impact on digit recall performance. The data pattern was identical when looking at tracking performance with and without concurrent digit recall: tracking performance declined when tracking demand increased, but tracking performance fixed at individual span was

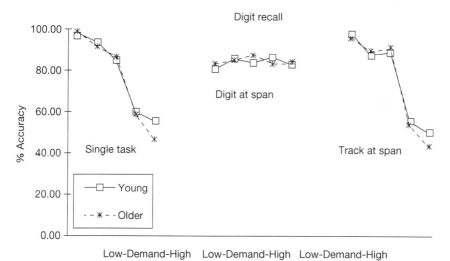

Figure 2.4 Immediate serial ordered recall of random digit sequences by younger and older healthy participants as a single task with increasing sequence length (left plot), with digit sequence length fixed at span concurrent with varying demand on a tracking task (middle plot), and with increasing sequence length concurrent with tracking fixed at tracking span (right plot)

Source: Data reproduced from Logie et al. (2004)

unaffected by changes in the demand of a concurrent digit recall task. That is, changing task demand only affected performance on the task for which demand was changed, and had no impact on performance of the concurrent task for which demand was fixed at each individual's span across trials for either age group.

There are two other important features of the data patterns depicted in Figure 2.4. First, comparing the left plot and the right plot, it is clear that digit recall performance was the same for each sequence length, regardless of whether or not people were performing a concurrent tracking task. This is also clear from the middle plot, which shows digit recall performance at a fixed sequence length (at span) for each level of tracking speed. Second, there was no difference in the performance of the younger and older participants, regardless of whether they were performing under single or dual-task conditions. That is, when dual-task demands are titrated (adjusted according to the maximum single task ability levels of each participant), and tasks are chosen to recruit different functions in working memory, then there is little or no dual task performance cost and no differential effect of dual task demands on older compared with younger healthy individuals. Therefore, the results reject the dull hypothesis by demonstrating conditions under which older people do not show poorer dual-task performance than younger people.

As with the Baddeley et al. (1986, 1991) studies, people suffering from Alzheimer's disease who took part in the Logie et al. (2004) experiments showed a substantial drop in performance under dual-task conditions, and this was true even when the demands of each task were set below the single task span for each patient. However, the Alzheimer's patients were no more sensitive to the effects of increasing single-task or dual-task demand than were the controls. That is, Alzheimer's disease is associated with a specific problem in carrying out two tasks concurrently, regardless of whether those tasks are low demand or high demand. This again points to a distinct working memory function for handling two concurrent tasks that is not simply based on overall task demand. Similar results to those found by Baddeley et al. (1986, 1991) and Logie et al. (2004) have been reported by Baddeley et al. (2001), Della Sala, Cocchini, Logie and MacPherson (2010), MacPherson et al. (2007), Ramsden et al. (2008), and Sebastian, Menor and Elosua (2006). Kilb and Naveh-Benjamin (Chapter 3 in this volume) review additional evidence consistent with these findings.

Although a detailed review is beyond the scope of this chapter, very similar results have been reported for tasks involving short-term memory for bindings of visual features. Specifically, retaining arbitrary combinations of colour and shape (e.g. a red cross, a blue circle and a green square) for periods of one or two seconds, shows little or no age-related decline in healthy adults (e.g. Brockmole & Logie, 2013; Parra et al., 2009; Parra et al., 2010a). So, as noted earlier, there is a clear age-related decline in general visual short-term memory (Brockmole & Logie, 2013; Johnson, Logie & Brockmole, 2010; Logie & Maylor, 2009), but the ability to hold temporary feature binding in working memory shows no additional effects of age over and above the ability to remember individual features. This contrasts with the well-established age-related decline in the ability to learn and retain new associations (see Kilb & Naveh-Benjamin, Chapter 3 in this volume).

So, older people can retain feature combinations for a few seconds, but have greater difficulty than younger people in learning feature combinations for longer-term retention. That is, feature binding in working memory appears to be rather different from learning of associations (see also Logie, Brockmole & Vandenbroucke, 2009), with the latter, but not the former, affected by age. Also consistent with the findings from the dual-task studies, although not affected by healthy ageing, temporary memory for arbitrary bindings of colour and shape is very severely affected in individuals suffering from, or who are likely to develop, Alzheimer's disease (e.g. Della Sala et al., 2011; Parra et al., 2009, 2010a, 2010b).

A possible reason for the apparent lack of closure or general agreement among researchers as to whether there are dual-task effects linked to healthy ageing is that many previous studies have used free recall or cued recall of word lists, and words are not repeated across lists (e.g. Naveh-Benjamin et al., 2005; see also Kilb & Naveh-Benjamin, Chapter 3 in this volume). These kinds of tasks are open to the use of elaborative semantic encoding or encoding strategies that could compensate for dual-task demands, and could do so differentially between older and younger groups. Such tasks therefore most likely engage long-term memory encoding and retrieval rather than heavy reliance on working memory. The use of random digit sequences for recall, with digits repeated in different orders across sequences in the Logie et al. (2004, 2007) studies reduces the possibility that participants use elaborative encoding strategies. It may therefore be the case that older adults have more difficulty than younger people in using elaborative encoding strategies for remembering word lists. Therefore, a task that does not lend itself to such elaborative strategies, such as recall of random digit sequences, may be less affected by age. This hypothesis gains some support from the Johnson, Logie and Brockmole (2010) finding that recall of random digit sequences is insensitive to the impact of age and appears to rely increasingly heavily on a domain-specific cognitive function that does not decline until people are well into their 70s. Johnson, Logie and Brockmole (2010) also demonstrated that tasks which showed a greater reliance on a more general cognitive ability in older people were also the tasks that showed the steepest decline across age, with that decline starting in the early 20s. So, in studies of cognitive ageing, and particularly in testing the 'dull' hypothesis, a key distinction is whether a task relies on relatively complex use of memory strategies for encoding and retrieval, and is therefore sensitive to age-related decline, or whether it relies on a single, domain-specific function in working memory that is much less sensitive to the effects of ageing.

Salthouse, Rogan and Prill (1984) argued that if individuals show slight performance differences on tasks performed on their own, they will almost certainly differ when they have to perform two tasks concurrently. By titrating tasks for individual ability levels, both age groups are performing at their own limits of ability under single-task conditions. Any changes in performance between single and dual-task conditions for either group can then be attributed specifically to the demands of performing two tasks concurrently rather than reflecting differences between groups in their ability to perform the two component tasks. Therefore, another possible source of the conflicting evidence with regard to dual-task costs and ageing is the tendency in many studies not to titrate single-task demand to allow for differences in single-task performance levels between older and younger groups. Moreover, tasks typically are selected largely on the assumption that they are placing demands on a single, limited capacity attentional resource, and that the level of demand is more important than the nature of that demand. If, instead, we assume multiple, domain-specific resources, then dual-task effects may reflect an overlap in the specific resource necessary to perform the tasks, or an increased burden on a specific resource required for dual task coordination. Likewise, a lack of age-related dual-task costs following individual titration of demand might be interpreted as reflecting the recruitment of different resources for each task, allowing parallel performance of the two tasks with little or no dual-task costs for younger or older healthy participants (e.g. Cocchini et al., 2002; Logie et al., 2004).

Dual task, ageing and processing speed

A further possible reason for the discrepancy in findings across studies is whether or not participants are required to perform a speeded response time task. It is well established that response time declines with age, starting in the early 20s (e.g. Fozard et al., 1994; Pierson & Montoye, 1958; Rabbitt, 1979). In studies of age-related dual-task costs, it is not uncommon to combine memory tasks with response time demands as a secondary task (e.g. see Naveh-Benjamin et al., 2005; Kilb & Naveh-Benjamin, Chapter 3 in this volume). In a study focused on healthy ageing, Logie et al. (2007) investigated dual-task costs when asking younger and older healthy participants to undertake immediate serial ordered verbal recall together with a response time task in which participants pressed a key as quickly as possible when a simple visual stimulus appeared. The dual-task combination avoided sensory input and output conflicts by using aural presentation and spoken recall of the digit sequences and a finger press response to a visual stimulus. Unlike in the previous dual-task studies carried out by our group, the demand of the response time task could not be adjusted to the ability of each participant, although, as before, the digit recall task demand was adjusted in this way. The main purposes of the study were to explore whether dual task costs occur with this combination of tasks, to investigate whether there are any greater dual-task costs for older than for younger people, and, when dual-task costs are observed whether they tend to occur during aural presentation of the digit sequence (i.e. encoding in memory) or during the retrieval stages of the memory task.

Logie et al. (2007) found that there was no overall effect on memory performance of carrying out a secondary response time task, and no interaction between age group and the comparison of single versus dual task. This result was consistent with previous findings of a lack of overall dual-task costs for two distinct tasks and a lack of an age-related dual-task cost. However, when memory performance was compared for concurrent response time only during encoding or only during retrieval, there was significantly poorer recall in the former than in the latter condition. This differential impact of dual task at encoding was greater for the older group than for the younger group. So, it appears that if the secondary task involves speeded responses to a visual stimulus then this disrupts encoding of aurally presented memory material and the effect of this disruption is greater for older than for younger healthy people. The analyses of the response time data showed that both groups were slower in responding under dual-task than under single-task conditions. This effect was greater under dual-task conditions at retrieval than at encoding, and greater in the older than in the younger participants. The overall pattern of data offers a contrast with previous (e.g. Baddeley et al., 1986, 1991; Logie et al., 2004) and subsequent results (e.g. Della Sala et al., 2010; MacPherson et al., 2007) showing a lack of a greater dual task cost for older participants when neither task involves speeded response times, and task demand for each task is titrated according to single-task ability for each participant.

Other studies that have investigated the effects of dual task at the encoding and retrieval phases of memory in younger and older adults (see Kilb & Naveh-Benjamin, Chapter 3 in this volume) have also found that dual-task performance during encoding disrupts the memory performance of older adults significantly more than younger adults (Park et al., 1989; Salthouse, Rogan & Prill, 1984), whereas others have not found any age-related disruption in memory performance at encoding (Anderson, Craik & Naveh-Benjamin, 1998; Naveh-Benjamin et al., 2005; Nyberg et al., 1997; Park, Puglisi & Smith, 1986; Park et al., 1987). A few studies of cognitive ageing have also reported the effects of dual task at encoding on secondary-task performance and the findings seem to suggest that secondary-task costs significantly increase with age (Anderson, Craik & Naveh-Benjamin, 1998; Duchek, 1984). Dual task at retrieval has been demonstrated to have little effect on memory performance in either younger or older adults (Anderson, Craik & Naveh-Benjamin, 1998; Macht & Buschke, 1983; Nyberg et al., 1997; Park et al., 1989), although significant age-related declines in secondary-task performance have been reported in previous studies (Anderson, Craik & Naveh-Benjamin, 1998; Craik & McDowd, 1987; Macht & Buschke, 1983), as well as by Logie et al. (2007). Naveh-Benjamin, et al. (2005) found a significant age-related dual-task impairment in a concurrent tracking task under time pressure, but only during the retrieval stages of the concurrent free recall task. Retrieval time was also slowed to a greater extent in the older adults by the requirement to undertake the tracking task. In contrast, Logie, et al. (2004) found no age-related dual-task impact on a tracking task when it was combined with concurrent recall of aurally presented digit sequences set at the span for each individual participant. Della Sala et al. (2010) reported a similar result, namely no age-related dual-task decrement in a tracking task in healthy older adults during encoding, maintenance or retrieval of a digit sequence set at the span for each participant, and when the tracking task was present throughout encoding, maintenance and retrieval of the digits. In a second experiment, Della Sala et al. (2010) required dual task only at encoding of the digit sequence, or only during a retention interval, or only during retrieval. Under these conditions, older healthy participants showed poorer tracking performance when concurrent with retention or retrieval of the digit sequence, but not when concurrent with encoding. However, when a combined measure was used to consider changes in the digit recall and changes in tracking together, there was no overall dual-task performance impairment.

An alternative approach to the study of response time under dual-task conditions was reported by Göthe, Oberauer and Kliegl (2007). This research team used a dual-tasking memory updating paradigm in which participants were presented with auditory-numerical and visual-spatial information. In the single task participants would respond to changes in either visual or auditory stimuli by selecting numbers or a specific part of the screen. In the dual-task condition participants were presented with concurrent auditory and visual information. Response times to changes were measured for both single and dual-task conditions. Efficient dual-tasking was said to be achieved when a participant's reaction time for responding to changes in simultaneously presented tasks was equal to their slowest performance on either single task. Participants were given a number of repeated trials. The authors found that the majority of younger adults reached the efficient dual-tasking stage, whereas none of the older adults did so. However, with the knowledge that we have from previous dual-task tests, it is likely that the methodology used by Göthe, Oberauer and Kliegl (2007) is actually displaying the same ability as that seen in the tasks used by Logie et al. (2004) and MacPherson et al. (2007). These studies demonstrated that some level of dual-tasking is possible, albeit with deficits in older adults when one of the tasks involved assessment of response time. However, Göthe, Oberauer and Kliegl's methodology led them to suggest that efficient dual-tasking is not possible in older adults, due to an inability in the older group to maintain single-task response times under dual-task conditions. Göthe, Oberauer and Kliegl found no effect of age on older participant's accuracy under dual-task conditions even if response times were longer, and this corresponds with the suggestions of Logie et al. (2007; see also Rabbitt, 1979) that older adults may trade speed for accuracy during dual-tasks.

Hartley, Maquestiaux & Butts (2011) used a similar paradigm to Göthe, Oberauer and Kliegl (2007) and found that within a group of eight older adults, five managed to show efficient dual-task performance as assessed from comparisons of response times in single and dual-task conditions. Both the older adults who did and those who did not demonstrate efficient dual-tasking showed significantly better auditory processing in the dual-task condition than in the single-task condition. Those who showed efficient dual-tasking did not have slower dual-task response times in the visual task. There was an increase in time taken to complete the visual task in those who did not demonstrate efficient dual-tasking. However, Hartley, Maquestiaux & Butts (2011) did not report accuracy data to allow an investigation of possible speed-accuracy trade-offs.

It therefore seems that the demands of dual-tasking at encoding can affect performance on the memory task when it is combined with a secondary-response time task, and dual task at retrieval can affect performance on a concurrent response time task. However, adjusting the task demands to the ability of each individual removes the dual-task impairment in older adults, and only when a secondary time-critical task is not or cannot be adjusted for individual ability do the age-related dual-task impairments appear. Therefore, the studies that show age-related dual-task effects might reflect the well-established general slowing of responses with increasing age, and could be explained by reference to the Salthouse,

Rogan and Prill (1984) argument that if younger and older groups differ in single-task performance then they will also differ in dual-task performance. This reinforces the need to equate single-task performance across groups by adjusting single-task demand according to the ability of each individual participant. The greater impact of response time demands on older compared with younger participants is also consistent with literature demonstrating that older adults tend to be strategic in tasks that require a speeded response, often sacrificing speed of responding in order to maintain levels of accuracy (e.g. Forstmann et al., 2011; Rabbitt, 1979).

Dual task with Visual Inspection Time

An alternative approach to examining the effect of age on processing time under dual-task conditions that would allow individual titration of demand is to use a task such as inspection time, which does not depend on a speeded response (see Deary & Stough, 1996 for a review). Here, the participant is asked to make a decision about a rapidly presented stimulus, but is not under time pressure to respond. The presentation duration of the stimulus is adjusted for each participant until they can maintain a criterion level of performance, and this can then be treated as a span for the task. In a recent study in our own laboratory (Pettit, 2014), 25 young (18–35), 25 middle-aged (36–64) and 25 older (65–85) healthy adults were asked to perform a Visual Inspection Time (VIT) task (adapted from Edmonds et al., 2008). This is a forced choice paradigm that requires participants to decide which side of a geometric figure has a longer tail. The task is illustrated in Figure 2.5a. Processing speed was investigated by manipulating the duration of the stimulus rather than recording reaction time data, thus eliminating potential confounds due to motor slowing in older people.

Participants attempted VIT trials with decreasing display duration until each individual's level of ability was established. All participants started at 85ms display time. If five out of six trials were completed accurately then VIT display duration was decreased. If participants failed more than one trial then VIT display duration was increased. Possible VIT durations were: 150ms, 125ms, 102ms, 85ms, 68ms, 51ms, 34ms, 17ms, and 10ms. The titrated level of demand was taken as the display duration which was one step longer than the shortest delay at which five out of six trials were correct. For example, if the latter was 68 ms, then the titrated display time was taken as 85 ms. Digit span was also assessed for each individual participant. All participants started with three trials, each with aural presentation and spoken recall of three random digits. On each trial, there was an unfilled delay of 15 seconds followed by oral recall of the digit sequence. If two out of three trials were recalled correctly, then the length of the digit sequence was increased by one. Titrated demand level was taken as the sequence length below the longest sequence at which two out of three trials were correct. For example, if the latter was seven digits, then the titrated demand was taken as six digits. The titrated demand levels for each task ensured that participants were performing close to their maximum levels of performance. So, we would expect a low error rate, but be confident that performance was not at ceiling. Next, participants were asked to perform each single task for eight trials at their titrated demand level, and this was followed by a dual-task condition, illustrated in Figure 2.5b.

As shown in Figure 2.5b, dual task involved a preload procedure so as to avoid input and output conflicts, following the general procedure used by Cocchini et al. (2002). During any one trial, participants were presented with digit sequences at their individually titrated span, followed immediately by 15 seconds of inspection time trials (also at titrated level). A cue then prompted recall of the digit sequences. Participants completed eight trials in total. Performance in each task was measured as described in the single task conditions and the mean percentage performance levels in single and dual task conditions for each task are shown in Table 2.1

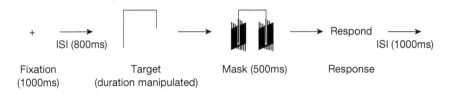

+   →   → Respond   →
    ISI (800ms)   ISI (1000ms)

Fixation   Target   Mask (500ms)   Response
(1000ms)   (duration manipulated)

Figure 2.5a The Visual Inspection Time task

Source: Pettit (2014)

Present digits   Recall digits
"2 6 4 7 1 9"   "2 6 4 7 1 9"

Titrated VIT trials – 15 secs

Figure 2.5b The procedure for combining Visual Inspection Time with a memory preload and subsequent recall of random digit sequences

Source: Pettit (2014)

Table 2.1 Mean percentage performance of younger, middle-aged and older healthy adults on digit recall and visual inspection time under single task and dual task conditions, and percentage dual task costs

	Young	*Middle*	*Older*
Digit Recall Single	97.5 (3.9)	98.1 (4.2)	96.1 (4.7)
VIT Single	95.0 (5.3)	95.3 (3.5)	91.4 (5.4)
Digit Recall Dual	94.4 (7.4)	93.7 (9.7)	89.0 (7.0)
VIT Dual	89.3 (9.4)	84.5 (12.6)	83.1 (7.2)
Digit Recall cost	3.2 (7.7)	4.5 (9.6)	7.3 (7.5)
VIT cost	6.1 (7.0)	11.3 (13.2)	8.9 (8.1)
Combined cost	4.7 (6.3)	7.9 (7.9)	8.1 (5.7)

Source: Pettit (2014)

The key question is whether the cost of dual-task demands varied across the three age groups. Dual-task cost was calculated following the formula used by Cocchini et al. (2002) and Logie et al. (2004) shown below:

$$\text{Percentage change} = \frac{\text{Dual task \% correct} - \text{Single task \% correct}}{\text{Single task \% correct}} \times 100$$

This formula ensures that each participant acts as their own control for comparing dual-task and single-task performance, and so provides a pure measure of dual-task cost that removes any differences between the groups in single-task performance. Finally, we also calculated a combined dual-task cost by taking the mean percentage cost across the two task types. The percentage dual-task cost for each task and the combined dual-task cost are shown in Table 2.1. An analysis revealed that the groups did not differ in the level of dual-task cost: Digit Recall $F(2.72) = 1.58$, $p = 0.213$; VIT $F(2.72) = 1.74$, $p = 0.183$, Combined $F(2.72) = 2.1$, $p = 0.134$.

Note that the scores shown in Table 2.1 arise from levels of task demand that are titrated to be challenging for each individual participant, and so high scores indicate the maximum performance that the participants can achieve; they do not indicate ceiling levels of performance or that participants could perform very much better if the task were to be made more challenging. Therefore, the lack of an age-related increase in dual-task cost cannot be interpreted by suggesting that the two tasks were simply too easy for the participants to perform. These results extend the previous findings showing that there is no age-related dual-task cost even when a memory task is combined with a task that involves demanding rapid cognitive processing but without requiring a speeded response. So, this offers a clear demonstration of rejecting the dull hypothesis.

Age differences in mental ability or in cognitive strategy?

Hartley, Maquestiaux and Butts (2011) reported that some older adults could maintain their speed of responding for an auditory-verbal task under dual-task compared with single-task conditions if they were given practice on the tasks and the two tasks avoided input and output conflicts. However, they had more difficulty with maintaining response speed for a visual task under dual-task conditions. Participants were explicitly told when they had achieved effectively parallel processing under dual-task conditions, and so would have been aware of the need to perform as efficiently as possible. They were also given a financial incentive to do so. Clearly they were able to automate some aspects of the auditory-verbal task or use some alternative strategy that allowed them to maintain their response speed. This fits with the findings from Johnson et al. (2010) and Park et al. (2002), suggesting that performance on tasks designed to test visuo-spatial short-term memory abililty declines with age much more rapidly than does performance on tasks designed to assess verbal short-term memory.

Johnson et al. (2010) showed further that a test widely used to assess visual short-term memory appears to rely more heavily on some general mental ability in older people than in younger people. Brown et al. (2012) found that visual short-term memory in older adults was associated with processing speed, spatial working memory and IQ adjusted for age. The link with IQ adds to the evidence that visual tasks rely on general mental ability in older people, and is consistent with the hypothesis that older people are attempting to use a range of strategies to perform the task, possibly in order to compensate for the decline in their visual short-term memory ability. However, those strategies appear to become less and less effective as people get older. Therefore, could the poorer performance of older compared with younger adults on some tasks reflect the use of a non-optimal strategy by the older group rather than reflecting the operation of a declining specific ability that those tasks were designed to assess? That is, do older and younger people perform the same tasks in qualitatively different ways? For example, older people might attempt to use verbal recoding of the visually presented patterns that happen to resemble familiar shapes or objects. Participants who use this strategy could maintain performance above floor with correct recall of the patterns that are easy to name, but generate poor overall performance because many of the patterns might not resemble a familiar shape and be very difficult to name, or naming some patterns might take more time than is available for each test item. The Brown et al. (2012) association between visual short-term memory and speed of processing in older adults is consistent with this latter possibility.

Related evidence was reported by Fox and Charness (2010) who found that performance of older but not younger adults on the Ravens Matrices task was improved by verbalisation. The concept of verbal recoding of visuospatial information by older adults has also been suggested by Bopp and Verhaegen (2007). They found that older adults performed more poorly than younger adults in both accuracy and response time measures in a visuospatial secondary task. Within their discussion they speculate on the possibility of verbal recoding being the basis for this increase. This is dismissed by the authors who suggest that the response times seen in older adults would not be long enough to allow for this recoding. However, Brown, Forbes and McConnell (2006) provided some evidence that verbal recoding might be used in visual memory tasks in a study with younger adults, in which the visual patterns were selected as being hard to name or easy to name. It was found that scores were significantly higher for the easy to name shapes. Therefore, participants in the Bopp and Verhaegen study would only have to use verbal recoding for those patterns which they could name rapidly for this to be viable basis for performance on some of the trials, whereas for other trials, participants might continue to attempt to retain the patterns as a visual representation (for a similar argument see Broadbent & Broadbent, 1981). Preliminary studies in our own laboratory have suggested that the positive effect of 'nameability' might be even stronger for older adults, although nameable patterns might also be easy for older and younger people to encode semantically if the patterns happen to depict recognisable objects, and we are currently exploring this possibility.

Other evidence that participants can maintain performance levels while using alternative strategies for a task comes from studies of individuals who have suffered cognitive impairments as a result of damage to the function of specific brain networks. For example, Zeman et al. (2010) reported the case of an older individual (MX – a retired building surveyor age 65) who developed a sudden complete loss of visual imagery. When asked to perform a visual mental imagery task in an fMRI study, he showed a dramatically different network of prefrontal cortical activation compared with age-matched and occupation-matched controls (surveyors and architects), who reported no loss of imagery and who showed more posterior activation for the same task. MX also failed to show the relationship between angle of rotation and time to respond typically found for mental rotation tasks and found in the control participants for this study. Nevertheless, MX performed at a high level of accuracy on all the visual processing, visual memory, and visual mental imagery tasks he was asked to perform. It appeared that he was using a combination of verbal, semantic and perceptual strategies to maintain performance levels despite his specific cognitive impairment in visual imagery.

A related functional neuroimaging study with younger healthy adults performing mental rotation (Logie et al., 2011) has shown that people who report poor imagery tend to show longer response times, and a steeper slope in the response time/angle of rotation plot than do people who report using vivid visual imagery in their daily lives. The two groups also generate activation patterns that overlap but are clearly different when performing mental rotation in fMRI. So, even among younger people, different individuals may perform the same tasks in different ways (see also Zacks, 2008).

There is further evidence to suggest that verbal recoding of visual information does occur in younger adults. Brandimonte, Hitch and Bishop (1992) found that the use of articulatory suppression to prevent sub-vocal recoding during mental image transformations improved the performance of younger adults. They also found that when use of a verbal code was encouraged, articulatory suppression had a negative effect on performance in the transformation task. In a different paradigm that involved visual presentation with written recall of sequences of English words and letters by English speakers and Japanese kanji characters by Japanese speakers, Saito et al. (2008) and Logie et al. (2000) showed that participants used visual codes as well as phonological codes to remember visually presented verbal sequences. This could also be true for a task that was designed to measure visual short-term memory, and that is open to the use of different strategies across trials for the same individual as well as between groups of individuals. The use of alternative strategies has also been demonstrated for tasks designed to assess verbal short-term memory with some participants showing evidence of using visual or semantic codes for retaining verbal sequences (Logie et al., 1996). In sum, individuals can and do recode information in ways that are not explicitly being tested. This also points to possible inherent behaviour to recode information that could be a factor in all visuospatial tasks, for younger as well as older adults.

Given this evidence that people of different ages perform tasks in ways that the tasks were not designed to assess, and the evidence that verbal abilities increase or are maintained across the lifespan compared with visual abilities, it appears reasonable to suggest that people might become more reliant on verbal and/or semantic recoding of visual material as they grow older.

An approach to formalising the use of strategies by older people has been proposed by Park and Reuter-Lorenz (2009) who are developing the Scaffolding Theory of Ageing and Cognition (STAC). They suggest that neural scaffolding is a process of healthy ageing that involves the development of compensatory and alternate neural circuitry to achieve cognitive goals within the ageing mind (for a similar argument see Baltes & Baltes, 1990; see also Nagel & Lindenberger, Chapter 6 in this volume). The essence of STAC is that as we age 'more' is required to do 'less'. The authors note that this compensatory recruitment is not purely the preserve of the ageing brain. It is suggested that the older adult's response to the intrinsic challenge of ageing is the same as a younger adult's response to the extrinsic challenge of increasing task difficulty (e.g. see Parra et al., 2014). Both cases result in the adaptive, but increasingly inefficient recruitment of multiple systems to perform tasks. Reuter-Lorenz, Stanczak and Miller (1999) showed that older adults increased bilateral processing at lower task demands than younger adults. STAC suggests that this highlights the recruitment of additional circuitry needed to shore up declining structures, the functions of which have become inefficient.

Conclusions

It appears that there is a broad range of evidence for rejecting the 'dull hypothesis' of cognitive ageing, that older adults perform more poorly than younger adults on any cognitive task or task combination. Under some circumstances, and on some tasks, older healthy people can generate levels of performance that are similar to those observed in younger adults. Until people reach advanced old age, there appears to be little or no age-related decline in verbal short-term memory. There also appears to be no age-related dual-task cost when the demands of the individual single tasks are titrated according to the ability of each participant, when tasks are chosen to require the use of different components of working memory, and neither of the tasks requires a speeded response. That is, older people are no more disrupted by dual-task requirements in working memory than are younger people, provided the older person is not under time pressure. It appears that previously observed age-related impairments in dual-task processes may be explained by the use of tasks that were not titrated according to the ability of each participant, or use of tasks that require speeded manual responses, or involve tasks such as free recall that rely more heavily on long-term memory rather than working memory for encoding and retrieval. It also appears that previous studies that have shown age-related dual-task impairments have been designed on the assumption that there is a single, general purpose, limited capacity working memory system constrained by attentional capacity. These studies therefore focus on the level of overall cognitive demand rather than the nature of the demand. We have argued in this chapter that the nature of the demand is crucial, as is the need to manipulate demand according to the measured ability of each individual participant. When studies are designed to allow for the possibility that there are multiple, domain-specific components of working memory, and demand is titrated for each individual, it appears that healthy older people are not at a disadvantage.

We have also reviewed evidence of variation among participants in the strategies that they use to perform cognitive tasks, and the fact that older adults may use different strategies than younger people when performing the same tasks. So, when comparing the cognitive performance of different age groups it seems crucial to investigate how the different groups are attempting to meet the task requirements. The qualitative differences in cognition between groups could provide a great deal more insight into the nature of age-related cognitive change than the scores obtained on tests or the degree of common variance across tests. There does appear to be increasing evidence that older people might attempt to use verbal recoding for tests designed to assess non-verbal ability, and this offers one possible explanation as to why older people might perform at equivalent levels to their younger counterparts. A related account could draw on the well-established finding that crystallised intelligence tends to increase during adulthood and be maintained in old age, allowing the use of highly practiced or automated cognitive skills that can support performance on some tasks.

Clearly, many aspects of cognition do decline as people get older, but there are several cognitive abilities that are relatively insensitive to the ageing process. Several components of a multiple-component working memory appear to be among those cognitive functions indicating that growing older is not wholly commensurate with cognitive decline.

References

Anderson, J. H. (1978). Arguments concerning representations for mental imagery. *Psychological Review, 85*, 249–277.

Anderson, N. D., Craik, F. I. & Naveh-Benjamin, M. (1998). The attentional demands of encoding and retrieval in younger and older adults: 1. Evidence from divided attention costs. *Psychology and Aging, 13*, 405–423.

Baddeley, A. D. (2007). *Working Memory, Thought, and Action*. Oxford, United Kingdom: Oxford University Press.

Baddeley, A. D. & Logie, R. H. (1999). Working memory: The multiple component model. In A. Miyake & P. Shah (Eds.), *Models of Working Memory* (pp. 28–61). New York: Cambridge University Press.

Baddeley, A. D., Baddeley, H. A., Bucks, R. S. & Wilcock, G. K. (2001). Attentional control in Alzheimer's disease. *Brain, 124*, 1492–1508.

Baddeley, A. D., Bressi, S., Della Sala, S., Logie, R. H. & Spinnler, H. (1991). The decline of working memory in Alzheimer's disease: A longitudinal study. *Brain, 114*, 2521–2542.

Baddeley, A., Logie, R., Bressi, S., Della Sala, S. & Spinnler, H. (1986). Senile dementia and working memory. *Quarterly Journal of Experimental Psychology, 38A*, 603–618.

Baltes, P. B. & Baltes, M. M. (1990). Psychological perspectives on successful aging: The model of selective optimization with compensation. In P. B. Baltes & M. M. Baltes (Eds.), *Successful Aging: Perspectives from the Behavioral Sciences*. Cambridge, UK: Cambridge University Press (pp. 1–34).

Barrouillet, P., Bernardin, S. & Camos, V. (2004). Time constraints and resource sharing in adult's working memory spans. *Journal of Experimental Psychology: General, 33*, 570–585.

Bopp, K. L. & Verhaeghen, P. (2007). Age-related differences in control processes in verbal and visuospatial working memory: Storage, transformation, supervision, and coordination. *Journals of Gerontology: Series B. Psychological Sciences and Social Sciences, 62*, 239–246.

Borst, G., Niven, E. H. & Logie, R. H. (2012). Visual mental image generation does not overlap with visual short-term memory: A dual task interference study. *Memory and Cognition, 40*, 360–372.

Brandimonte, M. A., Hitch, G. J. & Bishop, D. V. M. (1992). Verbal recoding of visual stimuli impairs mental image transformations. *Memory & Cognition, 20*(4), 449–455.

Broadbent, D. E. & Broadbent, M. H. P. (1981). Recency effects in visual memory. *Quarterly Journal of Experimental Psychology, 33A*, 1–15.

Brockmole, J. R. & Logie, R. H. (2013). Age-related change in visual working memory: A study of 55,753 participants aged 8 to 75. *Frontiers in Perception Science, 4*(12). doi: 10.3389/fpsyg.2013.00012

Brown, L. A., Forbes, D. & McConnell, J. (2006) Limiting the use of verbal coding in the Visual Patterns Test. *Quarterly Journal of Experimental Psychology, 59*(7), 1169–1176.

Brown, L. A., Brockmole, J. R., Gow, A. J. & Deary, I. J. (2010). Processing speed and visuo-spatial executive function predict visual working memory in older adults. *Experimental Aging Research, 38*, 1–19.

Cocchini, G., Logie, R. H., Della Sala, S., MacPherson, S. E. & Baddeley, A. D. (2002). Concurrent performance of two memory tasks: Evidence for domain-specific working memory systems. *Memory & Cognition, 30*, 1086–1095.

Cowan, N. (2005). *Working Memory Capacity*. Hove, UK: Psychology Press.

Craik, F. I. & McDowd, J. M. (1987). Age differences in recall and recognition. *Journal of Experimental Psychology: Learning, Memory, and Cognition, 13*, 474–479.

Deary, I. J. & Stough, C. (1996). Intelligence and inspection time: Achievements, prospects, and problems. *American Psychologist, 51*, 599–608.

Deary, I. J., Batty, G. D. & Gale, C. R. (2008). Bright children become enlightened adults. *Psychological Science, 19*, 1–6.

Deary, I. J., Whalley, L. J. & Starr, J. M. (2009). *A Lifetime of Intelligence: Follow-Up Studies of the Scottish Mental Surveys of 1932 and 1947*. Washington, DC: American Psychological Association.

Deary, I. J., Yang, J., Davies, G., Harris, S. E., Tenesa, A., Liewald, D., Luciano, M., Lopez, L. M., Gow, A. J., Corley, J., Redmond, P., Fox, H. C., Rowe, S. J., Haggarty, P., McNeill, G., Goddard, M. E., Porteous, D. J., Whalley, L. J., Starr, J. & Visscher, P. M. (2012). Genetic contributions to stability and change in intelligence from childhood to old age. *Nature, 482*(7384), 212–215.

Della Sala, S., Cocchini, G., Logie, R. H. & MacPherson, S. E. (2010). Dual task during encoding, maintenance and retrieval in Alzheimer's disease and healthy ageing. *Journal of Alzheimer's Disease, 19*, 503–515.

Della Sala, S., Foley, J. A., Beschin, N., Allerhand., M. & Logie, R. H. (2010). Assessing dual-task performance using a paper-and-pencil test: Normative data. *Archives of Clinical Neurology, 25*, 410–419.

Della Sala, S., Foley, J. A., Parra, M. A. & Logie, R. H. (2011). Dual tasking and memory binding in Alzheimer's. *Journal of Alzheimer Disease, S23*, 22–24.

Duchek, J. M. (1984). Encoding and retrieval differences between young and old: The impact of attentional capacity usage. *Developmental Psychology, 20*, 1173–1180.

Edmonds, C. J., Isaacs, E. B., Visscher, P. M., Rogers, M., Lanigan, J., Singhal, A., Lucas, A., Gringras, P., Denton, J. & Deary, I. J. (2008). Inspection time and cognitive abilities in twins aged 7 to 17 years: Age-related changes, heritability and genetic covariance. *Intelligence, 36*, 21–225.

Emerson, M. J. & Miyake, A. (2003). The role of inner speech in task switching: A dual-task investigation. *Journal of Memory and Language, 48*, 148–168.

Forstmann, B. U., Tittgemeyer, M., Wagenmakers, E.-J., Derrfuss, J., Imperati, D. & Brown, S. (2011). The speed-accuracy trade off in the elderly brain: A structual model-based approach. *The Journal of Neuroscience, 31*, 17242–17249.

Fox, M. C. & Charness, N. (2010). How to gain eleven IQ points in ten minutes: Thinking aloud improves Raven's Matrices performance in older adults. *Aging, Neuropsychology, and Cognition, 17*(2), 191–204.

Fozard, J. L., Vercruyssen, M., Reynolds, S. L., Hancock, P. A. & Quilter, R. E. (1994). Age differences and changes in reaction time: The Baltimore longitudinal study of aging. *Journal of Gerontology, 49*, 179–189.

Göthe, K., Oberauer, K. & Kliegl, R. (2007). Age differences in dual-task performance after practice. *Psychology and Aging, 22*, 596–606. doi: 10.1037/0882-7974.22.3.596

Gow, A., Johnson, W., Pattie, A., Whiteman, M., Whalley, L. J., Starr, J. M. & Deary, I. J. (2008). Mental ability in childhood and cognitive aging. *Gerontology, 54*, 177–186.

Hartley, A. A., Maquestiaux, F. & Butts, S. (2011). A demonstration of dual-task performance without interference in some older adults. *Psychology and Aging, 26*(1), 181–187. doi: 10.1037/a0021497

Johnson, W., Logie, R. H. & Brockmole, J. R. (2010). Working memory tasks differ in factor structure across age cohorts: Implications for dedifferentiation. *Intelligence, 38*, 513–528.

Li, S., Lindenberger., U. & Sikstrom, S. (2001). Aging cognition: From neuromodulation to representation to cognition. *Trends in Cognitive Sciences, 5*, 479–486.

Logie, R. H. (1986). Visuo-spatial processing in working memory. *Quarterly Journal of Experimental Psychology, 38A*(2), 229–247.

Logie, R. H. (1995). *Visuo-Spatial Working Memory*. Hove, UK: Erlbaum.

Logie, R. H. & Maylor, E. A. (2009). An Internet study of prospective memory across adulthood. *Psychology and Aging, 24*, 767–774.

Logie, R. H. & Niven, E. H. (2012). Working memory: An ensemble of functions in on-line cognition. In V. Gyselinck and F. Pazzaglia (Eds.), *From Mental Imagery to Spatial Cognition and Language. Essays in Honour of Michel Denis* (pp. 77–105). Hove, UK: Psychology Press.

Logie, R. H. & van der Meulen, M. (2009). Fragmenting and integrating visuo-spatial working memory. In J. R. Brockmole (Ed.), *The Visual World in Memory* (pp. 1–32). Hove, UK: Psychology Press.

Logie, R. H., Brockmole, J. R. & Vandenbroucke, A. (2009). Bound feature combinations in visual short-term memory are fragile but influence long-term learning. *Visual Cognition, 17*, 160–179.

Logie, R. H., Cocchini, G., Della Sala, S. & Baddeley, A. (2004). Is there a specific executive capacity for dual-task coordination? Evidence from Alzheimer's disease. *Neuropsychology, 18*, 504–513.

Logie, R. H., Della Sala, S., Laiacona, M., Chalmers, P. & Wynn, V. (1996). Group aggregates and individual reliability: The case of verbal short-term memory. *Memory and Cognition, 24*(3), 305–321.

Logie, R. H., Della Sala, S., MacPherson, S. E. & Cooper, J. (2007). Dual-task demands on encoding and retrieval processes: Evidence from healthy adult ageing. *Cortex, 43*, 159–169.

Logie, R. H., Della Sala, S., Wynn, V. & Baddeley, A. D. (2000). Visual similarity effects in immediate verbal serial recall. *Quarterly Journal of Experimental Psychology, 53A*, 626–646.

Logie, R. H., Pernet, C. R., Buonocore, A. & Della Sala, S. (2011). Low and high imagers activate networks differentially in Mental Rotation. *Neuropsychologia, 49*, 3071–3077.

Macht, M. L. & Buschke, H. (1983). Age differences in cognitive effort in recall. *Journal of Gerontology, 38*, 695–700.

MacPherson, S. E., Della Sala, S., Logie, R. H. & Wilcock, G. K. (2007). Specific AD impairment in concurrent performance of two memory tasks. *Cortex, 43*, 858–865.

Maylor, E. A. & Logie, R. H. (2010). A large-scale comparison of prospective and retrospective memory development from childhood to middle age. *Quarterly Journal of Experimental Psychology, 63*, 442–451.

Miyake, A., Friedman, N. P., Emerson, M. J., Witzki, A. H., Howerter, A. & Wager, T. D. (2000) The unity and diversity of executive functions and their contributions to complex "frontal Lobe" tasks: A latent variable analysis. *Cognitive Psychology, 41*(1), 49–100.

Naveh-Benjamin, M., Craik, F. I. M., Guez, J. & Kreuger, S. (2005). Divided attention in younger and older adults: Effects of strategy and relatedness on memory performance and secondary costs. *Journal of Experimental Psychology: Learning, Memory, and Cognition, 31*, 520–537.

Nyberg, L., Nilsson, L.-G., Olofsson, U. & Backman, L. (1997). Effects of division of attention during encoding and retrieval on age differences in episodic memory. *Experimental Aging Research, 23*, 137–143.

Park, D. C. & Reuter-Lorenz, P. A. (2009). The adaptive brain: Ageing and neurocognitive scaffolding. *Annual Review Psychology, 60*, 173–196.

Park, D. C., Puglisi, J. T. & Smith, A. D. (1986). Memory for pictures: Does an age-related decline exist? *Psychology and Aging, 1*, 11–17.

Park, C., Lautenschlager, G., Hedden, T., Davidson, N. S., Smith, A. D. & Smith, P. K. (2002). Models of visuospatial and verbal memory across the adult life span. *Psychology and Aging, 17*(2), 299–320. doi: 10.1037/0882-7974.17.2.299

Park, D. C., Puglisi, J. T., Smith, A. D. & Dudley, W. (1987). Cue utilization and encoding specificity in picture recognition by older adults. *Journal of Gerontology, 42*, 423–425.

Park, D. C., Smith, A. D., Dudley, W. N. & Lafronza, V. N. (1989). Effects of age and a divided attention task presented during encoding and retrieval on memory. *Journal of Experimental Psychology: Learning, Memory, and Cognition, 15*, 1185–1191.

Parra, M. A., Abrahams, S., Fabi, K., Logie, R., Luzzi, S. & Della Sala, S. (2009). Short-term memory binding deficits in Alzheimer's Disease. *Brain, 132*, 1057–1066.

Parra, M. A., Abrahams, S., Logie, R. H. & Della Sala, S. (2010a). Visual short-term memory binding in Alzheimer's disease and depression. *Journal of Neurology, 257*, 1160–1169.

Parra, M. A., Abrahams, S., Logie, R. H., Mendez, L. G., Lopera, F. & Della Sala, S. (2010b). Visual short-term memory binding deficits in Familial Alzheimer's Disease. *Brain, 133*, 2702–2713.

Parra, M. A., Della Sala, S., Logie, R. H. & Morcom, A. (2014). Neural correlates of shape-color binding in visual working memory. *Neuropsychologia, 52C*, 27–36.

Perfect, T. J. & Maylor, E. A. (2000). Rejecting the dull hypothesis: The relation between method and theory in cognitive aging research. In T. J. Perfect & E. A. Maylor (Eds.), *Models of Cognitive Aging.* Oxford: Oxford University Press.

Pettit, L. (2014). White matter integrity, executive dysfunction, and processing speed in Amyotrphic Lateral Sclerosis. Unpublished PhD thesis, University of Edinburgh, UK.

Pierson, W. R. & Montoye, H. J. (1958). Movement time, reaction time, and age. *Journal of Gerontology, 13*, 418–421.

Rabbitt, P. (1979). How old and young subjects monitor and control responses for accuracy and speed. *British Journal of Psychology, 70*, 305–311.

Ramsden, C. M., Kinsella, G. J., Ong, B. & Storey, E. (2008). Performance of everyday actions in mild Alzheimer's disease. *Neuropsychology, 22*, 17–26.

Reuter-Lorenz, P. A., Stanczak, L. & Miller, A. (1999). Neural recruitment and cognitive ageing: Two hemispheres are better than one especially as you age. *Psychological Science, 10*, 494–500.

Salthouse, S. (1996). The processing-speed theory of adult age differences in cognition. *Psychological Review, 103*, 403–428.

Salthouse, T. A. (1998). Independence of age-related influences on cognitive abilities across the life span. *Developmental Psychology, 34*, 851–864.

Salthouse, T. A. Steps toward the explanation of adult age differences in cognition. Models of cognitive aging. In Perfect, T. J. & Maylor, E. A. (Eds.) (2000). *Models of Cognitive Aging: Debates in Psychology* (pp. 19–49). New York: Oxford University Press.

Salthouse, T. A., Rogan, J. D. & Prill, K. A. (1984). Division of attention: Age differences on a visually presented memory task. *Memory & Cognition, 12*, 613–620.

Saito, S., Logie, R. H., Morita, A. & Law, A. (2008). Visual and phonological similarity effects in verbal immediate serial recall: A test with kanji materials. *Journal of Memory and Language, 59*, 1–17.

Sander, M. C., Werkle-Bergner, M. & Lindenberger, U. (2011). Binding and strategic selection in working memory: A lifespan dissociation. *Psychology & Aging, 26*(3), 612–624.

Sebastian, M. V., Menor, J. & Elosua, M. R. (2006). Attentional dysfunction of the central executive in AD: Evidence from dual task. *Cortex, 42*, 1015–1020.

van der Meulen, M., Logie, R. H. & Della Sala, S. (2009). Selective interference with image retention and generation: Evidence for the workspace model. *Quarterly Journal of Experimental Psychology, 62*, 1568–1580.

Wilson, R. S., Beckett, L. A., Barnes, L. L., Schneider, J. A., Bach, J., Evans, D. A. & Bennett, D. A. (2002). Individual differences in rates of change in cognitive abilities of older persons. *Psychology & Aging, 17*, 179–193.

Zacks, J. M. (2008). Neuroimaging studies of mental rotation: A meta analysis and review. *Journal of Cognitive Neuroscience, 20*, 1–19.

Zeman, A., Della Sala, S., Torrens, L., Gountouna, E., McGonigle, D. & Logie, R. H. (2010). Loss of imagery phenomenology with intact visual imagery performance. *Neuropsychologia, 48*, 145–155.

3 The effects of divided attention on long-term memory and working memory in younger and older adults

Assessment of the reduced attentional resources hypothesis

Angela Kilb and Moshe Naveh-Benjamin

What causes age-related memory decline?

Even though both anecdotal evidence and systematic research indicate that memory abilities decline with age, there is currently no definitive explanation for what causes such deficits. Over the years, several theoretical explanations have been provided, including (but not limited to) reduced speed of processing (Salthouse, 1996), reduced processing resources (Craik, 1982, 1983), reduced inhibition (Zacks & Hasher, 1994), reduced binding/associative ability (Naveh-Benjamin, 2000), failures of metamemory, semantic deficits, and impairment of deliberate recollection (Jennings & Jacoby, 1993; see Old & Naveh-Benjamin, 2008a, for a review).

In this chapter, we will primarily focus on the reduced (attentional) processing resources explanation by reviewing representative studies from relevant research on divided attention in younger and older adults and the resulting memory performance in tasks reflecting both long-term memory (LTM) and working memory (WM). We will first elucidate studies that attempt to simulate aging effects by placing younger adults under divided attention (DA), and then determine whether older adults are more affected by DA than younger adults.

Craik's reduced processing resources hypothesis and divided attention simulations in younger adults

As mentioned above, one prominent explanation of age-related changes in cognition in general, and memory in particular, is the reduced (attentional) processing resources hypothesis, suggested by Fergus Craik (1982, 1983). According to this hypothesis, older adults do not have as many available processing resources as younger adults, leading to less efficient encoding and retrieval of information. In one way of testing this hypothesis, younger adults can be required to perform two simultaneous tasks – one that involves memory and an unrelated secondary task whose purpose is to experimentally reduce the processing resources that would ordinarily be devoted to the memory task. For instance, one common secondary task is digit monitoring, which entails listening to a series of numbers and responding when a particular target string is heard (e.g. three consecutive odd digits); this might be performed while visually encoding a list of words. As discussed below, several studies were conducted to assess whether adding a secondary task makes younger adults under divided attention conditions (young-DA) perform similarly to older adults under full attention.

Tasks reflecting LTM performance: DA at encoding as a simulation of older adults' declined attentional resources

The similarity between LTM performance of a young-DA group and older adults under full attention has been observed in a diverse assortment of methodologies. Rabinowitz, Craik & Ackerman (1982) in which unique aspects of the context are integrated with the target item, requires a substantial amount of attentional resource but that the core semantic features of words are encoded relatively automatically. Thus, under conditions of reduced processing resource, a general, stereotyped encoding is predicted. The effectiveness of general, categorical retrieval cues was compared to the effectiveness of contextually specific retrieval cues in 3 experiments with 84 undergraduates and 60 elderly (approximately 66–69 yrs old found that older adults were less successful than young adults in cued recall when the cues matched the originally studied material, but the groups performed equally well when non-studied semantic cues were presented at test, indicating that older adults tend to encode information in a more general way, whereas their younger counterparts encode context-specific information. Such reliance on gist-based processing was mimicked in younger adults when they carried out a simultaneous digit monitoring task at encoding. Likewise, Anderson et al. (2000) showed impairment in cued recall for young-DA and old under full attention compared to young in full attention conditions. Jennings & Jacoby (1993) provided evidence for similar contextual deficits in an adapted recognition paradigm. Participants were asked to discriminate between moderately famous names and non-famous names that were repeatedly shown prior to the test. Whereas younger adults under full attention had little difficulty in this task, young-DA and older adults under full attention had trouble distinguishing between names that previously had been learned outside of the laboratory and names that were first encountered in the context of the experiment, demonstrating a "false fame" effect for repeated, non-famous names. Repetition was also seen to interfere with remembering contextual information in the DRM false memory paradigm, which requires participants to discriminate between studied items and closely related (but not studied) lures (see Roediger & McDermott, 1995, for the procedure). With repetition, young-DA and older adults under full attention produced more false recollections, signifying their confusion between the context-specific and gist-based information, whereas young adults under full attention had reduced false recollections with repetition. Taken together, these findings illustrate that dividing attention at encoding reduces younger adults' ability to encode contextual details, likening them to older adults.

In a different line of research, Chen & Blanchard-Fields (2000) demonstrated that in contrast to younger adults under full attention conditions, both young-DA and older adults under full attention are less able to inhibit the encoding of irrelevant information. Participants read criminal reports but were told to ignore all words displayed in a red font. Critically, the words in red changed the tone of the passage (e.g. "Tom was *shouting obscenities at pedestrians* while hitching a ride" or "Tom was *stopping to chat with some old friends* while hitching a ride"). When later asked to recommend a prison term, young-DA and older adults allowed the irrelevant information to affect their judgments, but the young under full attention did not.

Tasks reflecting LTM performance: DA at retrieval as a simulation of older adults' declined attentional resources

Other studies have supported Craik's hypothesis by focusing on retrieval. Jacoby, Woloshyn & Kelley (1989) found that DA at retrieval elicited a false fame effect in younger adults that was larger than that observed under full attention and similar to that observed in older adults, indicating that recollection can be impaired by DA at retrieval as well as DA at encoding. Similarly, Troyer et al. (1999) in comparison with item memory, is more sensitive to frontal lesions and may require more strategic processing. Divided attention was used to restrict attentional resources and strategic processing on memory tasks. Participants encoded and retrieved items (i.e., words divided the attention of younger adults at retrieval to show a greater impairment in source memory for voice and spatial location than in item recognition. Since it has been shown separately that age differences are larger for context than focal information (Spencer & Raz, 1995), this is yet another situation in which young-DA and older adults under full attention demonstrate similar memory performance patterns. Extending these results, Luo & Craik (2009) showed that older adults have a particular deficit in source memory when discriminating between similar sources. Specifically, older adults had a larger impairment in deciding whether a word was earlier presented with a photo or with a line drawing compared to deciding between a picture and a word shown alone. These researchers then showed that this pattern can also be seen in younger adults when attention is divided at retrieval. Evidence from these studies suggests that source memory tests require a substantial amount of processing resources, which seems to be lacking in both older adults and young-DA groups.

A related aspect of Craik's attentional resources hypothesis is that older adults have fewer processing resources to expend on demanding memory tests that require a great deal of "self-initiated processing" (e.g. free recall). Instead, they must rely on environmental support (i.e. cues) in order to meet the performance level of younger adults. Given Craik's ideas about the necessity of environmental support for older adults, we can make some predictions about the expected age differences as a function of cue type. For example, item recognition involves more environmental support than cued recall, which provides more support than free recall. Therefore, we should expect the smallest age differences in item recognition and the largest age differences in free recall. As predicted, Craik & McDowd (1987) with recognition performance as the covariate, showed a reliable age decrement in recall. It was therefore concluded that older people perform more poorly on recall tasks than they do on recognition tasks. Performance on the secondary reaction time observed no age differences in an item recognition test, despite an age-related impairment in cued recall (see left panel of Figure 3.1). In order to assess whether the processing demands were the same for each test, participants were asked to perform a secondary task during retrieval. The secondary task "costs" of completing a memory task can be calculated as the difference between performance in the baseline and DA conditions of the secondary task, where a higher cost reflects a more demanding memory task. Craik & McDowd showed higher secondary task costs for cued recall than recognition, in younger and especially in older adults, indicating that cued recall is particularly resource-demanding for older adults (see right panel of Figure 3.1).

Additional perceptual cues beyond the reinstatement of a studied item can further enhance older adults' memory. Naveh-Benjamin & Craik (1995) presented younger and older adults with words in different contexts (different fonts or different voices) to show that old benefited at least as much as young in word recognition when words were shown in the same perceptual context compared to a different one. This is in line with the notion that by providing the original context at retrieval as environmental support, older adults do not need to use self-initiation processes that require substantial processing resources at retrieval, resulting in as good a memory performance as that of younger adults. Craik & Schloerscheidt

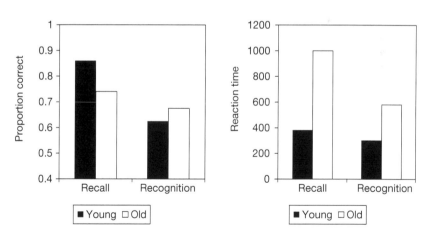

Figure 3.1 Left panel: Cued recall scores (proportion correct) and recognition scores (hits minus false alarms) as a function of age. Right panel: RT costs (in milliseconds; mean dual-task RT minus mean baseline RT) as a function of age and retrieval task

Source: Reproduced from Craik & McDowd (1987). Reprinted with permission from APA.

(2011) reported similar results when presenting both age groups with words in the context of unrelated landscape pictures. At test, participants were asked to recognize the words when shown in the same or a different context, and older adults showed more sensitivity to context changes than did younger adults. These studies further support Craik's notion that older adults' memory deficits are the result of reduced processing capacity, which is required for effective encoding and retrieval.

There are, however, some studies that do not seem to be directly in line with the claim that older adults' memory decline is due to reduced attentional resources at retrieval. For example, while the results of Naveh-Benjamin & Craik (1995) as well as Craik & Schloerscheidt (2011) indicate that older adults are less impaired in item recognition when the context is reinstated at test, both studies also included explicit associative tests requiring participants to remember the word-context combinations. If older adults can take advantage of contextual reinstatement in the item test, then they should also show spared performance in the explicit associative test. However, their performance on the associative test was impaired relative to younger adults (in line with an age-related associative memory deficit hypothesis, see below). One possibility is that younger adults can use their abundant processing resources to bind together individual pieces of information (e.g. a word and a context), whereas older adults lack the resources necessary for binding. We will examine this possibility in the section below.

Can reduced resources explain the associative deficit of older adults?

Craik's notion of environmental support makes specific predictions about age differences in item recognition, cued recall, and free recall. However, Naveh-Benjamin (2000; Experiment 4) found that older adults were actually more impaired in cued recall than free recall tasks for unrelated pairs, despite cued recall providing more environmental support (see Figure 3.2). An alternative way of categorizing these tasks is in terms of their need for binding. Both item recognition and free recall require that a word is bound to the studied context, but cued recall requires another layer of binding in order to associate the cue word with its target. Accordingly, Naveh-Benjamin's results were interpreted as evidence for the associative deficit hypothesis – the notion that age differences in memory are due to a decline in the ability to encode and retrieve links between unrelated pieces of information. The major evidence for this hypothesis comes from studies in which young and old participants learned unrelated word pairs and later received item and associative recognition tests (e.g. see Naveh-Benjamin, 2000; Experiment 2). While item tests include old and new words and ask which words were studied, associative tests only include studied words, appearing either in old or recombined pairs, and ask which pairs were studied. Because associative tests require more binding than item tests, the associative deficit hypothesis predicts greater age differences in associative tests. Several sets of studies confirm this prediction (Kilb & Naveh-Benjamin, 2007; Naveh-Benjamin, 2000; Naveh-Benjamin, Brav & Levy, 2007; Naveh-Benjamin et al., 2003; Old & Naveh-Benjamin, 2008b; see a meta-analysis by Old & Naveh-Benjamin, 2008c).

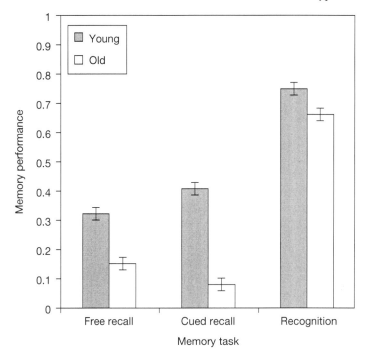

Figure 3.2 Proportion of hit rates in the free-recall and cued-recall tests and proportion of hits minus false alarm rates in the recognition test (± *SEs*) for the younger and older participants

Source: Reproduced from Naveh-Benjamin (2000; Experiment 4). Reprinted with permission from APA.

Since Craik's reduced processing hypothesis has been shown to explain a wide variety of age-related memory differences, an interesting question in the context of the topic discussed in this chapter is whether reduced processing may mediate older adults' binding deficit. In other words, encoding and retrieving associations may require more processing resources than encoding and retrieving individual items, causing older adults to display an associative deficit. To test this hypothesis, a young-DA group was again used for comparison, but in the context of the associative deficit paradigm – i.e. separate item and associative recognition tests. Findings show that dividing the attention of younger adults at encoding indeed reduced memory performance; however, it did not reduce their associative memory more than item memory (see Figure 3.3), thereby demonstrating that older adults have a unique deficit in binding beyond a reduction in processing resources (Kilb & Naveh-Benjamin, 2007; Naveh-Benjamin et al., 2004; Craik, Luo & Sakuta, 2010; for similar results in a WM paradigm, see Cowan et al., 2006). The fact that DA does not cause differential binding deficits in the young is in line with the suggestion that older adults' binding deficit might be somewhat

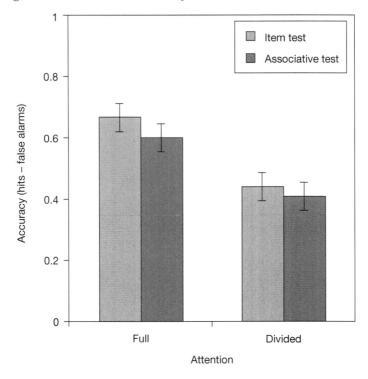

Figure 3.3 Mean memory accuracy as a function of attention and test

Source: Reproduced from Kilb & Naveh-Benjamin (2007). Reprinted with permission of The Psychonomic Society.

automatic and mediated by hippocampal structures (see Naveh-Benjamin, 2000, for a more detailed explanation).

Interestingly, newer findings from Kelly Giovanello's laboratory did identify cases in which DA impaired associative memory more than item memory. Kim and Giovanello (2011) gave younger adults two separate DA tasks while learning unrelated word pairs. In the item DA task, participants either identified which of two faces was male (Experiment 1) or identified which of two digits was odd (Experiment 2). In order to disrupt associative processing, the respective relational DA tasks required participants to choose which of two faces was older or which of two digits was larger. In both experiments, all DA tasks equally affected item memory, but the relational DA tasks reduced associative memory significantly more than the item DA tasks did, simulating the pattern seen in older adults. This latter result provides some evidence that even older adults' associative deficit may be tied to their having reduced processing resources once we consider declines in specific domain-based resources rather than declines in a pool of general resources. For example, Kim & Giovanello (2011) suggest that older adults have reduced resources in relational processing (but not item processing), which may explain their binding deficit.

Overall, the majority of studies reveal that reducing the processing resources of younger adults can simulate the patterns seen in older adults' long-term memory performance (e.g. Rabinowitz, Craik & Ackerman, 1982), supporting the suggestion that older adults' available cognitive/attentional resources are more limited than those of younger adults and that this reduction contributes to their memory deficits. However, reduced resources cannot fully explain all of older adults' memory deficits, especially those related to their associative memory decline (e.g. Kilb & Naveh-Benjamin, 2007). While the experiments performed by Kim & Giovanello (2011) show promise in specifying the type of processing necessary for carrying out particular tasks, future research is needed to investigate this notion further.

Age-related memory differences under divided attention

While some earlier work on DA and aging did not involve memory tasks, it can still help us understand how older adults' processing resources compare to those of younger adults. For example, Somberg & Salthouse (1982) asked younger and older adults to type visually presented numbers while completing a tone-response task (i.e. press a key as soon as a tone is heard). It was no surprise that older adults performed more slowly than the young overall, but no age differences were found in the effect of DA on task accuracy or in the effect on reaction times (after adjusting for older adults' slower baseline performance). Baddeley et al. (1986) observed similar effects of DA for young and old on tracking performance when they were asked to follow a moving target with a cursor while carrying out a tone-response task or articulatory suppression. In contrast, McDowd & Craik (1988) found larger age differences in reaction time under DA when participants performed two continuous reaction time tasks (one visual and one auditory). A meta-analysis reported by Verhaeghen et al. (2003) indicates that older adults are typically no more impaired by DA than are younger adults when measuring their accuracy; however, they are more impaired than younger adults when looking at latency measures. Interestingly, this pattern is somewhat mirrored in studies of memory performance, as we will see below.

Based on the above DA studies (which are not limited to memory), it seems that there is at least some additional evidence for older adults having reduced processing resources, as suggested by Craik. Next, we will turn to studies involving memory processing for further clarification.

Divided attention effects: The asymmetry between encoding and retrieval in younger adults

In our own work, we have focused primarily on the effects of DA in the context of LTM, and it became clear that different results could be seen depending on whether attention was divided during encoding or retrieval. Baddeley et al. (1984)

were among the first to highlight a dissociation between results based on paradigms involving DA at encoding and DA at retrieval. In a series of nine experiments using middle-aged women, participants viewed words and completed free recall tests. To divide their attention, they simultaneously performed a card sorting task or digit recall during either encoding or retrieval. The results show that dividing attention at encoding consistently impaired memory performance, whereas dividing attention at retrieval did not. However, dividing attention at retrieval still had a negative impact on memory performance by lengthening retrieval latency (i.e. the time it takes for a participant to respond to a test probe), though dividing attention at encoding did not. Years later, Craik et al. (1996) published a series of experiments designed to further observe and understand the dissociation between DA at encoding and DA at retrieval, using several methodological advances. The results showed that divided attention at encoding (DAF) conditions produced a substantial impairment to memory performance relative to full attention (FF), while divided attention at retrieval (FDA) was associated with only a minimal impairment, if any. However, examination of performance on the secondary task yielded the opposite pattern – now larger impairments were the result of FDA conditions when compared to baseline and DAF (for free recall tests in particular).

One possibility is that even though participants were explicitly asked to pay equal attention to each task, they may have allocated their attention differently between encoding and retrieval, giving priority to the secondary task during encoding and to the primary task during retrieval. However, further investigation by Craik et al. (1996) ruled out this possibility by providing participants with three different instruction conditions pertaining to the amount of attention to be directed toward each task (equal emphasis, memory emphasis, and secondary task emphasis) and showed predictable trade-offs in their dual-task performance when attention was divided at encoding. When attention was divided at retrieval, the results were not in line with a trade-off pattern: secondary task performance predictably decreased with increased memory emphasis, but memory performance was unaffected by the instructions (see Figure 3.4). These results seem to suggest that memory retrieval is somewhat automatic; however, it still takes a substantial toll on secondary task performance, creating even higher secondary task costs for FDA than DAF conditions relative to baseline, suggesting that retrieval is obligatory rather than automatic.

A few studies indeed showed a large impact of FDA on memory performance when the secondary task required similar processing to the primary memory task. Fernandes & Moscovitch (2002) manipulated whether the secondary task was verbal or pictorial and found a substantially larger decline in word recall when paired with the verbal secondary task that required phonological processing, suggesting that retrieval is not obligatory and that material-specific interference creates a deficit beyond any arising from the combination of two unrelated tasks (see also Fernandes & Guild, 2009). These findings are somewhat consistent with those of Kim & Giovanello in that resources may be domain-specific, and impairments are observed when the primary and secondary tasks require the same types of processing.

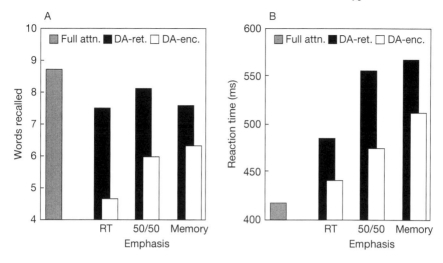

Figure 3.4 (A) Numbers of words recalled (free recall) under conditions of full attention (Full Attn.) and divided attention at retrieval (DA-Ret.) and encoding (DA-Enc.). Instructions emphasized the reaction-time (RT) task, the memory task, or both tasks equally (50/50). (B) Performance on the continuous RT task under full and divided attention conditions

Source: Reprinted from Craik et al. (1996). Reprinted with permission of APA.

Taken together, these findings suggest that both encoding and retrieval are resource-demanding processes. Dual-task conditions elicit impaired performance in one or both tasks when attention is divided at encoding and retrieval, particularly when the type of information in each task is highly similar. We will turn now to studies that include older adults when dividing attention at encoding and retrieval.

Are older adults more impaired by divided attention than young adults when memory tasks are used?

Given Craik's (1982, 1983) notion that older adults have fewer processing resources than younger adults, we might expect them to be more impaired by divided attention than younger adults. Earlier, we observed that a young-DA group can sometimes simulate older adults' memory deficits, but we have not yet assessed how older adults behave under divided attention during memory tasks. In the following sections, we will investigate both DAF and FDA conditions to determine whether or not older adults are more impaired than younger adults when attention is divided.

Age-related differences under divided attention at encoding

One prediction is that if encoding is under conscious control and older adults have fewer available processing resources, then we would see greater impairments of DA at encoding on memory performance for older than younger adults. Past research has established that age differences are relatively large for controlled processes. For example, in a meta-analysis investigating age differences in the ability to divide attention, Riby, Perfect & Stollery (2004) concluded that older adults were much more impaired in tasks that require conscious effort (e.g. episodic memory) compared to tasks that are more automatic (e.g. perceptual tasks). Therefore, we might expect to see greater effects of divided attention for older than younger adults for DAF compared to full attention conditions.

However, studies involving aging have been somewhat inconsistent in terms of the effect of DA at encoding on memory performance. Anderson, Craik & Naveh-Benjamin (1998) replicated the findings from Craik et al. (1996), displaying an asymmetry between encoding and retrieval, and included a group of older adults to show that older adults were no more impaired by DAF than their younger counterparts in free recall, cued recall, or recognition (see Figure 3.5, left panel). Converging evidence comes from a number of studies using different paradigms. For example, Nyberg et al. (1997) had 1,000 participants learn words for later recall while sorting cards and reported that age was not a significant predictor of dual-task performance when examined using hierarchical regression. Evidence also shows that older adults are no more impaired under DAF conditions than young adults when learning pictures with a simultaneous digit monitoring task (Park, Puglisi & Smith, 1986). More recently, Naveh-Benjamin et al. (2005) showed equal impairments in cued recall for young and old when learning word pairs while tracking a moving target, and Kilb & Naveh-Benjamin (2007) found no greater effects of DA at encoding for older than younger adults on item or associative recognition tests. All of these results indicate that older adults' memory performance is no more affected by DA at encoding than that of younger adults.

In contrast, several studies have found that older adults are *more* impaired by DA at encoding than young adults. Park et al. (1989) showed a larger impairment for old in free and cued recall tests after learning words with digit monitoring as the secondary task. One possible explanation for the discrepancy between the results of this study and those described above is that the participants in this study were asked to focus their attention on the digit monitoring task, further reducing the attention paid to the learning task; however, Anderson, Craik and Naveh-Benjamin (1998) manipulated such instructions and showed no greater age-related effect of attention when either the primary or secondary task was emphasized. Also, Li et al. (2001) and Lindenberger, Marsiske & Baltes (2000) showed greater effects of DA for old than young on a memory task when encoding was done while walking around a track (relative to while standing), probably because older adults were more concerned about protecting their walking performance, allowing word learning to suffer. This explanation will be examined again below, when describing secondary task performance at encoding.

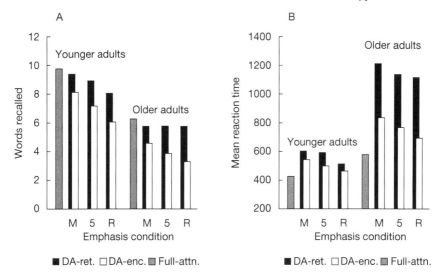

Figure 3.5 (A) Number of words recalled (free recall) under conditions of full attention (Full-Attn.), divided attention at encoding (DA-Enc.), and divided attention at retrieval (DA-Ret.). Instructions emphasized the memory task (M), the reaction time task (R), or the two tasks equally (5). (B) Performance on the reaction time task under full and divided attention conditions

Source: Reproduced from Anderson, Craik & Naveh-Benjamin (1998). Reprinted with permission of APA.

Beyond factors specific to some of the studies described above, one possible explanation for the discrepancy between studies showing no age differences in the effect of DAF on memory performance and those that show greater impairments for older adults might be a methodological one. The work of Somberg and Salthouse (1982) illustrates the importance of comparing task costs to a baseline in order to obtain relative scores since age differences often exist in single-task conditions. These researchers showed that older adults had a higher absolute cost than young adults (measured as the difference between single-task and dual-task performance). Critically, though, their *relative* cost was equivalent to younger adults, as measured by each individual's absolute cost divided by their own single-task score. While this procedure has been widely adopted in the examination of secondary task costs in different domains, the standard way of reporting memory impairment in the literature is in absolute scores, which does not take into consideration age-related differences under full attention. However, if there are any age differences in memory performance under full attention conditions, it could impact the interpretation of performance under DA conditions. For example, let us assume that under full attention conditions a younger adult group scored 8/10 on average, and an older group scored 6/10 on a memory test. When attention is divided, both scores are reduced by two points. In absolute terms, it seems that the reductions are equivalent; however, the scores decreased by 25% and 33% for young and old, respectively, demonstrating that older adults' DA impairment is larger than that of younger adults in relative terms, considering their full attention baseline memory performance levels.

Some researchers have already looked at relative memory accuracy. For example, after Fernandes and Grady (2008) reported no age differences in the effect of DA at retrieval on absolute scores, they turned to percentage decline in memory (a relative score) and determined that older adults were more impaired than young adults in certain situations. To investigate the possibility that age differences in the effect of DA at encoding will emerge when examining relative scores, we looked at all the experiments that appear in the top portion of Table 3.1 (N = 13), which provided enough information to assess memory performance effect sizes (using Cohen's d) in younger and older adults under full and divided attention, and we calculated both absolute and relative decline scores under divided attention at encoding. As Figure 3.6 shows, both types of scores showed only slightly larger declines under DA in older adults than in younger ones (see Figure 3.6, A and B for absolute and relative scores, respectively), and in both cases the 95% confidence intervals overlapped, indicating no significant differences between younger and older adults. While these calculations are based on relatively few studies, they do not clearly show larger age-related declines under DA at encoding than under full attention.

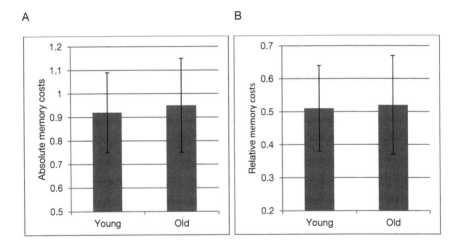

Figure 3.6 LTM-divided attention at encoding. (A) Absolute memory costs for young and old, calculated as the difference between full and divided attention memory performance divided by the estimated standard deviations of the two groups. (B) Relative memory costs for young and old calculated as the difference between full and divided attention memory performance divided by full attention performance, which is then divided by the estimated standard deviations of the two groups for the studies in Table 3.1 that used divided attention at encoding. Error bars represent 95% confidence intervals

Table 3.1 Studies assessing LTM-divided attention at encoding, LTM-divided attention at retrieval, and WM-divided attention

Category	Article reference
LTM-divided attention at encoding	Kilb & Naveh-Benjamin (2007); Experiment 1
	Kilb & Naveh-Benjamin (2007); Experiment 2
	Li, Lindenberger, Freund & Baltes (2001)
	Light & Prull (1995); Experiment 1
	Light & Prull (1995); Experiment 2
	Lindenberger, Marsiske & Baltes (2000)
	Naveh-Benjamin, Craik, Guez & Kreuger (2005)
	Park, Puglisi & Smith (1986)
	Park, Smith, Dudley & Lafronza (1989); Experiment 1
	Park, Smith, Dudley & Lafronza (1989); Experiment 2
	Puglisi, Park, Smith & Dudley (1988)
	Schmitter-Edgecombe (1999)
	Tun, Wingfield & Stine (1991)
LTM-divided attention at retrieval	Fernandes & Grady (2008)
	Fernandes & Moscovitch (2003)
	Fernandes, Pacurar, Moscovitch & Grady (2006)
	Mellinger, Lehman, Happ & Grout (1990)
	Naveh-Benjamin, Craik, Guez & Kreuger (2005)
	Park, Smith, Dudley & Lafronza (1989); Experiment 1
	Park, Smith, Dudley & Lafronza (1989); Experiment 2
	Skinner & Fernandes (2008)
	Veiel & Storadt (2003); Experiment 1
	Veiel & Storadt (2003); Experiment 2
	Veiel & Storadt (2003); Experiment 3
WM-divided attention	Brown & Brockmole (2010)
	Knott, Harr & Mahoney (1999)
	Logie, Cocchini, Della Sala & Baddeley (2004); Experiment 2
	Logie, Della Sala, MacPherson & Cooper (2007); Experiment 1
	Logie, Della Sala, MacPherson & Cooper (2007); Experiment 2
	MacPherson, Della Sala, Logie & Wilcock (2007)

Turning now to age differences in secondary task costs when attention is divided at encoding, the majority of studies seem to suggest larger secondary task costs for older than for younger adults (e.g. Anderson, Craik & Naveh-Benjamin, 1998; Kilb & Naveh-Benjamin, 2007; Lindenberger, Marsiske & Baltes, 2000; Naveh-Benjamin et al., 2005). A representative study of those showing such larger costs in older adults is the one by Naveh-Benjamin et al. (2005), who used a tracking secondary task in which younger and older participants learned unrelated word pairs or completed a cued recall task while following a constantly moving target. Accuracy on the secondary task was measured as the distance between the moving target and the cursor, which was recorded every 20 ms, allowing for a micro-level analysis. Although there were no differential age-related differences in cued recall under dual task conditions, secondary task performance indicated that the attentional costs were larger in older than in younger adults (see Figure 3.7, left panel), and this was particularly so as participants continuously processed the pairs under instructions to use an elaborative encoding strategy (see Figure 3.7, right panel).

At least one study (Li et al., 2001) shows no age differences in attentional costs during encoding. One possible explanation for such a result (mentioned earlier) is that older adults prioritize the tasks differently, depending on their demands. In Li et al. (2001), younger and older participants were asked to memorize a list of words using a mnemonic strategy while walking on a track. Although there were no greater age differences in walking performance when attention was divided, DA impaired the memory performance of older adults more than the young, suggesting that older adults prioritized the secondary task, presumably since avoiding a fall is more important to them than failing to encode a word. Although it seems reasonable that older adults would prioritize their secondary task

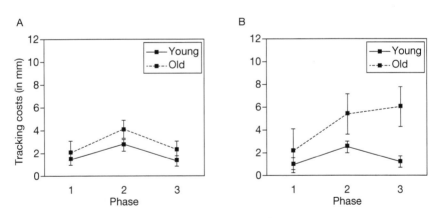

Figure 3.7 Temporal distribution of performance on the secondary tracking task for younger and older adults for the three phases of the encoding period in the no-strategy (A) and strategy (B) conditions, aggregated over 6-s encoding segments after subtraction of single-task tracking performance (distance in millimeters)

Source: Reproduced from Naveh-Benjamin et al. (2005). Reprinted with permission of APA.

performance in such a situation, Lindenberger, Marsiske and Baltes (2000) reported greater age differences in walking performance when using a very similar paradigm in addition to greater memory costs, indicating age-related declines in both tasks rather than a trade-off between them.

Overall, the age differences in dual-task costs associated with encoding seem to indicate larger secondary task costs in older adults with no such differential costs in memory performance. In the following section, we will discuss age differences associated with retrieval.

Age-related differences under divided attention at retrieval

The predicted patterns associated with DA at retrieval for young and old may be expected to depend on task demands. For example, it has been found that DA at retrieval in younger adults impairs source memory more than item memory (Troyer et al., 1999) and recollection more than familiarity (Jacoby, Woloshyn & Kelley, 1989), and is impaired more by material-specific interference than by an unrelated secondary task (Fernandes & Guild, 2009; Fernandes & Moscovitch, 2002). Thus, one possibility is that only retrieval tasks that elicit memory impairments in younger adults will further impair older adults' memory performance. This is not necessarily the case. There is a general lack of studies examining DA in older adults that are directly analogous to the especially demanding retrieval tasks mentioned above, but we can at least explore the findings using material-specific interference. Myra Fernandes and her colleagues have repeatedly shown that older adults are no more impaired by material-specific interference than younger adults, even when looking at relative scores (Fernandes & Grady, 2008; Fernandes & Moscovitch, 2002; Fernandes et al., 2006; Skinner & Fernandes, 2008). However, at least one study shows a greater impairment in old for DA at retrieval. While investigating material-specific interference, Fernandes & Grady (2008) also looked at whether unrelated or categorizable words would be more affected by DA. No differences could be observed for younger adults, but older adults were more affected by both word- and digit-based secondary tasks for categorizable rather than unrelated words. The authors concluded that older adults do not have the necessary processing resources required to engage in organizational strategies at retrieval.

In general, researchers report either no age differences on memory accuracy due to the effect of DA at retrieval (Craik & Naveh-Benjamin, 1998; Fernandes et al., 2006; Logie et al., 2007) or very minimal differences (Naveh-Benjamin et al., 2005). However, as mentioned earlier in the context of DA at encoding, studies assessing age-related differences under DA at retrieval mostly do so in absolute scores. To investigate the possibility that age differences in the effect of DA at retrieval will emerge when examining relative scores, we looked at all the studies in the middle portion of Table 3.1 that provided enough information to assess memory performance effect sizes (using Cohen's d) in younger and older adults under full and divided attention at retrieval (N = 11) and calculated both absolute and relative decline scores. The results indicated no differential effects of DA at retrieval in younger and older adults, either for absolute scores (Figure 3.8, left panel) or for relative scores (Figure 3.8, right panel), as in both cases the 95% confidence intervals overlapped.

As we have already seen from Craik et al. (1996), the larger impact of DA at retrieval is typically shown on the secondary task rather than the memory task, and extensive evidence demonstrates that this effect is amplified in older adults. More specifically, both age groups have slowed reaction times to the secondary task during retrieval, but older adults' slowing is more severe than for the young, even after adjusting for baseline levels (Anderson, Craik & Naveh-Benjamin, 1998 [see Figure 3.5, right panel]; Fernandes et al., 2006; Kilb & Naveh-Benjamin, 2007; Logie et al., 2007; McDowd & Craik, 1988; Salthouse, Rogan & Prill, 1984; Tun, McCoy & Wingfield, 2009; Whiting & Smith, 1997, but see Fernandes & Grady, 2008).

As an alternative to looking at reaction times, Naveh-Benjamin & Guez (2000) investigated secondary task costs through the use of a tracking task. While other researchers had already used tracking tasks to divide attention (e.g. see Baddeley et al., 1986), Naveh-Benjamin and Guez devised a sophisticated way of examining the costs of different stages of retrieval. As mentioned earlier, younger participants learned unrelated word pairs or completed a cued recall task while following a constantly moving target. Accuracy on the secondary task was measured as the distance between the moving target and the cursor, which was recorded every 20ms, allowing for a micro-level analysis. In addition to replicating the asymmetry of

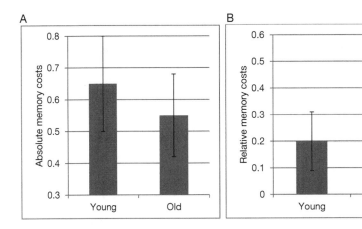

Figure 3.8 LTM-divided attention at retrieval. (A) Absolute memory costs for young and old, calculated as the difference between full and divided attention memory performance divided by the estimated standard deviations of the two groups. (B) Relative memory costs for young and old calculated as the difference between full and divided attention memory performance divided by full attention performance, which is then divided by the estimated standard deviations of the two groups for the studies in Table 3.1 that used divided attention at retrieval. Error bars represent 95% confidence intervals

encoding and retrieval and showing that the effects of FDA are limited to secondary task costs, they separated retrieval into three stages: (1) perception and encoding of the cue word, (2) cue elaboration or search for the target word, and (3) time between successful retrieval and the next cue. They found that the source of the secondary task costs was limited to the cue elaboration/search phase, implicating that as the primary resource-demanding aspect of retrieval.

Naveh-Benjamin et al. (2005) later explored age differences in memory performance when a tracking task was used as the secondary task. Attention was divided during retrieval using a similar procedure as Naveh-Benjamin and Guez (2000). As seen in several earlier studies, age differences under DA were limited to secondary task costs. After the three stages of retrieval were segmented, greater costs were seen for older adults in all stages, with the largest cost occurring in stage 2 (cue elaboration/search – see Figure 3.9, left panel). Moreover, older adults showed larger tracking task impairments relative to the young when asked to use a strategy (e.g. sentence generation or mental imagery – see Figure 3.9, right panel), suggesting that compensatory mechanisms associated with effortful strategies during retrieval require more resources for old than young, which is in agreement with the work of Fernandes & Grady (2008).

To summarize age differences under DA, most studies reflect only small differences in the effects of DA on memory performance, whether attention is divided at encoding or at retrieval. The age differences in DA appear, however, when looking at secondary task performance. Most studies show larger age-related secondary task costs at encoding, and older adults consistently show larger costs for DA at retrieval than younger adults.

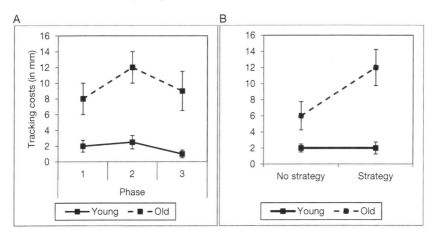

Figure 3.9 Temporal distribution of performance on the secondary tracking task for younger and older adults (A) for the three phases of the retrieval period for successful retrievals, and (B) in the no-strategy and strategy conditions, aggregated over 6-s retrieval segments after subtraction of single-task tracking performance (distance in millimeters)

Source: Reproduced from Naveh-Benjamin et al. (2005). Reprinted with permission of APA.

Why are age differences in DA largely limited to secondary task costs?

Overall, there is a general asymmetry between encoding and retrieval such that DAF impairs memory performance, and FDA impairs secondary task performance in both younger and older adults. Interestingly, behavioral evidence does not suggest that this pattern is the outcome of a trade-off between the memory and secondary tasks, especially when attention is divided at retrieval (Anderson, Craik & Naveh-Benjamin, 1998; Craik et al., 1996).

Since encoding and retrieval each require processing resources, it is somewhat surprising that older adults do not always show a greater impairment to memory performance from DAF when compared to younger adults, particularly since they consistently show a greater disadvantage in secondary task costs at retrieval. Several possibilities might explain these results. The first possibility is that older adults typically prioritize their memory performance under DA, which produces a larger secondary task cost than that of the younger adults. Just as older adults might prioritize walking performance over memory in order to avoid falling (Li et al., 2001), they might prioritize memory performance over a reaction time task to avoid social stigma regarding their poor memory and ensure an appropriate level of performance in a memory task. Research on stereotype threat identifies negative stereotypes surrounding aging as one of the sources of older adults' memory impairments (e.g. Hess, Emery & Queen, 2009). In other words, societal beliefs that older adults have poor memories can create increased anxiety for older adults when performing a memory task, which will cause them to prioritize this task. Although findings indicate that older adults' increased stereotype threat is associated with decreased memory performance (Chasteen et al., 2005; Hess et al., 2003; Hess, Emery & Queen, 2009), no study has investigated how stereotype threat might affect DA performance. In proposing prioritized memory performance, it might be argued that the results described earlier are not in line with a trade-off in task performance for both younger and older adults (Anderson, Craik & Naveh-Benjamin, 1998); however, a trade-off does not necessarily implicate full symmetrical mobility of resources between two tasks. It might be the case that older adults prioritize the memory task (especially under test conditions at retrieval), resulting in larger secondary task costs, which constitutes an asymmetrical trade-off.

A second possibility for the observed pattern of performance under DA is that age differences in DA tasks are merely a function of age differences in the speed of processing. Since it has been largely shown that older adults display reduced processing speed compared to younger adults (Salthouse, 1996), perhaps it should be no surprise that the biggest age decrement for DA is in a measure of reaction time (i.e. the length of time that is required to respond to the secondary task). This was seen in studies of DA at retrieval (e.g. Anderson, Craik & Naveh-Benjamin, 1998) as well as in a meta-analysis of DA performance that was not limited to memory tasks (Verhaeghen et al., 2003). Perhaps older adults are capable of doing everything that younger adults can do, only at a slower rate. If they require more time than the young in the primary memory task, then they have less time to devote to the secondary task. Similarly, the performance decline in the tracking task used by Naveh-Benjamin et al. (2005) possibly reflects the fact that older adults needed more time to retrieve the information, and hence were slower to react to changes in the position of the moving target, resulting in larger distance measures in this task.

At a different level of analysis, it might be that older adults use less efficient neural mechanisms to retrieve information under DA than younger adults, resulting in slower reaction times in the secondary task. Evidence from neuroimaging research supports the notion that younger and older adults approach memory tasks differently. Cabeza (2002, 2004) argues for a Hemispheric Asymmetry Reduction in Older Adults (known as the HAROLD model). Younger adults typically show lateralized brain activation when performing various tasks (e.g. verbal WM), but older adults have activation in both brain hemispheres for the same tasks (see also Fernandes et al., 2006; Madden et al., 1999). Such increases in activation for older adults have been linked to increased memory performance. Cabeza et al. (2002) studied the brain activation of younger adults, high-functioning older adults, and low-functioning older adults at retrieval with the prediction than only the high-functioning older adults would show bilateral activity. This is precisely what was observed during a source memory test showing no behavioral differences between the young and the high-functioning old group. Davis et al. (2008) extended this work and specified the posterior-anterior shift in aging (PASA), signified by an age-related decrease in occipitotemporal activity combined with an increase in frontal activity at retrieval. Critically, this age-related shift to increased frontal activation was positively correlated with word recognition memory. These findings clearly indicate that the increased frontal activation observed in older adults is a compensatory mechanism. Although such patterns of activation may minimize age differences on a memory task, it may also cause less efficient processing that incurs a greater secondary task cost at encoding and retrieval. Further research is needed to determine the validity of the above explanations or whether additional explanations are better suited for the observed general lack of age differences in long-term memory tasks performed under DA, coupled with an increase in secondary task costs, especially at retrieval.

In conclusion, we have summarized the results of DA tasks as they pertain to aging and long-term memory. Although Craik's reduced processing hypothesis predicts greater dual-task costs in older than younger adults, these costs are not consistently seen in memory performance. However, older adults were reliably more impaired than younger adults in the costs associated with various secondary tasks, especially at retrieval.

The effects of divided attention on Working Memory tasks

Compared to the literature on long-term memory, there have been many fewer studies looking either at (1) whether the effects of divided attention in young adults mimic the performance of older adults in WM tasks or (2) whether the effects of DA in WM tasks are larger for older than for younger adults. This is especially so for tasks that assessed storage and maintenance of information in WM.

To address the former, Cowan et al. (2006) included a young-DA group to simulate older adults' WM performance in a change detection task. Their results indicated some similarity between young-DA and older adults, though reducing younger adults' attentional resources could not fully explain the differential patterns shown by older adults in item and associative memory. In a different paradigm, Naveh-Benjamin et al. (2007) had young, young-DA, and older adults view short lists of word pairs for immediate serial recall and again showed only partial similarity between young-DA and older adults. Murphy et al. (2000) also presented participants with words for immediate serial recall. In the full attention version, the words were presented auditorily without any background noise; under DA conditions, the words to be learned were presented along with babble to be ignored. Their results showed that the memory performance of younger adults in the noise condition very closely matched the results of older adults in the quiet condition.

Several studies addressed the second issue, examining whether older adults are more affected by DA than their younger counterparts in WM paradigms, and most of them showed results consistent with the findings from LTM. For example, Baddeley et al. (1986) used a serial digit recall task based on each participant's own span size but did not show greater memory impairments for a healthy group of older adults than young adults when attention was divided with a tracking task throughout the encoding, maintenance, and retrieval periods. Likewise, MacPherson et al. (2007) used serial digit recall (also adjusted for span size) with tracking, visual pattern recall, or articulatory suppression as the secondary task during the maintenance phase (after digits were encoded but before they were retrieved) and found effects of DA on memory accuracy but no greater impairment of DA in older adults than young adults for any of the task combinations.

A study that looked at the ability to retain information in WM in the context of a dual-task procedure that showed somewhat different results was conducted by Logie et al. (2007), who paired an auditory digit span task with a visual simple RT task (which was manipulated separately at encoding and retrieval). Results of Experiment 1 were only partially consistent with the LTM literature. As seen in studies described earlier, older adults demonstrated greater secondary task costs than the young adults when attention was divided at retrieval (and to some degree at encoding, too), even when baseline performance was equated across age groups. However, older adults were now also affected more than the young adults in their memory performance under divided attention at encoding. Experiment 2 of this report manipulated the difficulty of the secondary task and indicated similar results. Logie et al. claim that their age-related DA effect at encoding may be related to the fact that the single digits to be learned did not allow older participants to use compensatory strategies, unlike many of the LTM studies. Alternatively, the differential age-related effect under DA at encoding might be related to the use of a verbal WM paradigm that requires rote rehearsal, which might be more easily disrupted in the old by the secondary task than in other paradigms. Another feature of this study is that each participant's digit span was individually assessed prior to the experimental trials and span score determined the level of difficulty for the primary task, placing each participant at their breaking point in the full attention conditions before adding a secondary task and making the digits especially difficult for older adults to remember under dual-task conditions (but see above for similar procedures). Finally, the results can also be due to the nature of the serial recall task itself, which involves memory for temporal order information – a type of memory shown to be especially disrupted in older adults (Naveh-Benjamin, 1990).

One potential reason for the differences between the above results and those reported by Logie et al. (2007) is that each of the studies that do not show greater impairment in WM for older adults under DA accounted for baseline performance in the secondary tasks at the individual level, whereas Logie et al.'s study did not. That is, each participant's secondary task performance was evaluated, and the subsequent conditions were designed according to each participant's ability level, thereby experimentally equating baseline secondary performance for all individuals. Given that single-task performance was equated between the age groups for both the memory *and* secondary task, this set of studies allows for a more precise measure of task coordination. In contrast, Logie et al. (2007) observed age differences in baseline performance for the secondary task. To equate the age groups, they compared older adults in an easier secondary task condition to younger adults in a harder condition, but such an adjustment is necessarily made at the group level rather than the individual level, unlike the WM studies showing no age differences (for further discussion see Chapter 2 in this volume).

Using a different primary and secondary task altogether, Brown and Brockmole (2010) also found no greater age differences under DA conditions in a WM paradigm. Participants counted backwards during the encoding, maintenance, and retrieval of a visual working memory task requiring participants to learn colored shapes. After testing participants on the colors, shapes, and color-shape associations, the researchers found that younger and older adults' memory performance were equally impaired by DA; furthermore, no age differences were observed in secondary task speed or accuracy. Although participants' baseline secondary task performance was not reported, individuals counted backwards at their own pace, allowing them to make adjustments for their own ability level under dual-task conditions. These findings are consistent with the argument that age differences in the effect of DA are not observed in WM when older adults are not already impaired in baseline secondary task conditions.

To investigate the effects of DA on WM performance in younger and older adults, we computed effect sizes (using Cohen's d) for both absolute and relative scores for studies that provided enough information to assess memory performance in younger and older adults under full and divided attention (N = 8, see bottom portion of Table 3.1). As shown in studies addressing LTM, the results indicated no differential effects of DA on WM performance in younger and older adults, either for absolute scores (Figure 3.10, left panel) or relative scores (Figure 3.10, right panel), as in both cases the 95% confidence intervals overlapped.

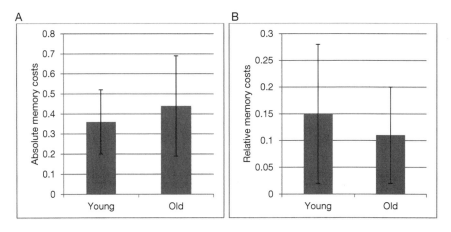

Figure 3.10   WM-divided attention. (A) Absolute memory costs for young and old, calculated as the difference between full and divided attention memory performance divided by the estimated standard deviations of the two groups. (B) Relative memory costs for young and old calculated as the difference between full and divided attention memory performance divided by full attention performance, which is then divided by the estimated standard deviations of the two groups for the studies in Table 3.1 that used divided attention for WM tasks. Error bars represent 95% confidence intervals

Another interesting feature concerning the WM studies discussed in this section is that, in contrast to the LTM studies, only one of them shows a greater secondary task cost for older adults. No age differences in secondary task costs were seen for a tracking task (Baddeley et al., 1986; Della Sala et al., 2010; MacPherson et al., 2007), a visual pattern task (MacPherson et al., 2007), articulatory suppression (MacPherson et al., 2007), or counting backwards (Brown & Brockmole, 2010), but Logie et al. (2007) showed that older adults were especially slow to respond to a visual simple RT task under DA conditions compared to the young adults. As suggested earlier, this could be because baseline performance was not experimentally equated between the two age groups.

It is interesting to note the lack of consistent larger secondary task costs for older adults in WM tasks, as these are not in line with results reported in a meta-analysis by Verhaeghen et al. (2003) on aging and dual-task performance, which was briefly described earlier, and which showed larger secondary task costs in older adults in tasks involving speed measures. One potential reason for this discrepancy is that most studies included in the meta-analysis were not related directly to memory performance. Recently, Verhaeghen (2012) proposed that this age-related deficit seen in speed measures can be due to the maintenance of the two distinct mental task sets required to carry out the divided attention procedure, taking the form of the coordination step itself or the reduced capacity of a WM framework that does not allow maintaining multiple sets simultaneously.

Overall, the results of the effects of DA on performance in WM tasks seem to indicate that younger adults under DA conditions generally mimic older adults' memory performance, as suggested by the reduced processing resources hypothesis. However, studies that look at the effects of DA in younger and older adults mostly show a lack of differentially larger age-related effects on WM performance, with patterns of performance on the secondary task varying as a function of performance in the baseline condition.

Summary

In this chapter, we have examined the reduced processing resources explanation suggested for the age-related declines in episodic memory by reviewing the relevant research on divided attention in younger and older adults and the resulting memory and secondary task performance in tasks reflecting both long-term memory (LTM) and working memory (WM). The review of representative studies on aging and DA seems to point to the following conclusions: Reviewing studies from the LTM literature, we have found that (1) dividing the attention of younger adults does simulate in some cases, but not in all, the specific memory impairments seen in older adults under full attention; (2) older adults do not consistently show greater impairments than young adults when attention is divided at encoding; and (3) older adults nearly always display greater secondary task costs than young adults when attention is divided, especially at retrieval. Of the selected studies examining divided attention and WM, most also showed that divided attention in younger adults did simulate older adults' performance to some degree. In addition, most of the WM studies also showed no greater age differences in memory performance under DA; however, they diverged from the LTM results in mostly showing no greater secondary task costs for older adults.

The fact that the observations regarding the age-related effects of DA on LTM and WM performance are somewhat similar is in line with claims that the two types of memory are at least partially subserved by similar cognitive mechanisms. It is also in line with the notion that encoding and retrieval in LTM are based to some degree on online WM processes and temporary storage involved in these operations (e.g. Baddeley, 2000; Cowan, 2005).

On the other hand, the fact that the observations regarding LTM and WM are not identical, especially with respect to secondary task costs, suggests that they each also underlie to some degree distinct processes with different encoding and retrieval mechanisms. For example, when processing verbal information in a WM task, people might rely on rote rehearsal to maintain information for a short period of time, whereas they might use more elaborative strategies when encoding and retrieving information in an LTM task. This scenario fits the observed patterns since rote rehearsal may not require enough resources to result in greater secondary task costs for old, but other strategies that are more commonly seen in LTM tasks would (see Naveh-Benjamin et al., 2005). Furthermore, the immediate retrieval of information in WM tasks seems to be less demanding for older adults, as this information, just recently presented, may be in a heightened state of activation

(Cowan, 2001), leading to the same secondary task costs in older and younger adults. This is in contrast to the delayed retrieval of information in LTM that requires further efforts by older adults in accessing it, resulting in increased secondary task costs.

The current findings suggest that older adults are less efficient than younger adults when performing dual tasks in LTM. This can best be observed when we compare baseline and divided attention conditions in the secondary task, indicating that older adults require more resources than young adults to meet the demands of encoding and especially retrieval processes. Although the memory patterns reveal that there are generally no age differences in the ability to divide attention, the results can still be compatible with Craik's notion of older adults having reduced resources. As Anderson, Craik and Naveh-Benjamin (1998) noted:

> The reduced attentional resource view ... suggests that an age-related loss of available resources impairs the ability to engage in demanding operations such as enlisting mnemonic strategies at encoding and generating appropriate cues at retrieval. That is, encoding and retrieval operations are more attention demanding for older adults than for younger adults, and we would therefore predict larger secondary task costs for older than for younger adults.
>
> (p. 406)

It is also possible that older adults may be giving priority to the memory task, leaving fewer resources available to complete the secondary task. Finally, this pattern could also be explained by older adults having a reduced processing speed or less efficient neural mechanisms, though the discussion of these topics is beyond the scope of the current review.

Consistent with models of WM, we have seen that when primary and secondary tasks are highly similar (therefore relying on the same pool of resources), dual-task performance is especially impaired (e.g. Fernandes & Moscovitch, 2002; Kim & Giovanello, 2011). However, we could not find much evidence to support the claim that such task combinations are especially problematic for older adults to complete, even when examining secondary task costs. For example, when combining a verbal retrieval task with a word-based secondary task, older participants' secondary task costs (as measured by RT) were not greater for the word-based task than a control task when compared to younger adults (Fernandes & Moscovitch, 2003; Fernandes et al., 2006; Skinner & Fernandes, 2008). Such a finding potentially suggests that specialized pools of resources (e.g. for a phonological buffer) are not reduced in older adults.

There is, however, a large body of evidence showing age-related declines in WM tasks. For example, Craik (1994) observed that age differences in short-term memory storage are quite small (e.g. when measured by digit span or the size of the recency effect), but when the task also involves active processing (e.g. backward digit span), older adults are at a disadvantage. Unlike short-term memory, WM involves both storage and processing, and numerous studies provide evidence that older adults have a lower WM span (when the task requires both storage and processing) than younger adults (Gick, Craik & Robin, 1988; Light & Anderson, 1985; Norman, Kemper & Kynette, 1992; Stine & Wingfield, 1990). In order to more carefully examine these differences, models of WM allow a further breakdown between storage and processing components of WM (e.g. Baddeley et al., 1986; Daneman & Carpenter, 1980; Miyake & Shah, 1999), and studies indicate age deficits in both, though larger in the latter (e.g. see Cowan et al., 2006; Naveh-Benjamin et al., 2007). Future research may look at the potential resolution of such age-related declines and the relative comparable effects of DA in older and younger adults shown here in WM tasks.

Overall, the literature on the effects of divided attention on memory performance in younger and older adults provides support for the claim that one potential factor in older adults' declining episodic memory performance is their reduced processing (attentional) resources. However, further research is needed to clarify some contradictory evidence reported in the literature, in particular the apparent lack of larger divided attention effects on memory performance in older rather than younger adults.

References

* Articles marked with an asterisk were included in the meta-analyses presented in Figures 3.6, 3.8 and 3.10

Anderson, N. D., Craik, F. I. M. & Naveh-Benjamin, M. (1998). The attentional demands of encoding and retrieval in younger and older adults: I. Evidence from divided attention costs. *Psychology and Aging, 13*(3), 405–423. doi:10.1037//0882-7974.13.3.405

Anderson, N. D., Iidaka, T., Cabeza, R., Kapur, S., McIntosh, A. R. & Craik, F. I. M. (2000). The effects of divided attention on encoding- and retrieval-related brain activity: A PET study of younger and older adults. *Journal of Cognitive Neuroscience, 12*(5), 775–792. Retrieved from http://www.ncbi.nlm.nih.gov/pubmed/11054920

Baddeley, A. (2000). The episodic buffer: A new component of working memory? *Trends in Cognitive Sciences, 4*(11), 417–423.

Baddeley, A. D., Lewis, V., Eldridge, M. & Thomson, N. (1984). Attention and retrieval from long-term memory. *Journal of Experimental Psychology: General, 113*(4), 518–540. doi:10.1037/0096-3445.113.4.518

Baddeley, A. D., Logie, R. H., Bressi, S., Della Sala, S. & Spinnler, H. (1986). Dementia and working memory. *Quarterly Journal of Experimental Psychology, 38*(4), 603–618. Retrieved from http://www.informaworld.com/10.1080/14640748608401616

*Brown, L. A. & Brockmole, J. R. (2010). The role of attention in binding visual features in working memory: Evidence from cognitive ageing. *Quarterly Journal of Experimental Psychology (2006), 63*(10), 2067–2079. doi:10.1080/17470211003721675

Cabeza, R. (2002). Hemispheric asymmetry reduction in older adults: The HAROLD model. *Psychology and Aging, 17*(1), 85–100. doi:10.1037//0882-7974.17.1.85

Cabeza, R. (2004). Task-independent and task-specific age effects on brain activity during working memory, visual attention and episodic retrieval. *Cerebral Cortex, 14*(4), 364–375. doi:10.1093/cercor/bhg133

Cabeza, R., Anderson, N. D., Locantore, J. K. & McIntosh, A. R. (2002). Aging gracefully: Compensatory brain activity in high-performing older adults. *NeuroImage, 17*(3), 1394–1402. doi:10.1006/nimg.2002.1280

Chasteen, A. L., Bhattacharyya, S., Horhota, M., Tam, R. & Hasher, L. (2005). How feelings of stereotype threat influence older adults' memory performance. *Experimental Aging Research, 31*(3), 235–260. doi:10.1080/03610730590948177

Chen, Y. & Blanchard-Fields, F. (2000). Unwanted thought: Age differences in the correction of social judgments. *Psychology and Aging, 15*(3), 475–482. doi:http://dx. doi.org/10.1037/0882-7974.15.3.475

Cowan, N. (2001). The magical number 4 in short-term memory. *Behavioral and Brain Sciences, 24*, 87–185.

Cowan, N. (2005). *Working Memory Capacity*. New York, NY: Psychology Press

Cowan, N., Naveh-Benjamin, M., Kilb, A. & Saults, J. S. (2006). Life-span development of visual working memory: When is feature binding difficult? *Developmental Psychology, 42*(6), 1089–1102. Retrieved from http://www.ncbi.nlm.nih.gov/pubmed/17087544

Craik, F. I. M. (1982). Selective changes in encoding as a function of reduced processing capacity. In F. Klix, J. Hoffman & E. Van der Meer (Eds.), *Cognitive Research in Psychology* (pp. 152–161). Berlin: Deutscher Verlag der Wissenschaffen.

Craik, F. I. M. (1983). On the transfer of information from temporary to permanent memory. *Philosophical Transactions of the Royal Society of London, Series B, 302,* 341–359.

Craik, F. I. M. (1994). Memory changes in normal aging. *Current Directions in Psychological Science, 3*(5), 155–158. doi:10.1111/1467-8721.ep10770653

Craik, F. I. M. & McDowd, J. M. (1987). Age differences in recall and recognition. *Journal of Experimental Psychology: Learning, Memory, and Cognition, 13*(3), 474–479.

Craik, F. I. M. & Schloerscheidt, A. M. (2011). Age-related differences in recognition memory: Effects of materials and context change. *Psychology and Aging, 26*, 671–677. doi:10.1037/a0022203

Craik, F. I. M., Luo, L. & Sakuta, Y. (2010). Effects of aging and divided attention on memory for items and their contexts. *Psychology and Aging, 25*(4), 968–979. Retrieved from http://www.ncbi.nlm.nih.gov/pubmed/20973605

Craik, F. I. M., Govoni, R., Naveh-Benjamin, M. & Anderson, N. D. (1996). The effects of divided attention on encoding and retrieval processes in human memory. *Journal of Experimental Psychology: General, 125*(2), 159–180.

Daneman, M. & Carpenter, P. (1980). Individual differences in working memory and reading. *Journal of Verbal Learning and Verbal Behavior, 19*(4), 450–466. Retrieved from http://linkinghub.elsevier.com/retrieve/pii/S0022537180903126

Davis, S. W., Dennis, N. A., Daselaar, S. M., Fleck, M. S. & Cabeza, R. (2008). Que PASA? The posterior-anterior shift in aging. *Cerebral cortex (New York, NY : 1991), 18*(5), 1201–1209. doi:10.1093/cercor/bhm155

Della Sala, S., Cocchini, G., Logie, R. H. & MacPherson, S. E. (2010). Dual task during encoding, maintenance and retrieval in Alzheimer disease and healthy ageing. *Journal of Alzheimer's Disease, 19*, 503–515.

*Fernandes, M. A. & Grady, C. L. (2008). Age differences in susceptibility to memory interference during recall of categorizable but not unrelated word lists. *Experimental Aging Research, 34*(4), 297–322. doi:10.1080/03610730802273860

Fernandes, M. A. & Guild, E. (2009). Process-specific interference effects during recognition of spatial patterns and words. *Canadian Journal of Experimental Psychology = Revue canadienne de psychologie expérimentale, 63*(1), 24–32. doi:10.1037/a0012870

Fernandes, M. A & Moscovitch, M. (2002). Factors modulating the effect of divided attention during retrieval of words. *Memory & Cognition, 30*(5), 731–744. Retrieved from http://www.ncbi.nlm.nih.gov/pubmed/12219890

*Fernandes, M. A. & Moscovitch, M. (2003). Interference effects from divided attention during retrieval in younger and older adults. *Psychology and Aging, 18*, 219–230.

*Fernandes, M. A., Pacurar, A., Moscovitch, M. & Grady, C. L. (2006). Neural correlates of auditory recognition under full and divided attention in younger and older adults. *Neuropsychologia, 44*(12), 2452–2464. Retrieved from http://www.ncbi.nlm.nih.gov/pubmed/16769093

Gick, M. L., Craik, F. I. M. & Robin, G. (1988). Task complexity and age differences in working memory. *Memory & Cognition, 16*(4). [originally cited as Gick (1988)]

Hess, T. M., Emery, L. & Queen, T. L. (2009). Task demands moderate stereotype threat effects on memory performance. *North*, 482–486. doi:10.1093/geronb/gbp044.

Hess, T. M., Auman, C., Colcombe, S. J. & Rahhal, T. A. (2003). The impact of stereotype threat on age differences in memory performance. *The Journals of Gerontology. Series B, Psychological Sciences and Social Sciences, 58*(1), 3–11. Retrieved from http://www.ncbi.nlm.nih.gov/pubmed/12496296

Jacoby, L. L., Woloshyn, V. & Kelley, C. M. (1989). Becoming famous without being recognized: Unconscious influences of memory produced by dividing attention. *Journal of Experimental Psychology: General, 118*(2), 115–125. doi:10.1037/0096-3445.118.2.115

Jennings, J. M. & Jacoby, L. L. (1993). Automatic versus intentional uses of memory: Aging, attention, and control. *Psychology and Aging, 8*(2), 283–293.

*Kilb, A. & Naveh-Benjamin, M. (2007). Paying attention to binding: Further studies assessing the role of reduced attentional resources in the associative deficit of older adults. *Memory & Cognition, 35*(5), 1162–1174. Retrieved from http://www.ncbi.nlm.nih.gov/pubmed/17910197

Kim, S.-Y. & Giovanello, K. S. (2011). The effects of attention on age-related relational memory deficits: Evidence from a novel attentional manipulation. *Psychology and Aging, 26*, 678–688. doi:10.1037/a0022326

*Knott, V. J., Harr, A. & Mahoney, C. (1999). Smoking history and aging-associated cognitive decline: An event-related brain potential study. *Neuropsychobiology, 40*(2), 95–106.

*Li, K. Z. H., Lindenberger, U., Freund, A. M. & Baltes, P. B. (2001). Walking while memorizing: Age-related differences in compensatory behavior. *Psychological Science, 12*(3), 230–237.

Light, L. L. & Anderson, P. A. (1985). Working-memory capacity, age, and memory for discourse. *Journal of Gerontology, 40*(6), 737–747. Retrieved from http://search.ebscohost.com/login.aspx?direct=true&db=psyh&AN=1986-24135-001

*Light, L. L. & Prull, M. (1995). Aging, divided attention, and repetition priming. *Swiss Journal of Psychology, 54*(2), 87–101.

*Lindenberger, U., Marsiske, M. & Baltes, P. B. (2000). Memorizing while walking: Increase in dual-task costs from young adulthood to old age. *Psychology and Aging, 15*(3), 417–436. Retrieved from http://www.ncbi.nlm.nih.gov/pubmed/11014706

*Logie, R. H., Cocchini, G., Della Sala, S. & Baddeley, A. D. (2004). Is there a specific executive capacity for dual task coordination? Evidence from Alzheimer's disease. *Neuropsychology, 18*(3), 504–513. doi:10.1037/0894-4105.18.3.504

*Logie, R. H., Della Sala, S., MacPherson, S. E. & Cooper, J. (2007). Dual task demands on encoding and retrieval processes: Evidence from healthy adult ageing. *Cortex, 43*(1), 159–169.

Luo, L. & Craik, F. I. M. (2009). Age differences in recollection: Specificity effects at retrieval. *Journal of Memory and Language, 60*(4), 421–436. doi:10.1016/j.jml.2009.01.005

McDowd, J. M. & Craik, F. I. M. (1988). Effects of aging and task difficulty on divided attention performance. *Journal of Experimental Psychology: Human Perception and Performance, 14*(2), 267–280. Retrieved from http://www.ncbi.nlm.nih.gov/pubmed/2967880

*MacPherson, S. E., Della Sala, S., Logie, R. H. & Wilcock, G. K. (2007). Specific impairment in concurrent performance of two memory tasks. *Cortex, 43*, 858–865.

Madden, D. J., Turkington, T. G., Provenzale, J. M., Denny, L. L., Hawk, T. C., Gottlob, L. R. & Coleman, R. E. (1999). Adult age differences in the functional neuroanatomy of verbal recognition memory. *Human Brain Mapping, 7*(2), 115–135. Retrieved from http://www.ncbi.nlm.nih.gov/pubmed/9950069

*Mellinger, J. C., Lehman, E. B., Happ, L. K. & Grout, L. A. (1990). Cognitive effort in modality retrieval by young and older adults. *Experimental Aging Research, 16*(1–2), 35–41. Retrieved from http://www.ncbi.nlm.nih.gov/pubmed/2265664

Miyake, A. & Shah, P. (1999). *Models of Working Memory*. New York, NY: Cambridge University Press.

Murphy, D. R., Craik, F. I., Li, K. Z. & Schneider, B. A. (2000). Comparing the effects of aging and background noise on short-term memory performance. *Psychology and Aging, 15*(2), 323–334. Retrieved from http://www.ncbi.nlm.nih.gov/pubmed/10879586

Naveh-Benjamin, M. (1990). Coding of temporal order information: An automatic process? *Journal of Experimental Psychology: Learning, Memory & Cognition, 16*(1), 117–126.

Naveh-Benjamin, M. (2000). Adult age differences in memory performance: Tests of an associative deficit hypothesis. *Journal of Experimental Psychology: Learning, Memory & Cognition, 26*(5), 1170–1187.

Naveh-Benjamin, M. & Craik, F. I. M. (1995). Memory for context and its use in item memory: Comparisons of younger and older persons. *Psychology and Aging, 10*(2), 284–293.

Naveh-Benjamin, M. & Guez, J. (2000). Effects of divided attention on encoding and retrieval processes: Assessment of attentional costs and a componential analysis. *Journal of Experimental Psychology: Learning, Memory & Cognition, 26*(6), 1461–1482.

Naveh-Benjamin, M., Brav, T. K. & Levy, O. (2007). The associative memory deficit of older adults: The role of strategy utilization. *Psychology and Aging, 22*(1), 202–208.

Naveh-Benjamin, M., Cowan, N., Kilb, A. & Chen, Z. (2007). Age-related differences in immediate serial recall: Dissociating chunk formation and capacity. *Memory & cognition, 35*(4), 724–737. Retrieved from http://www.pubmedcentral.nih.gov/articlerender.fcgi?artid=1995413&tool=pmcentrez&rendertype=abstract

*Naveh-Benjamin, M., Craik, F. I. M., Guez, J. & Kreuger, S. (2005). Divided attention in younger and older adults: Effects of strategy and relatedness on memory performance and secondary task costs. *Journal of Experimental Psychology: Learning, Memory, and Cognition, 31*(3), 520–537.

Naveh-Benjamin, M., Guez, J., Kilb, A. & Reedy, S. (2004). The associative memory deficit of older adults: Further support using face-name associations. *Psychology and Aging, 19*(3), 541–546. Retrieved from http://www.ncbi.nlm.nih.gov/pubmed/15383004

Naveh-Benjamin, M., Hussain, Z., Guez, J. & Bar-On, M. (2003). Adult age differences in episodic memory: Further support for an associative-deficit hypothesis. *Journal of Experimental Psychology: Learning, Memory, and Cognition, 29*(5), 826–837.

Norman, S., Kemper, S. & Kynette, D. (1992). Adults' reading comprehension: Effects of syntactic complexity and working memory. *Journals of Gerontology, 47*(4), 258–265. Retrieved from http://search.ebscohost.com/login.aspx?direct=true&db=psy h&AN=1993-01162-001

Nyberg, L., Nilsson, L. G., Olofsson, U. & Bäckman, L. (1997). Effects of division of attention during encoding and retrieval on age differences in episodic memory. *Experimental Aging Research, 23*(2), 137–143. Retrieved from http://www. informaworld.com/openurl?genre=article&doi=10.1080/03610739708254029&magic= crossref

Old, S. R. & Naveh-Benjamin, M. (2008a). Age-related changes in memory: Experimental approaches. In S. M. Hofer & D. F. Alwin (Eds.), *Handbook of Cognitive Aging: Interdisciplinary Perspectives* (pp. 151–1670.) Thousand Oaks, CA: Sage Publications, Inc.

Old, S. R. & Naveh-Benjamin, M. (2008b). Memory for people and their actions: Further evidence for an age-related associative deficit. *Psychology and Aging, 23*(2), 467–472. doi:http://dx.doi.org/10.1037/0882-7974.23.2.467

Old, S. R. & Naveh-Benjamin, M. (2008c). Differential effects of age on item and associative measures of memory: A meta-analysis. *Psychology and Aging, 23*(1), 104–118.

*Park, D. C., Puglisi, J. T. & Smith, A. D. (1986). Memory for pictures: Does an age-related decline exist? *Psychology and Aging, 1*(1), 11–7. Retrieved from http://www.ncbi.nlm. nih.gov/pubmed/3267373

*Park, D. C., Smith, A. D., Dudley, W. N. & Lafronza, V. N. (1989). Effects of age and a divided attention task presented during encoding and retrieval on memory. *Journal of Experimental Psychology. Learning, Memory, and Cognition, 15*(6), 1185–1191. Retrieved from http://www.ncbi.nlm.nih.gov/pubmed/2530311

*Puglisi, J. T., Park, D. C., Smith, A. D. & Dudley, W. N. (1988). Age differences in encoding specificity. *Journal of Gerontology, 43*(6), 145–150.

Rabinowitz, J. C., Craik, F. I. M. & Ackerman, B. P. (1982). A processing resource account of age differences in recall. *Canadian Journal of Psychology, 36*(2), 325–344.

Riby, L., Perfect, T. & Stollery, B. (2004). The effects of age and task domain on dual task performance: A meta-analysis. *European Journal of Cognitive Psychology, 16*(6), 863–891. doi:10.1080/09541440340000402

Roediger, H. L. & McDermott, K. B. (1995). Creating false memories: Remembering words not presented in lists. *Journal of Experimental Psychology: Learning, Memory, and Cognition, 21*(4), 803–814. doi:10.1037/0278-7393.21.4.803

Salthouse, T. A. (1996). The processing speed theory of adult age differences in cognition. *Psychological Review, 103*, 403–428.

Salthouse, T. A., Rogan, J. D. & Prill, K. A. (1984). Division of attention: Age differences on a visually presented memory task. *Memory & Cognition, 12*(6), 613–620. Retrieved from http://www.ncbi.nlm.nih.gov/pubmed/6533430

*Schmitter-Edgecombe, M. (1999). Effects of divided attention and time course on automatic and controlled components of memory in older adults. *Psychology and Aging, 14*(2), 331–345. Retrieved from http://www.ncbi.nlm.nih.gov/pubmed/10403719

*Skinner, E. I. & Fernandes, M. A. (2008). Interfering with remembering and knowing: Effects of divided attention at retrieval. *Acta Psychologica, 127*(2), 211–221. Retrieved from http://www.ncbi.nlm.nih.gov/pubmed/17599796

Somberg, B. L. & Salthouse, T. A. (1982). Divided attention abilities in young and old adults. *Journal of Experimental Psychology. Human Perception and Performance, 8*(5), 651–663. Retrieved from http://www.ncbi.nlm.nih.gov/pubmed/6218227

Spencer, W. D. & Raz, N. (1995). Differential effects of aging on memory for content and context: A meta-analysis. *Psychology and Aging, 10*(4), 527–539.

Stine, E. A. & Wingfield, A. (1990). How much do working memory deficits contribute to age differences in discourse memory? *European Journal of Cognitive Psychology, 2*(3), 289–304. Retrieved from http://search.ebscohost.com/login.aspx?direct=true&db=psyh&AN=1992-30732-001

Troyer, A. K., Winocur, G., Craik, F. I. M. & Moscovitch, M. (1999). Source memory and divided attention: Reciprocal costs to primary and secondary tasks. *Neuropsychology, 13*(4), 467–474. Retrieved from http://www.ncbi.nlm.nih.gov/pubmed/10527055

Tun, P. A., McCoy, S. & Wingfield, A. (2009). Aging, hearing acuity, and the attentional costs of effortful listening. *Psychology and Aging, 24*(3), 761–766. doi:10.1037/a0014802

*Tun, P. A., Wingfield, A. & Stine, E. A. (1991). Speech-processing capacity in young and older adults: A dual-task study. *Psychology and Aging, 6*(1), 3–9. Retrieved from http://www.ncbi.nlm.nih.gov/pubmed/18759261

*Veiel, L. L. & Storandt, M. (2003). Processing costs of semantic and episodic retrieval in younger and older adults. *Aging, Neuropsychology, and Cognition (Neuropsychology, Development and Cognition: Section B), 10*(1), 61–73. Retrieved from http://www.tandfonline.com/doi/abs/10.1076/anec.10.1.61.13458

Verhaeghen, P. (2012). Working memory still working: Age-related differences in working-memory functioning and cognitive control. In M. Naveh-Benjamin (Ed.), *Memory and Aging: Current Issues and Future Directions* (pp. 3–30). New York, NY: Psychology Press.

Verhaeghen, P., Steitz, D. W., Sliwinski, M. J. & Cerella, J. (2003). Aging and dual-task performance: A meta-analysis. *Psychology and Aging, 18*(3), 443–460. Retrieved from http://www.ncbi.nlm.nih.gov/pubmed/14518807

*Whiting, W. L. & Smith, A. D. (1997). Differential age-related processing limitations in recall and recognition tasks. *Psychology and Aging, 12*(2), 216–224. Retrieved from http://www.ncbi.nlm.nih.gov/pubmed/9189981

Zacks, R. T. & Hasher, L. (1994). Directed ignoring: Inhibitory regulation of working memory. In D. Dagenbach & T. H. Carr (Eds.), *Inhibitory Processes in Attention, Memory, and Language* (pp. 241–264). San Diego, CA: Academic Press, Inc.

4 Working memory training in late adulthood

A behavioral and brain perspective

Anna Stigsdotter Neely and Lars Nyberg

A wealth of evidence has shown that aging is associated with decline in various cognitive abilities. For decades, cognitive aging research has focused on explaining age-related cognitive decline with less emphasis on how to support the aging mind and brain. Recently, this has changed noticeably where issues related to how cognitive functions can be successfully maintained and improved throughout the adult life span have entertained increased interest (see Hertzog et al., 2009, for a comprehensive review). This is certainly welcomed from both a theoretical and a practical standpoint. In the face of an aging population the motivation has grown to find methods to support cognitive health, vital for coping with the challenges of everyday life. This chapter will provide an overview of the efforts that have been undertaken to ameliorate decline in cognitive functions in healthy older adults through practice and training with a particular focus on working memory and its processes. Working memory has long been viewed as a memory system not amendable in any significant way by training or practice. However, recent studies are questioning this trait-like view of working memory by showing that training can improve working memory performance in ways that may suggest more general alterations in working memory capacity (Klingberg, 2010). This field is rapidly developing and the results to date are promising but also mixed. We will begin this review by discussing the multitude of training paradigms that have been used to address working memory and related processes as well as the theoretical motivations behind them. This is followed by findings from neuroimaging studies concerning the neural underpinnings of working memory plasticity and age-related differences thereof. The success of working memory training lies in its ability to give rise to generalized gains that are maintained over time: the question is whether it does.

Early cognitive training studies

It has not been until quite recently that more focused attempts to train working memory have become the very topic of cognitive training for both young and old adults. In a well-cited review article by Verhaeghen, Marcoen and Goossens (1992) it was shown that the majority of cognitive training studies undertaken up to that point focused predominately on episodic memory and fluid intelligence.

The motivation in many of these studies was to teach strategies such as the method of loci to support encoding and retrieval of words or reasoning skills to help solve problems (Stigsdotter, Neely & Bäckman, 1993; Verhaeghen, 2000). This line of work has generally demonstrated that older adults show substantial and long-lasting improvements in the tasks trained, but more limited gain in tasks not trained (Lustig et al., 2009; Rebok, Carlson & Langbaum, 2007). Also, when training gains have been compared to those of young adults, older adults show less gain after training suggesting that age differences are magnified not reduced after training. Overall, these studies have shown that learning after strategy training in old age is possible but rather task-specific in nature.

The lack of more generalized gain after strategy-based training programs has sparked an interest in issues related to the scope and nature of transfer effects (Lövdén et al., 2010). Is it so that cognitive training mainly fosters acquisition of skills beneficial to the specific tasks used in training with limited applicability outside that context (Owen et al., 2010), as results from strategy-training studies may imply? Or can training also affect more general cognitive mechanisms and capacities targeted in training? If so, the training may stand a greater chance to affect a wider range of tasks. To find ways to alter more fundamental ability levels through training has been the driving force behind the recent interest in working memory training and more process-oriented training approaches to cognition in old age.

As this volume attests, working memory can be conceptualized in several ways but is commonly referred to as a limited multicomponent memory system that actively holds and manipulates information over brief periods of time (Baddeley & Hitch, 1974; Miyake & Shah, 1999). The centrality of working memory to human cognition and behavior has been illustrated extensively (Unsworth, Heitz & Engle, 2005). Working memory capacity as measured by complex span tasks has been found to correlate with higher order cognition such as episodic memory, reading comprehension, multi-tasking, reasoning and measures of fluid intelligence to name but a few (Unsworth & Engle, 2007). Moreover, working memory performance is sensitive to many conditions affecting the brain, such as Alzheimer's and Parkinson's disease, but is also negatively affected by normal aging (Gabrieli et al., 1996; Kempler et al., 1998; McCabe et al., 2010). As a matter of fact, one prominent theory of cognitive aging suggested that decline in working memory capacity underlies much of the observed negative relationship between age and cognitive performance (Hasher, Lustig & Zacks, 2007). Hence, a person's working memory capacity is essential for successfully being able to carry out a wide variety of cognitive tasks important for everyday life. Given the importance of working memory for cognition and the aging mind it is surprising that working memory plasticity (here defined as positive change in performance as a function of training) has not until recently enjoyed more scientific interest.

We will present the behavioral studies that have been conducted with older adults to address whether prolonged practice and training of working memory leads to improved, maintained and widespread effects on trained and untrained tasks.

Working memory intervention studies: Behavioral results

As will be evident from this review, working memory performance has been trained in many different ways. There are most likely many reasons for this, one being that researchers in this field have used different conceptualizations of working memory as well as holding different views on what specific processes need to be addressed in old age. As mentioned above, perhaps one of the most influential models of the working memory system was proposed by Baddeley and Hitch in 1974. The model comprises three components for brief storage and maintenance of verbal, visuo-spatial and integrated episodic information (the phonological loop, the visuo-spatial sketchpad and the episodic buffert) as well as a domain-general component (the central executive) responsible for coordinating use of the storage systems and for controlling attention. This model has inspired many of the working memory training studies that will be reviewed here and will help classify the reviewed training protocols according to their main focus: is the purpose of the training to expand the capacity to store and maintain information, or is the focus to improve the central executive abilities for controlled attention and the coordination of information in the storage systems, or are the protocols addressing both aspects of working memory function?

The main focus for this review is to evaluate whether working memory training gives rise to improvements in the ability level and not only in the particular task used in training. In other words, the training should foster skilled performance outside the immediate context of the training. In order to be able to draw such a conclusion the benefits of the training should be assessed on three dimensions. First, the magnitude of task-specific gains should be addressed, that is, did the training lead to improvements in the trained tasks? Second, the generalizability or transfer of positive gains to tasks not trained needs to be investigated. The battery of transfer tests should optimally tap both near- and far-transfer tests, where near-transfer tests commonly refer to tasks measuring the ability of interest (here working memory and its processes) and far-transfer tests tap other ability domains related to working memory such as fluid intelligence or everyday life skills. And finally, the durability or maintenance of positive task-specific as well as transfer effects over time should be assessed to evaluate whether there have been more fundamental effects on the cognitive system. Furthermore, to protect against several sources of potential confounds such as test-retest and Hawthorne effects, a pretest-training-posttest design with random assignment of participants to a treatment group and to one or more control groups is recommended in order to minimize alternative explanations. Hence working memory intervention studies designed accordingly provide a controlled way to assess the nature of cognitive training effects.

Training executive cognitive control processes: Dual-tasking

As pronounced age differences have commonly been observed in various processes related to the central executive, several training paradigms have specifically addressed one or more of these cognitive control abilities such as dual tasking, updating, inhibition and shifting. As has been made clear since the original Baddeley and Hitch (1974) proposal, the central executive is not a unitary system and can be subdivided into several component processes. Miyake and colleagues (2000) provided evidence for a division of the central executive into three separate but moderately correlated processes, namely updating, shifting and inhibition. This model has influenced some of the training studies below.

In the mid 1990s Kramer and colleagues started off a series of studies that examined the effects of dual-task training in young and old adults (Kramer, Larish & Strayer, 1995; Kramer et al., 1999). A number of research questions have been addressed in this research and here we will only focus on the issues related to training gains, maintenance and transfer in old and young adults.

The dual-task training protocol used in this research has varied slightly between studies but generally consists of two tasks performed concurrently such as a tracing task combined with an alphabet-arithmetic task or letter discrimination combined with tone discrimination (Bherer et al., 2005, 2006, 2008; Kramer, Larish & Strayer, 1995). Several of their studies have assessed the impact of variable-priority strategy training in which the participants were to vary their response priorities between the two tasks by prioritizing one task over the other as compared to a fixed-priority strategy where both tasks were to be equally emphasized. The variable-priority strategy is thought to foster different ways to perform a complex task, which may be beneficial for learning and transfer of skill (see also Schmidt & Bjork, 1992). Also, adaptive individual feedback on performance is an integral part of their protocol. The number of training sessions provided has usually been around five one-hour sessions. The results from these studies have convincingly shown that both young and old adults can improve substantially in the trained dual-task, measured as lower task-set costs and dual-task costs after training. The results are, however, mixed concerning the benefits of the variable-priority strategy over the fixed priority instruction, with some showing clear benefits (Kramer, Larish & Strayer, 1995) and others not (Bherer et al., 2005). A possibility that has been suggested to resolve the discrepant findings may be that different dual tasks have been used in these studies where the variable-priority strategy seems more beneficial when applied to more complex dual tasks. Long-term effects have been addressed in two studies showing maintenance for one and two months respectively following training, indicating that the effects show some stability and do not wear off immediately (Bherer et al., 2005; Kramer et al., 1999). The transfer of positive gains to tasks not trained has usually been addressed by including two near-transfer dual tasks, where results have consistently shown positive effects. Far transfer effects have been addressed to a lesser extent – although, in two recent studies on older adults the effects of dual-task training on simulated driving performance as well as on motoric performance were examined. In both studies positive effects of dual-task training were demonstrated suggesting that far transfer is possible in task domains requiring the coordination of multiple sub-skills (Li et al., 2010; Cassavaugh & Kramer, 2009). But no far transfer to mental speed was seen in a study by MacKay-Brandt (2011) using a dual-task training protocol similar those in the above studies. More studies are clearly needed to examine a broader range of transfer effects after dual-task training. Finally, age-related differences in dual-task training gains have been addressed in several studies most of which have shown parallel gains or an advantage for the older adults (Kramer, Larish & Strayer, 1995; Bherer et al., 2006). This pattern of similar or a reduction of age differences as a function of training is at odds with much of strategy-training research, which more often yields a magnification of age differences following training (Verhaeghen & Marcoen, 1996).

In sum, dual-task training shows promise as a viable method to train one critical aspect of working memory, namely dual-tasking, by showing substantial immediate and near transfer effects in both young and old adults. However, the evidence is more limited concerning long-lasting and far-transfer effects. Maintenance has only been observed after a couple of months and transfer has only been addressed with a limited transfer battery. For example, no measures of working memory capacity has been included in these studies making it hard to draw firm conclusions about whether working memory capacity in a more general sense has been improved. Hence strong conclusions about whether these effects indicate a more general improvement of working memory or dual-task ability rather than just strengthen a stimulus-response relationship specific to the trained task cannot be convincingly made and need further scientific attention.

Training in updating, shifting and inhibition

Another line of research that in recent years has enjoyed increased interest is training that targets updating of information in working memory. Updating refers to the ability to monitor incoming information for relevance to the task in hand and when necessary updating old no longer relevant information with newer more relevant information. Previous research has implicated the importance of updating for learning (Collette & Van der Linden, 2002) and intelligence (Friedman et al., 2006).

A study by Jaeggi and colleagues (2008) with young adults has attracted a high degree of attention as it was one of the first studies reporting far transfer to a measure of intelligence after updating working memory training (see also Olesen, Westerberg & Klingberg, 2004). In this study updating was trained in four groups receiving 8, 12, 17, or 19 sessions respectively using a dual n-back task. This task required participants to attend to a changing stream of information (here positions and numbers) and to decide if the items currently shown were the same as n-items ago. The results showed, in a dose-response manner, greater gains with more practice in the trained dual n-back task and in an untrained non-verbal reasoning task but not in a complex working memory task (Jaeggi et al., 2008). As far as we know these results have not been replicated nor has the stability of these effects across time been established. The study has also been criticized due to its unconventional way of administering the far transfer test (see Moody, 2009). The fact that no effects were seen in complex working memory task performance makes it hard to argue that the training has improved working memory capacity more broadly. Therefore the mechanism by which dual-updating training may enhance intelligence remains somewhat unclear. Nevertheless, the findings are encouraging and deserve further attention.

In two studies we have used a slightly different approach in training updating of working memory in both young and old adults (Dahlin et al., 2008a; Dahlin et al., 2008b). Our program provided training in four running span tasks where the task was to constantly update a stream of single items in order to be able to remember the four last presented items in correct order. Also a keep-track task was used where the participant had to associate a stream of words to categories and to be able to remember the most recently presented word associated with the categories. Fifteen sessions of adaptive practice over a five-week period were given. A large transfer battery was given covering tasks tapping mental speed, short-term memory, working memory, inhibition, episodic memory and intelligence. In contrast to the Jaeggi study, our findings (Dahlin et al., 2008a) were more limited for the young adults showing near-transfer to an untrained updating task (n-back) and far-transfer to an episodic memory task, where only the near-transfer effect was maintained 18 months later (Dahlin et al., 2008a). We have interpreted the finding of a maintained transfer effect to n-back to suggest that transfer is facilitated only when the trained task and the untrained transfer task overlap in terms of shared processes (e.g updating) and may reflect an ability-specific effect for updating, which will be further discussed below in relation to brain data. Moreover, the older adults only showed improvement in the trained task that was maintained 18 months later. Hence no transfer effects were seen in the old. With regard to age-related differences in gain after training both young and old improved to a similar degree in the trained task. Despite equal gains, the performance level for the older adults was significantly below that of the young adults at post-test. This may suggest that not only the magnitude of gain but also the level of performance obtained after training may be one important aspect behind transfer.

Also a study by Li and colleagues (2008) has examined the effects of updating training with older and younger adults. Here 45 daily practice sessions of 15 min were given and a limited transfer battery of two untrained updating tasks as well as two complex working memory span tasks were administered. Also a follow-up assessment was made after three months. The program focused on a spatial n-back task with two levels of difficulty that was not adaptive to performance. In line with our study above, only near transfer effects were seen to the two untrained updating tasks for both age groups. These effects were maintained three months later. Hence, no evidence for far-transfer effects were obtained for young or for old. Also, the older adults showed a pattern of equal and slightly greater gains as a function of training. This pattern, however, may be explained by a functional ceiling effect for the young adults.

In an ongoing study, we have addressed the question of whether a training program that taps the central executive more broadly by addressing three critical executive control processes – updating, inhibition, and shifting – would give rise to more broad transfer effects in both young and old adults (Sandberg et al., 2013).

Our assumption is that a training program focused on several critical cognitive control functions, and assumed to engage a common core of domain-general executive processes, may give rise to more generalized transfer effects. The experimental set-up was the same as in the Dahlin et al. (2008a) studies in which 15 sessions of training over a five-week period were given. The same transfer battery was also employed. Six different tasks were used in training that increased in difficulty. Two tasks were used to train updating, inhibition and shifting respectively. The results showed pronounced gains in the trained tasks, where both the young and old gained equally across training. Also, near transfer was seen for both the young and old adults to non-trained updating and inhibition tasks. However, only the young adults showed transfer to two complex working memory tasks suggesting greater transfer effects in the young. No far-transfer effects were seen to episodic memory or to intelligence. Maintenance effects have so far only been examined for the older adults and suggest stability of task-specific and near transfer effects 18 months after completion of training. Our data suggest that when the training is focused on a wider range of process, here three instead of one executive process as in the Dahlin study (2008a), more generalized improvements occur at least for the young adults. At the same time transfer was limited to the working memory domain and did not affect measures of intelligence, reflecting a highly selective effect.

A notable exception to the finding of limited transfer in old adults after executive process training has recently been shown in a study by Karbach and Kray (2009). In this study task-shifting was trained which taps the ability to flexibly switch between two simple tasks such as deciding whether a picture is a fruit or a vegetable (task A) or if it is small or large (task B). Four different training groups were compared to address potential benefits of self-instructions (e.g. verbalize the upcoming task vs not) and of variable training (one vs several tasks) in groups of children, and young and old adults (Karbach & Kray, 2009; see also Karbach, Mang & Kray, 2010). The training was not adaptive in terms of difficulty and an active control group was used. A broad transfer battery was administered tapping shifting, inhibition, verbal and spatial working memory, and fluid intelligence. The findings yielded near-transfer to an untrained shifting-task, but more striking was the transfer to all far-transfer tasks and across all age groups and training conditions. This suggests that far-transfer was broad and similar for young and old and not related to type of training. One reason for the broad transfer effects offered by the authors was that the trained shifting task engaged a multitude of critical processes, such as goal maintenance, interference control, and task-set selection, as well as the ability to switch between tasks. This explanation is not easy to accept when contrasted with the above study by Sandberg et al., where shifting was trained in a similar fashion over 15 sessions and did not result in broad transfer effects. A replication of these findings is desirable to further cast light on what factors might drive the far-transfer effects.

In sum, the dominant finding from the studies presented above on executive process training in older adults was strong and long-lasting task-specific and near-transfer effects to the trained ability. Only one study (Karbach & Kray, 2009) showed broad far-transfer effects in older as well as younger adults after executive process training. Based on these data the evidence is not in favor of broad improvements after training in updating, shifting or inhibition in older adults. As for dual-task training, gains across training were similar for both young and old adults in the above studies (Dahlin et al., 2008a; Li et al., 2008; Sandberg et al., 2013).

Training in maintenance and cognitive control: The complex working memory span task

Another task that has been used in the working memory training literature is the complex working memory span task introduced by Daneman and Carpenter (1980). In the original version the subjects had to read sentences while remembering the final words of all the sentences for later serial recall. Since then many versions of the complex working memory task have been developed but core features are that these tasks jointly tap storage and processing in working memory. Moreover this task has served as the foundation of many studies linking working memory capacity to complex cognition (e.g. Unsworth, Heitz & Engle, 2005) making it an interesting task as a target for training.

In a study by Borella and colleagues (2010) they offered three sessions of training to a group of older adults in a categorization working memory span task. Here, the participants were presented with lists of words and had to tap their hand if the presented word belonged to the category of animals (processing) while trying to remember the last word presented in each list (storage). The training increased in difficulty and was adaptive to the performance of the subject. No feedback was provided. A contact control group was used, filling in questionnaires related to autobiographical memory and well-being. The test-battery included near and far-transfer tests tapping mental speed, short-term memory, working memory, inhibition, and fluid intelligence. Follow-up assessment was carried out eight months after completion of training. The results were impressive, showing transfer effects to all tasks administered to assess short-term memory, working memory, inhibition, mental speed and fluid intelligence. These effects were still present for fluid intelligence and mental speed eight months later. One factor raised by the authors as critical for obtaining the positive effects was, besides focusing on critical WM processes, that the training was variable and flexible (Borella et al., 2010).

A slightly different version of the complex span task was used in a recent study by Richmond and colleagues (2011). Here they provided 20 sessions of training in one verbal and one visuo-spatial complex span task to a group of older adults. The training was adaptive to the participant's performance level and feedback was provided. Also an active control group, engaged in solving trivia quizzes, was used. The results indicated performance gains in both trained complex span tasks and near transfer to a similar complex working memory span task (reading span). Far transfer was only seen in an episodic memory task where fewer repetitions of recalled items were made after training (Richmond et al., 2011). Moreover the results of the older trained group were also compared to younger adults who had been part of an earlier study receiving a very similar training protocol (see Chein & Morrison, 2010). In line with the above results, older adults performed at a lower level but the magnitude of gain as function of training was similar for young and old adults.

Finally, a study by Buschkuehl and colleagues (2008) used a training protocol with three tasks to train working memory – one simple span task and two complex span tasks. They also included two simple reaction time tasks mainly to make the training more variable and attractive. The participants were 80 years old and took part in 23 sessions. As for the above studies they used an active control group receiving light physical training. The results only showed a near-transfer effect to an untrained simple span task similar to the task used in training but no far transfer effects to episodic memory. A one-year follow-up assessment did not reveal any maintenance effects. Hence the results indicate slim transfer effects with limited durability in older samples.

First of all, these studies enjoy several positive design characteristics by including active control groups, adaptive training protocols and the use of more extensive transfer batteries to evaluate training effects. However, given that all three studies offered training in rather similar complex working memory span tasks in healthy older adults, the finding of impressive far transfer effects after three practice sessions reported in the Borella et al. (2010) study is intriguing in relation to the more humble near-transfer effects seen after 20 sessions or more of training in the studies by Richmond et al. (2011) and Buschkuehl et al. (2008) respectively. As mentioned above, Borella et al. (2010) offered two tentative explanations for their positive far transfer effects, namely that the training was challenging and variable and that the short time frame of the training phase had a facilitating effect on performance. However, the training protocols used in both the Richmond et al. (2011) and Buschkuehl et al. (2008) studies were also challenging and variable in that several training tasks were used and the training was adaptive to the performance of the subjects. Hence training variability does not seem like a strong candidate for driving the effects. Also it is hard to reconcile that few practice sessions should have a more facilitating effect on performance over several sessions (see Jaeggi et al., 2008). Clearly more research is needed on the factors important to foster far-transfer effects as well as the replication and extension of successful training protocols.

Conclusions: The behavioral training studies of working memory

The main question for this review was whether working memory training for healthy older adults produces generalized gains that are maintained over time. As evidenced by the review of the literature, the support for a broad generalized improvement is limited. The majority of studies show near-transfer to the same ability trained reflecting a restricted view on transfer. This is very much in line with a study by Owen and colleagues (2010) where over 11,000 participants took part in an online training program focusing on several cognitive functions. The study showed that on average 25 sessions of online cognitive training distributed over a six-week period did not result in any transfer effects as compared to an active control group. Needless to say this is an impressive demonstration of the lack of generalized improvements. Why this may be the case will be the topic of the next section.

However, two studies have been successful in obtaining broad generalization following working memory training in older adults (Borella et al., 2010; Karbach & Kray, 2009). What may account for these positive effects? Here, it is interesting to note that in both studies the training was short and limited to one task. Is it so that a brief and focused approach to training leads to greater gains? This seems highly unlikely since it runs contrary to many findings within the field suggesting that both task-specific and transfer gains are more evident after longer training periods (see Jaeggi et al., 2008) and that more variable and complex training experiences tend to optimize transfer (see Schmidt & Bjork, 1992). The driving force behind these positive far-transfer effects remains unclear.

The relatively recent interest in working memory training in aging has resulted in a body of literature that is very diverse. Type of training, the number of sessions, the duration of sessions and spacing of practice sessions provided are just a few of the many characteristics of training programs which have varied between studies – making it a challenge when reviewing the entire body of work to understand how these factors may contribute to positive training effects (see also Morrison & Chein, 2011; Shipstead, Redick & Engle, 2010). Hopefully, however, the field has started to mature to a point where critical training characteristics can be more systematically examined in order to find out how to best support the aging mind.

Finally, it is interesting to note that most studies did not find age differences in the magnitude of training-related improvements in the trained tasks. This finding is at odds with much earlier research showing that training more often amplifies preexisting age differences in performance (Verhaeghen & Marcoen, 1996). One reason for similar age trajectories as a function of working memory training may be due to fewer demands on self-initiated processing, as most training tasks employed require very little strategy acquisition and application (Craik & Byrd, 1982).

Working memory plasticity: Brain imaging studies

To the best of our knowledge, the first functional brain imaging study of the neural correlates of cognitive training in adulthood and aging targeted the method of LOCI mental imagery mnemonic (Nyberg et al., 2003). In keeping with previous behavioral studies (Baltes & Kliegl, 1992), age differences in memory performance were found to be magnified after as compared to before the intervention. Analyses of functional brain activity patterns, based on positron emission tomography (PET) recordings, revealed that one basis for the age-related difference implicated putative task-specific processes such as creating visual images and binding of cue-target information. These processes were related to occipito-temporal cortex and medial-temporal lobe regions, and significant age differences were observed in these regions (Nyberg et al., 2003; see also Jones et al., 2006). A second basis for the observed age differences and their magnification following training was found to be age-related processing deficits (e.g. executive), which affected the older adults' ability to effectively make use of the LOCI mnemonic (Nyberg et al., 2003; see also Jones et al., 2006). The apparent age-related processing deficit was linked to diminished frontal brain activity.

Thus, age-related differences in fronto-parietal brain activity, and associated executive processes, seem to underlie constraints in benefiting from mnemonic support. In a subsequent project, we therefore targeted training of executive processes (cf. section above, Dahlin et al., 2008a). The basic idea was that if we could strengthen executive processes and related fronto-parietal circuits, then older adults might show similar training-related gains to those of younger adults. A second motivation behind targeting general executive processes was to test the hypothesis that training of executive functions might lead to stronger and potentially broader transfer effects than more domain-specific interventions such as the method of LOCI. Numerous brain-imaging studies converge to show that a common characteristic of many cognitive tasks is that they engage fronto-parietal networks (for reviews, see Cabeza & Nyberg, 2000; Naghavi & Nyberg, 2005). At least in part, this commonality may reflect shared executive processes (Collette et al, 2006; Marklund et al., 2007). Hence, by strengthening executive processes and associated fronto-parietal networks by a certain type of cognitive training program, transfer to non-trained tasks that also rely on fronto-parietal regions might be expected (cf. Klingberg et al., 2005). However, as was reviewed above, cognitive transfer effects are typically weak or non-existent (e.g. Owen et al., 2010; Lee et al., 2012), which apparently conflicts with the notion that training a specific executive task and associated fronto-parietal recruitment will benefit other executive (fronto-parietal) tasks. An alternative possibility, then, is that training affects much more specific processes and brain systems, which accounts for the general finding of limited transfer.

Figure 4.1a schematically outlines our experimental protocol for testing whether executive functions training might broadly enhance the performance of older adults and lead to transfer via fronto-parietal networks. We targeted *updating* of information in working memory, a process related to fronto-parietal cortical regions as well as the striatum (Collette et al., 2006; Marklund et al., 2007; O'Reilly, 2006). Before and after five weeks of updating training (Dahlin et al., 2008b), functional magnetic resonance imaging (fMRI) was used to assess training-related changes in functional brain activity. Three different tasks were scanned: a letter memory updating task which served as the criterion task and two transfer tasks; an n-back working memory task; and a Stroop inhibition task. All three tasks were expected to engage executive control processes and fronto-parietal circuits (Collette et al., 2006; Miyake et al., 2000), and our fMRI findings supported this prediction (Figure 4.1b). The letter-memory task and the n-back task were expected to involve updating and engage the striatum (Miyake et al., 2000; O'Reilly, 2006), whereas the Stroop inhibition task was not, and the fMRI results confirmed this prediction (Fig 4.1b). Thus, to the degree that transfer was based on a shared fronto-parietal network, we would expect to find transfer from letter memory to both n-back and Stroop, whereas if transfer instead was based on the striatal updating network we would expect transfer to n-back only. The findings showed a highly selective behavioral transfer effect to n-back along with a training-related modulation of the fMRI signal in the striatum. These results confirm the hypothesis that a prerequisite for transfer is that the transfer task taxes the same basic process as supported by the intervention and related brain areas (Jonides, 2004; Thorndike & Woodworth, 1901) – in the present case updating and basal ganglia circuits.

An additional goal of the experiment was to examine whether executive processing training would lead to similar training-related gains for older as for younger adults. The results were positive by showing parallel gains for both age groups, i.e. there was no magnification of age differences. However, the older adults' level of performance on the letter-memory criterion task after five weeks of training was similar to the level reached by younger adults after two weeks. Moreover, the older adults did not show a significant transfer effect to the n-back task. The age-related constraints on learning and transfer after updating training were related to age-related changes in the striatum, thereby providing further support for a critical role of this brain region for updating.

Theoretical and computational models of the role of striatum in updating of information in working memory indicate that dopaminergic neurotransmission is a key factor (Drustewitz, 2006; O'Reilly, 2006). A recent PET study provided empirical support for this prediction (Bäckman et al., 2011). PET was used to assess dopamine D2 binding potential before and after five weeks of updating training, and an extensive neuropsychological battery was administered before and after the training period (cf. the fMRI protocol above). The behavioral results replicated the findings from the fMRI study by showing highly selective transfer to an n-back task only. The PET recordings were done during a baseline task as well as during a period when information was updated in working memory. Updating processing was found to affect bilateral striatal dopamine binding. Critically, a training-related influence on dopaminergic activity was observed in the left striatum, closely overlapping the region where a training-related effect was seen in the fMRI study. These findings extend related observations for the dopamine D1 system (McNab et al., 2009), and show that the dopamine system is modifiable by directed training. Physical activity (exercise) has been demonstrated to have beneficial effects on learning and cognition (Hillman et al., 2009), and the exercise-induced cognitive facilitation may in part be mediated by stimulation of dopaminergic neurotransmission by physical activity (Winter et al., 2007).

Taken together, the brain-imaging findings converge with behavioral findings of weak transfer effects, and indicate that a critical underlying factor is that the criterion and transfer tasks must engage overlapping *specific* processes and brain regions (cf. Boot et al., 2010), such as updating and the striatum as focused on here. Quite likely, other forms of training will critically depend on other processes and related brain circuits, but together with the rich set of behavioral studies showing limited transfer effects the imaging data reviewed here predict that attempts at developing training programs that lead to broad transfer effects are likely to fail.

A

FMRI session I	Five weeks of	FMRI session II
- letter memory	updating training	- letter memory
- n-back		- n-back
- Stroop		- Stroop

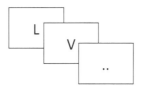

B

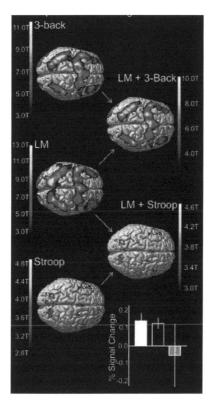

Figure 4.1 (A) An outline of the experimental protocol. (B) To the left, brain maps showing activation of common fronto-parietal circuits for all three tasks. The bar graph shows overlapping activation at pretest for both updating tasks (letter memory and 3-back) but not for the Stroop task

Source: Reproduced with permission from Dahlin et al. (2008b)

Important questions for future research

A central message of the present chapter is that transfer-of-learning effects are highly selective and limited in magnitude. At the same time, it is important to stress that reliable and reproducible transfer can be demonstrated, as in the original study by Dahlin et al. (2008a) and in the independent replication by Bäckman et al. (2011). Thus, for the future, an important task will be to determine what training conditions lead to best transfer effects (Jaeggi et al., 2011).

Relatedly, the transfer to everyday activities requires further examination. Based on the experimental findings, broad transfer seems unlikely (cf. Ball et al., 2002), indicating that analyses of key component processes underlying the targeted everyday behavior is vital for setting up an optimal training program.

The durability of training effects is a key issue that warrants further examination (Dahlin et al., 2008a; also Dahlin et al., 2009). As for physical activities, there are reasons to believe that cognitive training needs to be maintained. At the same time, some long-lasting effects have been reported (Dahlin et al., 2008a). The determining factor may be the length of the initial training program, as longer programs are more likely to establish new cognitive skills of substantial durability.

In conclusion, the present review indicates that cognitive training in general and working-memory training in particular cannot be expected to have very broad and general effects. At the same time, by now it seems firmly established that training of working memory is possible, and that some such effects do transfer. Therefore, although caution is warranted in view of commercial claims of training being a "low-hanging fruit" (cf. Owen et al., 2010), we are optimistic about future intervention studies.

References

Bäckman, L., Nyberg, L., Soveri, A., Johansson, J., Andersson, M., Dahlin, E., Stigsdotter Neely, A., Virta, J., Laine, M. & Rinne J. (2011). Effects of working-memory training on striatal dopamine release. *Science, 333*, 718.

Baddeley, A. D. & Hitch, G. (1974). Working memory. In G. H. Bower (Ed.), *The psychology of learning and motivation* (Vol. 8, pp. 47–89). New York: Academic Press.

Ball, K., Berch, D. B., Helmers, K. F., Jobe, J. B., Leveck, M. D., Marsiske, M. … Willis, S. L. (2002). Effects of cognitive training interventions with older adults: A randomized controlled trial. *Journal of the American Medical Association, 288*, 2271–2281.

Baltes, P. B. & Kliegl, R. (1992). Testing-the-limits research suggests irreversible aging loss in memory based on mental imagination. *Developmental Psychology, 28*, 121–125.

Bherer, L., Kramer, A. F., Peterson, M. S., Colcombe, S., Erickson, K. & Becic, E. (2005). Training effects on dual-task performance: Are there age-related differences in plasticity of attentional control? *Psychology and Aging, 20*, 695–709.

Bherer, L., Kramer, A. F., Peterson, M. S., Colcombe, S., Erickson, K. & Becic, E. (2006). Testing the limits of cognitive plasticity in older adults: Application to attention control. *Acta Psychologica, 123*, 261–278.

Bherer, L., Kramer, A. F., Peterson, M. S., Colcombe, S., Erickson, K. & Becic, E. (2008). Transfer effects in task-set cost and dual-task set cost after dual-task training in older and younger adults: Further evidence for cognitive plasticity in attentional control in late adulthood. *Experimental Aging Research, 34*, 188–219.

Boot, W. R., Basak, C., Basak, C., Erickson, K. I., Neider, M., Simons, D. J. … Kramer, A. F. (2010). Transfer of skill engendered by complex task training under conditions of variable priority. *Acta Psychologica, 135*, 349–357.

Borella, E., Carretti, B., Riboldi, F. & De Beni, R. (2010). Working memory training in older adults: Evidence of transfer and maintenance effects. *Psychology and Aging, 25*, 767–778.

Buschkuehl, M., Jaeggi, S., Hutchinson, S., Perrig-Chiello, P., Sapp, C., Muller, M. … Perrig, W. (2008). Impact of working memory training on memory performance in old-old adults. *Psychology and Aging, 23*, 743–753.

Cabeza, R. & Nyberg, L. (2000). Imaging cognition II: An empirical review of 275 PET and fMRI studies. *Journal of Cognitive Neuroscience, 12*, 1–47.

Cassavaugh, N. D. & Kramer, A. F. (2009). Transfer of computer-based training to simulated driving in older adults. *Applied Ergonomics, 40*, 943–952.

Chein, J. M. & Morrison, A. B. (2010). Expanding the mind's workspace: Training and transfer effects with a complex working memory span task. *Psychonomic Bulletin & Review, 17*, 193–199.

Collette, F. & Van der Linden, M. (2002). Brain imaging of the central executive component of working memory. *Neuroscience & Biobehavioral Reviews, 26*, 105–125.

Collette, F., Hogge, M., Salmon, E. & Van der Linden, M. (2006). Exploration of the neural substrates of executive functioning by functional neuroimaging. *Neuroscience, 139*, 209–221.

Craik, F. I. M. & Byrd, M. (1982). Aging and cognitive deficits: The role of attentional resources. In F. I. M. Craik & S. E. Trehub (Eds.), *Aging and cognitive processes* (pp. 191–211). New York: Plenum Press.

Dahlin, E., Bäckman, L., Stigsdotter Neely, A. & Nyberg, L. (2009). Training of the executive component of working memory: Subcortical areas mediate transfer effects. *Restorative Neurology and Neuroscience, 27*, 405–419.

Dahlin, E., Nyberg, L., Bäckman, L. & Stigsdotter Neely, A. (2008a). Plasticity of executive functioning in young and older adults: Immediate training gains, transfer and long-term maintenance. *Psychology and Aging, 23*, 720–730.

Dahlin, E., Stigsdotter Neely, A., Larsson, A., Bäckman, L. & Nyberg, L. (2008b). Transfer of learning after updating training mediated by the striatum. *Science, 320*, 1510–1512.

Daneman, M. & Carpenter, P. A. (1980). Individual difference in working memory and reading. *Journal of Verbal Learning and Verbal Behavior, 19*, 450–466.

Drustewitz, D. (2006). A few important points about dopamine's role in neural network dynamics. *Pharmacopsychiatry, 39*, 72–75.

Friedman, N. P., Miyake, A., Corley, R. P., Young, S. E., DeFries, J. C. & Hewitt, J. K. (2006). Not all executive functions are related to intelligence. *Psychological Science, 17*, 172–179.

Gabrieli, J. D. E., Singh, J., Stebbins, G. T. & Goetz, C. G. (1996). Reduced working memory span in Parkinson's disease: Evidence of the role of a frontostriatal system in working and strategic memory. *Neuropsychology, 10*, 322–332.

Hasher, L., Lustig, C. & Zacks, R. T. (2007). Inhibitory mechanisms and the control of attention. In A. R. A. Conway, C. Jarrold, M. J. Kane, A. Miyake & L. N. Towse (Eds.), *Variations in working memory*. New York: Oxford University Press.

Hertzog, C., Kramer, A. F., Wilson, R. S. & Lindenberger, U. (2009). Enrichment effects on adult cognitive development: Can the functional capacity of older adults be preserved and enhanced? *Psychological Science, 9*, 1–65.

Hillman, C. H., Pontifex, M. B., Raine, L. B., Castelli, D. M., Hall, E. E. & Kramer, A. F. (2009). The effect of acute treadmill walking on cognitive control and academic achievement in preadolescent children. *Neuroscience, 159*, 1044–1054.

Jaeggi, S. M., Buschkuehl, M., Jonides, J. & Perrig, W. J. (2008). Improving fluid intelligence with training on working memory. *Proceedings of the National Academy of Sciences, 105*, 6829–6833.

Jaeggi, S. M., Buschkuehl, M., Jonides, J. & Shah, P. (2011). Short- and long-term benefits of cognitive training. *Proceedings of the National Academy of Sciences, 108*, 10081–10086.

Jones, S., Nyberg, L., Sandblom, J., Stigsdotter Neely, A., Ingvars, M., Peterssons, K. M. & Bäckman, L. (2006). Cognitive and neural plasticity in aging: General and task-specific limitations. *Neuroscience & Biobehavioral Reviews, 30*, 864–871.

Jonides, J. (2004). How does practice makes perfect? *Nature Neuroscience, 7*, 10–11.

Karbach, J. & Kray, J. (2009). How useful is executive control training? Age differences in near and far transfer of task-switching training. *Developmental Science, 12*, 978–990.

Karbach, J., Mang, S. & Kray, J. (2010). Transfer of task-switching training in older age: The role of verbal processes. *Psychology and Aging, 25*, 677–683.

Kempler, D., Almor, A., Tyler, L. K., Andersen, E. S. & MacDonald, M. C. (1998). Sentence comprehension deficits in Alzheimer's disease: A comparison of off-line and on-line processing. *Brain and Language, 64*, 297–316.

Klingberg, T. (2010). Training and plasticity of working memory. *Trends of Cognitive Sciences, 14*, 317–324.

Klingberg, T., Fernell, E., Olesen, P. J., Johnson, M., Gustafsson, P., Dahlström, K., Gillberg, C. G., Forssberg, H., Westerberg, H. (2005). Computerized training of working memory in children with ADHD – a randomized, controlled trial. *Journal of the American Academy of Child & Adolescence Psychiatry, 44*, 177–186.

Kramer, A. F., Larish, J. F. & Strayer, D. L. (1995). Training for attentional control in dual task settings: A comparison of young and old adults. *Journal of Experimental Psychology: Applied, 1*, 50–76.

Kramer, A. F., Larish, J. F., Weber, T. A. & Bardell, L. (1999). Training for executive control: Task coordination strategies and aging. In D. Gopher & A. Koriat (Eds.), *Attention and performance XVII: Cognitive regulation of performance: Interaction of theory and application* (pp. 617–652). Cambridge, MA: The MIT Press.

Lee, H., Boot, W. R., Basak, C., Voss., M. W., Prakash, R. S., Neider, M. ... Kramer, A. F. (2012). Performance gains from direct training do not transfer to untrained tasks. *Acta Psychologica, 139*, 146–158.

Li, K. Z. H., Roudaia, E., Lussier, M., Bherer, L., Leroux, A. & McKinley, P. A. (2010). Benefits of cognitive dual-task training on balance performance in healthy older adults. *Journal of Gerontology: Medical Sciences, 12*, 1344–1352.

Li, S.-C., Schmiedek, F., Huxhold, O., Röcke, C., Smith, J. & Lindenberger, U. (2008). Working memory plasticity in old age: Transfer and maintenance. *Psychology and Aging, 23*, 731–742.

Lustig, C., Shah, P., Seidler, R. & Reuter-Lorenz, P. A. (2009). Aging, training, and the brain: A review and future directions. *Neuropsychological Review, 19*, 504–522.

Lövdén, M., Bäckman, L., Lindenberger, U., Schaefer, S. & Schmiedek, F. (2010). A theoretical framwork for the study of adult cognitive plasticity. *Psychological Bulletin, 136*, 659–676.

McCabe, D. P., Roediger III, H. L., McDaniel, M. A., Balota, D. A. & Hambrick, D. Z. (2010). The relationship between working memory capacity and executive functioning: Evidence for a common executive attention contruct. *Neuropsychology, 24*, 222–243.

MacKay-Brandt, A. (2011). Training attentional control in older adults. *Aging Neuropsychology and Cognition, 18*, 432–451.

McNab, F., Varrone, A., Farde, L., Jucaite, A., Bystritsky, P., Forssberg, H. & Klingberg, T. (2009). Changes in cortical dopamine D1 receptor binding associated with cognitive training. *Science, 323*, 800–802.

Marklund, P., Fransson, P., Cabeza, R., Larsson, A., Ingvar, M. & Nyberg, L. (2007). Unity and diversity of tonic and phasic executive control components in episodic and working memory. *NeuroImage, 36*, 1361–1373.

Miyake, A. & Shah, P. (1999). *Models of working memory: Mechanisms of active maintenance and executive control*. Melbourne, Australia: Cambridge University Press.

Miyake, A., Friedman, N. P., Emerson, M. J., Witzki, A. H., Howerter, A. & Wager, T. D. (2000). The unity and diversity of executive functions and their contributions to complex "Frontal Lobe" tasks: A latent variable analysis. *Cognitive Psychology, 41*, 49–100.

Moody, D. E. (2009). Can intelligence be increased by training on a task of working memory? *Intelligence, 37*, 327–328.

Morrison, A. B. & Chein, J. M. (2011). Does working memory training work? The promise and challenges of enhancing cognition by training working memory. *Psychonomic Bulletine Review, 18*, 46–60.

Naghavi, H. R. & Nyberg, L. (2005). Common fronto-parietal activity in attention, memory, and consciousness: Shared demands on integration? *Consciousness and Cognition, 14*, 390–425.

Nyberg, L., Sandblom, J., Jones, S., Stigsdotter Neely, A., Petersson, K. M., Ingvars, M. & Bäckman, L. (2003). Neural correlates of training-related memory improvement in adulthood and aging. *Proceedings of the National Academy of Sciences, 100*, 13728–13733.

Olesen, P. J., Westerberg, H., Klingberg, T. (2004). Increased prefrontal and parietal activity after training of working memory. *Nature Neuroscience, 7*, 75–79.

O'Reilly, R. C. (2006). Biologically based computational models of high-level cognition. *Science, 314*, 91–94.

Owen, A. M., Hampshire, A., Grahn, J. A., Stenton, R., Dajani, S., Burns, A. S., Howard, R. J. & Ballard, C. G. (2010). Putting brain training to the test. *Nature, 465*, 775–778.

Rebok, G. W., Carlson, M. C. & Langbaum, J. B. S. (2007). Training and maintaining memory abilities in healthy older adults: Traditional and novel approaches. *Journal of Gerontology: Series B, 62b*, 53–61.

Richmond, L. L., Morrison, A. B., Chein, J. M. & Olson, I. R. (2011). Working memory training and transfer in older adults. *Psychology and Aging, 26*, 813–822.

Sandberg, P., Rönnlund, M., Nyberg, L. & Stigsdotter Neely (2013). Executive process training in young and old adults. *Aging, Neuropsychology, and Cognition* [Epub ahead of print]. DOI: 10.1080/13825585.2013.839777

Schmidt, R. A. & Bjork, R. A. (1992). New conceptualizations of practice: Common principals in three paradigms suggest new concepts for training. *Psychological Science, 3*, 207–217.

Shipstead, Z., Redick, T. S. & Engle, R. W. (2010). Does working memory training generalize? *Psychologica Belgica, 50,* 245–276.

Stigsdotter Neely, A. & Bäckman, L. (1993). Long-term maintenance of gains from memory training in older adults: Two 3 ½ year follow-up studies. *Journal of Gerontology: Psychological Sciences, 48,* 233–237.

Thorndike, E. L. & Woodworth, R. S. (1901). The influence of improvement in one mental function upon the efficiency of other functions. *Psychological Review, 8,* 247–261.

Unsworth, N. & Engle, R. W. (2007). The nature of individual differences in working memory capacity: Active maintenance in primary memory and controlled search from secondary memory. *Psychological Review, 114,* 104–132.

Unsworth, N., Heitz, R. P., Engle, R. W. (2005). Working memory capacity in hot and cold cognition. In R. W. Engle, G. Sedek, U. Hecker & D. N. McIntosh (Eds.), *Cognitive limitations in aging and psychopathology: Attention, working memory, and executive functions* (pp. 19–43). New York: Oxford University Press.

Verhaeghen, P. (2000). The interplay of growth and decline: Theoretical and empirical aspects of plasticity of intellectual and memory performance in normal aging. In R. D. Hill, L. Bäckman & A. Stigsdotter Neely (Eds.), *Cognitive rehabilitation in old age* (pp. 3–22). New York: Oxford University Press.

Verhaeghen, P. & Marcoen, A. (1996). On the mechanisms of plasticity in young and older adults after instruction in the method of loci: Evidence for an amplification model. *Psychology and Aging, 11,* 164–178.

Verhaeghen, P., Marcoen, A. & Goossens, L. (1992). Improving memory performance in the aged through mnemonic training: A meta-analytic study. *Psychology and Aging, 7,* 242–251.

Winter, B., Breitenstein, C., Mooren, F. C., Voelker, K., Fobker, M., Lechtermann, A. … Knecht, S. (2007). High impact running improves learning. *Neurobiology of Learning and Memory, 87,* 597–609.

5 Associations between working memory and white matter integrity in normal ageing

Rebecca A. Charlton and Robin G. Morris

The chances of developing brain pathologies are much greater beyond middle age, along with an increase in causally related risk factors. As part of this neurobiological scenario there are changes that crucially reduce the integrity of brain white matter. In particular, neurovascular damage affects the small vessels that intricately supply blood to the white matter axons that are necessary for efficient neuronal transmission throughout the brain (Brown & Thore, 2011; Duprez et al., 2001). Whilst vascular damage can progress to the extent that it produces a clinical syndrome, as the focus of this book is 'normal ageing', we limit consideration of white matter damage to people defined as 'typical' individuals. Here it is acknowledged that the brain may still show significant levels of white matter damage. In normal ageing, there are distinct profiles of cognitive decline, and as the title of this book implies, a main feature of cognitive ageing is reduced working memory ability. Thus we explore the extent to which working memory performance can be explained specifically by neurovascular white matter damage and the potential risk factors that make this more likely.

Over the last decade the role of white matter in supporting complex cognitive functions that rely on distributed neural networks, such as working memory, has been explored (Charlton et al., 2006; O'Sullivan, Jones et al., 2001; Kennedy & Raz, 2009). It has been shown that in normal ageing, even relatively small amounts of white matter damage – largely thought to be vascular in nature – accumulate, disrupting communication between cortical regions and leading to disconnection. We have hypothesised that this damage might not be enough to disrupt, at a gross level, Shannonian Communication Transfer in which there is a high degree of redundancy, such as in visual perception. On the other hand it is sufficient to impact the efficiency of what we call here *Dynamic Connectivity*, neurocognitive control processes that are dynamic and reiterative, such as executive function and working memory (Charlton et al., 2008; Charlton, Barrick, Lawes, Markus & Morris, 2010; O'Sullivan, Jones et al., 2001).

To explore this hypothesis, different methods for measuring white matter integrity have been utilised. Since the degree to which functional integrity can be predicted by different methods has been found to vary, we start by considering these methods in turn. In outline, the measurement techniques include whole brain and regional volumes, rating scales and volume measurements for presence of white matter hyperintensities (WMH), and the more recently developed measures such as diffusion tensor imaging (DTI) and magnetisation transfer (MT) that quantify white matter efficiency. These measures and their associations with age will be briefly described before we discuss their relationship to working memory. In reviewing this literature, we make reference to our own studies as part of the GENIE (St George's Neuropsychology and Imaging in the Elderly) project, a large-scale longitudinal investigation of the relationship between white matter integrity and cognition in normal ageing.

Magnetic resonance imaging measures of white matter

White matter volume

Initially, neuroimaging white matter volume (WMV) was the only *in vivo* white matter measure. WMV was expressed either as total white matter volume or as volume of white matter within specified regions, often expressed as a percentage of total intracranial volume or total brain tissue volume to control for individual differences in head size (Davatzikos & Resnick, 2002; Resnick et al., 2000). Generally white matter volume has been shown to decline as age increases, but at a lower rate than occurs in degenerative conditions such as dementia (Carlson et al., 2008; van der Flier et al., 2005).

Age-related changes in white matter volume

White matter volume has generally been found to be fairly stable in adulthood until midlife, with an almost linear decline in volume being observed thereafter (Ge, Grossman, Babb, Rabin, Mannon & Kolson, 2002a). Data from the Baltimore Longitudinal Study of Aging demonstrated cross-sectionally that age correlated significantly with brain volumes in all areas, with age differences the greatest in the parietal lobe (Resnick et al., 2000). Longitudinally, brain volume was found to be fairly stable over one year (Resnick et al., 2000), but after four years white matter volume declined significantly in the frontal, parietal, and temporal regions (Davatzikos & Resnick, 2002). It is important to note that the rates at which white matter volume declined did not differ with age, i.e. decline was not 'faster' in the older adult age range (Davatzikos & Resnick, 2002), although some suggest accelerated decline in specific regions such as the thalamus and frontal white matter (Good et al., 2001).

In terms of regional differences in ageing, it has been suggested that the frontal lobes are particularly at risk of age-related decline (West, 1996; Raz et al., 1997). Several studies have identified reduction in prefrontal white matter volume with ageing, when other brain regions including parietal white matter did not show significant decline (Salat, Kaye & Janowsky, 1999; Raz et al., 1997).

White matter hyperintensities

In addition it has been noted that white matter hyperintensities (WMH), also known as white matter lesions (WML) are visible during stuctural MRI scanning, the appearance on scanning images termed *leukoaraiosis* by Hachinski (O'Sullivan, 2008). Readily observable hyperintense signals (white appearance) are seen on T2-weighted MRI images in the brains of normal older adults, with degree of WMH varying by individual (See Figure 5.1). Initially WMH were measured using observer rating scales that graded the presence of lesions according to location and severity (see Table 5.1) (Scheltens et al., 1993; Scheltens et al., 1998; Wahlund et al., 2001). More recently, WMH have been quantified as volume present in the brain, requiring lesions to be drawn either by hand or with the use of automatic segmentation software (Charlton, Schiavone, Barrick, Morris & Markus, 2010; Ramirez et al., 2011; Raz et al., 2007). Such volumes are often reported as proportion of total tissue volume.

Age-related changes in white matter hyperintensities

As well as WMH being readily apparent in old age (Charlton, Barrick, Markus & Morris, 2010; Sachdev et al., 2007; Scheltens, Barkhof, & Fazekas, 2003) there is strong evidence that they reflect vascular damage accumulating across the lifespan (Knopman et al., 2011; Young, Halliday & Kril, 2008), accentuated in people with vascular risk factors such as hypertension and diabetes (Enzinger et al., 2005; Marquine et al., 2010; Raz et al., 2007). WMH are most frequently located adjacent to the ventricles (periventricular: PVWMH) or in the deep white matter (DWMH) where small perforating arteries end (Enzinger et al., 2006; Wen &

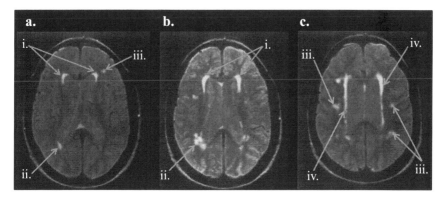

Figure 5.1 Example of WMH

Source: Reprinted from Scheltens et al. (1993) with permission from Elsevier.

Key: i.) = frontal 'caps'; ii.) = occipital 'caps'; iii.) = deep WMH; iv.) = periventricular bands. Frontal 'caps' score = 2; occipital 'caps' score = 2; periventricular bands score = 2; frontal WMH score = 4; parietal WMH score = 4. Note the distinction between the 'caps' and the deep WMH, most clearly seen in a.) The terms 'caps' and 'bands' refer to characteristic hyperintense regions around the lateral ventricles.

Table 5.1 Semiquantative rating scale for WMH

Visual rating of signal hyperintensities		
Periventricular Hyperintensities (PVWMH 0–6)		
Caps occipital	0 / 1 / 2	0 = absent
Caps frontal	0 / 1 / 2	1 = <5mm
Bands lateral ventricles	0 / 1 / 2	2 = >5mm and <10mm
White Matter Hyperintensities (WMH 0–24)		
Frontal	0 / 1 / 2 / 3 / 4 / 5 / 6	0 = n/a
Parietal	0 / 1 / 2 / 3 / 4 / 5 / 6	1 = <3mm, n ≤5
Occipital	0 / 1 / 2 / 3 / 4 / 5 / 6	2 = <3mm, n >6
Temporal	0 / 1 / 2 / 3 / 4 / 5 / 6	3 = 4–10mm, n ≤5
		4 = 4mm, n >6
		5 = >11mm, n>1
		6 = confluent
Basal Ganglia Hyperintensities (BG 0–30)		
Caudate nucleus	0 / 1 / 2 / 3 / 4 / 5 / 6	
Putamen	0 / 1 / 2 / 3 / 4 / 5 / 6	
Globus pallidus	0 / 1 / 2 / 3 / 4 / 5 / 6	
Thalamus	0 / 1 / 2 / 3 / 4 / 5 / 6	
Internal capsule	0 / 1 / 2 / 3 / 4 / 5 / 6	
Infra-tentorial foci of Hyperintensity (ITF 0–24)		
Cerebellum	0 / 1 / 2 / 3 / 4 / 5 / 6	
Mesencephalon	0 / 1 / 2 / 3 / 4 / 5 / 6	
Pons	0 / 1 / 2 / 3 / 4 / 5 / 6	
Medulla	0 / 1 / 2 / 3 / 4 / 5 / 6	

Source: Reprinted from Scheltens, Barkhof, Leys, Pruvo, Nauta,Vermersch, Steinling & Valk (1993) with permission from Elsevier.

Key: Semiquantative rating of signal hyperintensities in separate regions, the range of the scale between brackets, n = number or lesions, n/a = no abnormalities.

Sachdev, 2004). Some studies have suggested that PVWMH and DWMH are heterogeneous (Spilt et al., 2006). DWMH have been shown to progress at a faster rate than PVWMH (Sachdev et al., 2007) although PVWMH have been hypothesised to have a greater impact on cognition (van den Heuvel et al., 2006). Nevertheless, other studies have identified no clear distinctions between DWMH and PVWMH. DeCarli et al. (2005) suggest that total WMH volume may reflect associations with cognition just as accurately as DWMH and PVWMH.

Diffusion tensor imaging

The development of diffusion tensor imaging (DTI) has been a significant advance that allows the direct quantification of white matter tissue integrity. DTI measurement is based on physical observation that water molecules in unbounded space will diffuse in random directions, termed isotropic diffusion. In the brain, this diffusion is restricted by cellular structures such as axons, neurons and glial cells and is said to be anisotropic. DTI enables the generation of maps that quantify the degree of anisotropy, the principle diffusion direction and other metrics that provide specific information about diffusion in the tissue present. The two most established measures from DTI are fractional anisotropy (FA) and mean diffusivity (MD). FA represents a ratio of the principle diffusion direction and reflects structural organisation; MD measures the overall magnitude of water diffusion.

More recently measures such as axial diffusivity ($\lambda_{\parallel}$, the magnitude of the principal diffusivity along gross white matter axonal structure, i.e. $\lambda_{\parallel} = \lambda_1$) and radial diffusivity ($\lambda_{\perp}$, the mean cross-sectional diffusivity perpendicular to λ_1, i.e. $\lambda_{\perp} = (\lambda_2 + \lambda_3)/2$) have been developed from animal models and are being used in humans (Song et al., 2002; Sun, Neil & Song, 2003). It has been suggested that increases in $\lambda_{\perp}$ reflect demyelination ($\lambda_{\perp}$ lower in healthy tissue), whereas increases in $\lambda_{\parallel}$ reflect axonal damage (Irvine & Blakemore, 2006; Song et al., 2002; Song et al., 2005). However, caution is advised when interpreting these measures as they are closely associated with each other and may reflect other damage to white matter in addition to these factors (Wheeler-Kingshott & Cercignani, 2009). Studies of $\lambda_{\parallel}$ measures in particular have shown inconsistent results across human and animal models of axonal degeneration (Budde et al., 2009; Metwalli et al., 2010). To what extent these differences in AD represent disease severity or issues translating this measure from animal to human models remains to be established.

Age-related changes in diffusion tensor imaging

MD has been found to increase with ageing, generally considered to reflect a reduction in white matter integrity (Nusbaum et al., 2001; Abe et al., 2002; O'Sullivan, Jones et al., 2001).FA has been shown to decline with age, despite no corresponding reduction in white matter volume (Pfefferbaum & Sullivan, 2003; Sullivan et al., 2001).

Although many studies comparing younger and older subjects cross-sectionally have supported the preferential decline of the frontal lobes (Abe et al., 2002; Head et al., 2004), other studies using a continuum from midlife onwards have demonstrated a reduction in white matter integrity across the whole brain (Charlton et al., 2006; Nusbaum et al., 2001). Recently, our GENIE longitudinal study has established that changes in white matter integrity can be observed in as little as two years, as demonstrated using MD and FA measurement across the whole brain (see Figure 5.2) (Barrick et al., 2010). FA results suggested that although change occurred across the whole brain it was more pronounced in frontal regions, whereas MD data suggested changes were equivalent regardless of brain region (Barrick et al., 2010; Charlton, Schiavone, Barrick, Morris & Markus, 2010).

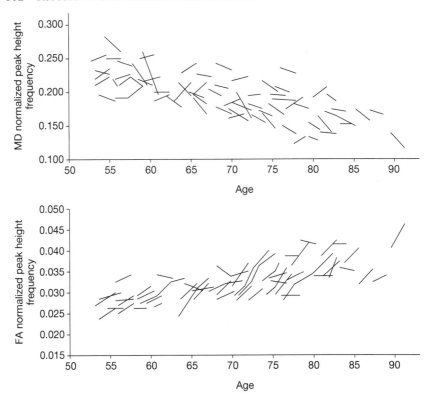

Figure 5.2 Decline in white matter integrity by age. Changes in mean diffusivity (MD) and fractional anisotropy (FA) normalised peak height frequency over two-year delay. Each line represents an individual participant

Source: Charlton, Schiavone, Barrick, Morris & Markus (2010).

Histological studies in humans have supported the association between $\lambda_\perp$ and myelin, with several studies identifying increases in $\lambda_\perp$ with older age (Sullivan, Rohlfing & Pfefferbaum, 2010; Vernooij et al., 2008; Zhang et al., 2010). Patterns of $\lambda_\parallel$ with increasing ageing are more complex with both increases and decreases observed in different brain regions (Sullivan, Rohlfing & Pfefferbaum, 2010; Vernooij et al., 2008; Zhang et al., 2010). It is important to note that caution should be still be exercised when interpreting these measures as they are not yet fully understood (Wheeler-Kingshott & Cercignani, 2009; see also Madden et al., 2012 for review of DTI methods).

Magnetisation Transfer

Magnetisation Transfer (MT) is based on a comparison of proton interactions in a 'free' environment (such as water) with proton interactions in an environment where motion is restricted, such as tissue (Ashburner & Friston, 2000; Molko et al., 2002). The most commonly used measure is the MT ratio (MTR), which reflects the efficiency of magnetisation exchange between protons in tissue compared with surrounding water. As such, MTR provides quantitative information and may allow distinction between different levels of lesion severity (Bastin et al., 2009; Grossman et al., 1994).

Age-related changes in Magnetisation Transfer

Most studies have found white matter MTR values to be lower in older adults compared to middle-aged adults and also to correlate with age (Fazekas et al., 2005; Ge, Grossman, Babb, Rabin, Mannon, & Kolson, 2002b), although some do not find this pattern (Benedetti et al., 2006). In a whole brain histogram analysis across the lifespan (11–76 years), MTR peak height correlated significantly with age (Rovaris et al., 2003). In a later study of middle-aged and older adults (50–90 years), a similar pattern was observed with both MTR peak height normalised frequency and median correlating highly significantly with age (Schiavone et al., 2009).

Associations between white matter measures and working memory

Definitions of working memory have been provided elsewhere in this book (See, for example, Chapter 1 and Chapter 2, this volume). Although the methods vary in terms of exploring working memory and white matter integrity, the main method has been to use span tasks, including different materials and modalities. In this sense the cognitive function explored concerns mainly the storage aspect of working memory, but other paradigms such as backward Digit Span or the N-back task, dual task processing, cognitive flexibility or response inhibition have also been examined.

White matter volume and working memory

Relatively few studies have examined associations specifically between white matter volume and working memory or indeed any other cognitive function. Those studies that have done so tend to incorporate this information with that of WMH and/or grey matter volume (covered on pp. 104–107).

In a recent study, total grey and white matter volume was examined controlling for total brain size (Taki et al., 2011). This study examined brain volume in a sample of 109 individuals aged over 69. Working memory was measured using the Wechsler Adult Intelligence Scale-III Digit Span task. After controlling for age, gender and education, grey matter volume correlated with working memory performance, but white matter volume did not. The same pattern was observed longitudinally. Raz and colleagues examined decline in working memory over five years, as well as white matter volume adjacent to the prefrontal cortex and the inferior parietal lobe, grey matter volumes and WMH (Raz et al., 2007). Although all three working memory tasks (Computation Span and Listening Span from Salthouse et al., 1998; Size Judgement Span from Cherry & Park, 1993) demonstrated age-related differences, only the Listening Span task demonstrated a longitudinal decline in performance. Furthermore, the decline in Listening Span was only present in a group with vascular risk factors and did not correlate with white matter volume or atrophy (Raz et al., 2007). Significant associations were noted in the grey matter of the fusiform gyrus and in DWMH (see the following section for more details).

A recent study that incorporates information about both blood pressure levels and apolipoprotein E (APOE) status demonstrates a complex pattern of associations (Bender & Raz, 2012). Although a working memory composite score (comprising Size Judgement Span, Listening Span, Spatial Recall and N-back) correlated with frontal white matter volumes in both APOE-ε4 carriers and APOE-ε3 homozygotes, different patterns of association were observed using structural equation modelling. For APOE-ε4 carriers, age-related variance in working memory composite score was explained by higher systolic blood pressure and smaller frontal white matter volumes, as well as slower information processing. In contrast, among APOE-ε3 homozygotes, age-related variance in working memory was explained by smaller frontal white matter and lateral prefrontal cortex grey matter volumes as well as slower information processing, but not systolic blood pressure (Bender & Raz, 2012). The authors discuss the important issue of cumulative effects from different risk factors. In this case, systolic blood pressure ratings within the high end of the normal range coupled with carrying the APOE-ε4 allele, was associated with smaller frontal volumes. Thus, these factors in combination may have more severe consequences in terms of both brain pathology and cognitive impairment than when they occur in isolation.

This latter study demonstrates the insightful conclusions that are possible by incorporating information about vascular risk and sophisticated statistics into cognitive ageing research. Nevertheless, the lack of straightforward association may also reflect the measurement technique, in which volume of tissue may be a fairly crude indication of tissue function. Alternative MRI methods may allow a more 'fine cuts' approach to understanding brain-cognition associations than relatively coarse white matter volume measures with divisions into regions often based only on large areas of brain.

White matter hyperintensities and working memory

The presence of white matter hyperintensities (WMH) has been associated with a range of different cognitive functions, with executive dysfunction being the most commonly described difficulty (Nitkunan et al., 2008; O'Sullivan et al., 2004). Given the strong association between vascular risk factors and WMH, many studies among older adults are in patient populations. Common patient groups include those with hypertension, diabetes, transient ischaemic attacks (TIA) or the neurological condition cerebral small vessel disease (Nitkunan et al., 2008; Raz, Rodrigue & Acker, 2003; Sachdev et al., 2004).

Cross-sectional

Using rating scales Oosterman and colleagues examined associations between WMH and working memory in normal middle-aged and older adults (Oosterman, Vogels et al., 2008; Oosterman, van Harten et al., 2008). In a sample of 54 adults aged over 65 years old, regression analyses were performed with age, sex and education as confounder variables, followed by vascular risk score (Framingham Stroke Risk Profile; FSRP) then WMH variables. Digit Span backwards, Paced Auditory Serial Addition Test (PASAT) or CANTAB spatial working memory task were assessed in turn as the dependent variable (Oosterman, van Harten et al., 2008). After confounder variables and FSRP were accounted for, DWMH explained a significant proportion of the variance in the PASAT and the CANTAB spatial working memory task. For the PASAT, confounders explained 21.7% of variance, FSRP explained non-significant increment of 2.2% and frontal DWMH explained a further 6.4% of the variance (total variance = 30.3%). For the CANTAB spatial working memory task, confounders explained 26.9% of variance, FSRP added a non-significant 1%, and total WMH significantly predicted 8.7% of the variance in performance – with DWMH particularly in frontal lobes the strongest predictor (total variance = 36.6%). Digit Span backwards performance was only explained by the confounder variables, and there was no significant correlation between Digit Span Backwards and CANTAB spatial working memory task. In contrast to these findings, in a larger sample of 160 adults aged over 50, PVWMH (as well as medial temporal lobe volume) but *not* DWMH were associated with performance on the CANTAB spatial working memory task (Oosterman, Vogels et al., 2008). It should be noted that the CANTAB spatial working memory paradigm has a large spatial learning component, as well as being sensitive in part to spatial working memory.

It is also possible that the complexity of the overall working memory task affect these WMH-working memory associations. In a study of 65 adults aged 65–84, prevalence of WMH correlated significantly with Digit Span Backwards and Word Span tasks, but not with the relatively simple Digit Span Forwards task (Rabbitt et al., 2007). However, in a study with a larger sample, significant correlations were also noted with Digit Span Forwards (Vannorsdall et al., 2009). Using WMH volumes rather than rating scales, a large community study (ABC Study) compared 121 adults aged over 60 (mean age = 74.2 yrs) and 132 adults aged under 60 (mean age = 42.7 yrs) (Vannorsdall et al., 2009). Volumes of both PVWMH and DWMH were associated with working memory performance measured using Digit Span Forwards and Backwards, and both Letters and Numbers from the Brief Test of Attention. Furthermore, among older adults, WMH accounted for a greater proportion of the variance than in the sample as a whole, which may be associated with their increased cardiovascular risk (Vannorsdall et al., 2009). In addition to a PVWMH-DWMH distinction, some studies have examined presence of WMH in each lobe. In such a study Raz, Rodrigue & Acker (2003) found that a working memory composite score (including Computation Span, Listening Span and Size Judgment Span tasks) was differentially associated with WMH across the brain. Frontal and Temporal WMH as well as DWMH in the Frontal lobe were significantly correlated with working memory, but PVWMH were not.

The relative impact of DWMH versus PVWMH or location of WMH on cognition is still debated and findings are mixed (van den Heuvel et al., 2006; DeCarli et al., 2005; Gunning-Dixon & Raz, 2003). It is unclear in the two studies by Oosterman and colleagues to what extent differences are due to the different age ranges assessed and/or sample size. Given that large periventricular lesions may infiltrate the deep white matter and that confluent lesions may be divided into PVWMH or DWMH by fairly arbitrary criteria, some authors have argued that the distinction between lesion types may be less important than originally thought (van den Heuvel et al., 2006; DeCarli et al., 2005). In addition, if we consider white matter tract, rather than a gross periventricular/deep white matter distinction, it is likely that it is the presence of a lesion *within* a functionally important tract that impacts cognitive performance, rather than the location of the lesion along the length of the tract (Duering et al., 2011; Gunning-Dixon & Raz, 2003).

This issue has been raised in a study exploring the relationship between executive function (measured using perseverative errors on the WCST), working memory (composite of Computation Span and Listening Span) and WMH, and brain volume using structural equation modelling. Whereas executive function performance was accounted for equally by prefrontal cortex volume and frontal WMH, decline in working memory performance was not explained by these measures and was only partially explained by age (Gunning-Dixon & Raz, 2003). These results show that working memory may implicate more diverse brain regions than the frontal lobes alone by activating a complex neural network (see also section from p. 115 on models). The authors acknowledged that WMH may not be the best measure for assessing integrity of diffuse networks, as the location of a WMH would have to be precise in order to disrupt the pathways that form the fronto-parietal connections which are implicated in working memory (Sauseng, Klimesch, Schabus & Doppelmayr, 2005; Carpenter, Just & Reichle, 2000). It is also important to note that not all studies have identified significant associations between WMH and working memory, although associations with executive function were observed (O'Brien et al., 2002).

Longitudinal

In addition to WMH measurements in cross-sectional studies, a potentially more discriminative technique is monitoring WMH longitudinally, allowing associations between lesion progression and cognitive decline to be assessed. In a study over five years, Raz and colleagues examined 46 individuals (aged 45–77), half of whom remained healthy during the study and half whom had baseline hypertension and/or developed vascular problems (Raz et al., 2007). Both PVWMH and DWMH were measured as well as regional grey matter volumes and three working memory tasks (Computation Span, Listening Span, Size Judgment Span). All three working memory measures demonstrated age-related differences, but only

Listening Span demonstrated a longitudinal decline in performance. This decline was only present in the vascular risk group and was associated with progression of DWMH and atrophy in the fusiform gyrus (Raz et al., 2007). The authors emphasise that modifiable risk factors such as vascular disease, even in a mild form, may contribute significantly to explaining age-related decline in working memory. Over a similar time-period, the ABC Study did not identify any associations between WMH volume and working memory performance although DWMH showed a trend towards significance (Vannorsdall et al., 2009).

Two further longitudinal studies, including our GENIE study, have measured WMH progression (Charlton, Schiavone, Barrick, Morris & Markus, 2010; Marquine et al., 2010). In the GENIE study, the mean WMH volume increased from 7.21% to 9% of brain volume after two years in a sample with a mean age of 71 years (age range 50–90). Over the same period working memory, measured using Digit Span Backwards and Letter-Number Sequencing from the Wechsler Memory Scale (WMS-III; Wechsler et al., 1998), also showed significant decline. We found that change in WMH did not explain any variance in working memory decline (Charlton, Schiavone, Barrick, Morris & Markus, 2010; but see p. 108 for details of associations with DTI). Furthermore, the volume of WMH at baseline did not predict the decline in working memory. Marquine and colleagues' (2010) study of 110 adults aged over 60 years of age divided WMH into anterior and posterior brain regions (divided by midline of corpus callosum). WMH in both anterior and posterior regions increased over the two-year period. Using Digit Span Backwards and Ascending Digit Span (modelled on the Digit Ordering Test) to create a composite score of working memory, Marquine and colleagues also report no significant association between change in working memory and increase in WMH volume (Marquine et al., 2010).

Despite cross-sectional associations between working memory performance and WMH volume, the longitudinal associations between decline in working memory and increase in WMH volume in healthy ageing are less robust. One reason that this has been put forward is the relatively small amount of WMH that can be seen in normal ageing compared to ageing with vascular disease or clinical conditions. In other words, WMH is too crude a measure of functional integrity to be straightforwardly associated with cognitive decline (Hannesdottir et al., 2009). Conversely, it has been argued that healthy brains can 'tolerate' a certain amount of vascular pathology and it is only once a threshold of damage has been reached that cognitive impairment is observed (Libon et al., 2008). Evidence does suggest that the same proportion of WMH has a greater impact on cognition when other brain pathology is present, i.e. in early Alzheimer's Disease compared to 'typical' older adults (Burns et al., 2005). However, in relation to normal ageing, the most likely explanation for the weak association is the lack of early visibility of WMH and the need to reach its own 'threshold' in order to be visible on MRI scans. Methods such as DTI and MTR, discussed in the following section, have been shown to detect 'damage' prior to the appearance of WMH (Spilt et al., 2006; O'Sullivan, Summers et al., 2001). Thus these methods are shown to be more sensitive in detecting white matter damage and may demonstrate stronger associations.

Diffusion tensor imaging and working memory

DTI studies have the advantage that they reflect more directly the physiological capability of neuronal tracts and can be used to explore either tracts or regions of interest (ROI). Also, by using sophisticated techniques, it is possible to use DTI data to plot specific tracts and analyse their integrity.

Region of interest studies

CROSS-SECTIONAL STUDIES

Two initial studies have described associations between working memory performance and DTI white matter integrity measures (Charlton et al., 2006; Deary et al., 2006). Although these studies used different cohorts – Charlton et al. examined 99 subjects aged 50–90; Deary et al. investigated 40 individuals all aged 79 – both studies identify associations between white matter integrity and working memory performance, among other findings. Prior studies had described associations between DTI and cognitive abilities including executive function (O'Sullivan, Jones et al., 2001; Shenkin et al., 2003), but working memory abilities were not examined.

The first study, by Charlton et al. (2006), was part of the GENIE project, which included a sample of 106 adults aged 50–90. This analysis used DTI measures of white matter integrity in a large ROI through the centrum semiovale and whole brain white matter histograms for both MD and FA. White matter integrity (MD and FA) was negatively correlated with age using both ROI and whole brain measures. Furthermore, within the ROI, both MD and FA correlated significantly with N-acetyl aspartate – a marker of neuronal and axonal integrity. Significant correlations were observed between white matter integrity and composite measures of working memory (Digit Span Backwards and Letter-Number Sequencing), executive function and information processing speed, using both ROI and whole brain histogram measures. However, after controlling for age and premorbid intelligence, only the correlations with working memory remained significant, regardless of the methodology used (see Figure 5.3) (Charlton et al., 2006). In a follow-up paper using structural equation modelling to explore aspects of the frontal-executive and the information processing speed hypotheses, a specific association between the large ROI and working memory was demonstrated. Specifically, age was associated with the variance in white matter integrity (measured using MD and FA), which in turn mediated working memory performance (Charlton et al., 2008). White matter integrity was not associated with information processing speed, executive flexibility or fluid intelligence. (See p. 115 for a discussion of modelling working memory decline in ageing.) Findings from both GENIE cohort studies suggest that working memory may be particularly susceptible to disruption of cortico-cortical and cortico-subcortical connections (Charlton et al., 2008).

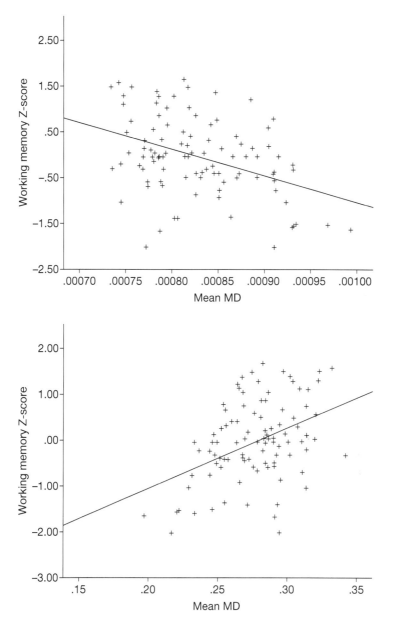

Figure 5.3 Association between working memory and white matter integrity. Correlation between working memory z-score and MD and FA values in a large ROI

Source: Created from Table 2 in Charlton et al. (2006).

Another study utilised the Scottish Mental Health Survey of 1932, where individuals had completed an IQ assessment at age 11 (Deary et al., 2006). The same individuals, now aged 83, completed a number of cognitive measures and white matter integrity was examined in small ROI. White matter integrity (MD and FA) in frontal and centrum semiovale regions correlated significantly with current working memory (Letter-Number Sequencing), as well as information processing speed, executive function and childhood IQ. Although hampered by not having either a younger control group or a spread of ages to explore ageing effects, this study also utilised the sample to explore the effect of childhood IQ on these associations. In a structural equation model analysis, current white matter integrity in the centrum semiovale was associated with both childhood IQ and current processing speed (simple reaction time task), with both cognitive variables being associated with current general mental ability (Deary et al., 2006). Significant working memory results were not observed and the authors suggest that correlations between white matter integrity and cognitive abilities may reflect a lifelong association, as has been demonstrated in previous white matter integrity-cognition investigation across the lifespan (Olesen et al., 2003).

These initial studies used ROI largely in the centrum semiovale and periventricular regions and identified associations with working memory. Thus it could be argued that working memory may be associated with white matter integrity in this general region. Further regional specificity was examined by Kennedy and Raz (2009) using small ROI throughout the brain in a sample of 52 adults aged between 19 and 81. White matter integrity of ROI placed in the prefrontal cortex, the genu of the corpus callosum, the anterior limb of the internal capsule and the temporal lobe were significantly associated with performance on a non-verbal N-back task, with no significant correlations with the posterior limb of the internal capsule, the splenium of the corpus callosum, or parietal or occipital white matter. A verbal N-back task and verbal and non-verbal span tasks demonstrated similar patterns although associations in some regions did not reach significance (p<.06–.09). This pattern of associations for working memory, spread throughout the brain, differed from other cognitive measures (see Figure 5.4 for representation of results). Executive function was associated with prefrontal, parietal and occipital white matter, episodic memory with white matter in the posterior limb of the internal capsule and temporal lobe, and processing speed largely with frontal white matter (Kennedy & Raz, 2009). The authors interpret the pattern of results as reflecting known age-related brain-cognition associations; in particular they state that working memory performance is associated with white matter integrity across a widely distributed network that may encompass 'most of the deep cerebral white matter' (Kennedy & Raz, 2009, p. 924). White matter damage across many fibre tracts may lead to decline across a number of cognitive domains and, through either compensation or dedifferentiation, may lead to the altered pattern of functional activation observed in ageing.

	Regions of interest								
	← Anterior ──────────────────── Posterior →								
Cognitive domain	PFC	CCg	ICa	ICg	ICp	Tmp	Par	CCs	Occ
Processing speed v	■	●□							
Processing speed nv	■	●□					●		
Working memory n-back v	□	□	○	□○	○			○	○
Working memory n-back nv	■○	■○	■	□		■			
Working memory Span v	□	■○	□	□		■	□		□
Working memory Span nv	■	■○	□	□	■	■	□		□●
Episodic memory CVLT				●	■	■	●		
Episodic memory LM			■		■	■			
Episodic memory MfN					■	□			
Executive functions Inh: Stroop							■	□	■
Executive functions Inh: WCST									
Executive functions Switch: 1	■○	□●					●		■
Executive functions Switch: 2	■○	●					●		■

Figure 5.4 Associations between regional white matter involvement and cognitive performance

Source: Reprinted from Kennedy & Raz (2009) with permission from Elsevier

Key: (■) = FA; (●) = ADC; (□) and (○) = non-significant trend for FA and ADC, respectively (p < .06–.09); PFC = superior frontal gyrus; CCg = corpus callosum genu; ICa = internal capsule anterior limb; ICg = internal capsule genu; ICp = internal capsule posterior limb; Tmp = temporal stem; Par = superior posterior parietal; Occ = occipital white matter; v = verbal; nv = nonverbal; Inh: Stroop = inhibition: Stroop interference; Inh: WCST = inhibition: Wisconsin Card Sort Test perseveration; Switch: 1 = single switching cost; Switch: 2 = dual switching cost; CVLT = list free recall; LM = story free recall; MfN = name–picture association recognition

LONGITUDINAL STUDIES

In the longitudinal study of the GENIE project, white matter integrity was shown to decline over a two-year period using a number of different DTI methods including 2D and 3D image analysis methods (Barrick et al., 2010). Regardless of the method, white matter integrity declined over this period, with observed decline typically greater than that predicted by baseline regressions with age. Using whole brain histograms, decline in white matter integrity correlated significantly with decline in working memory performance, independent of change in WMH volumes (Charlton, Schiavone, Barrick, Morris & Markus, 2010). Moreover decline in white matter integrity explained approximately 11% of the variance in working memory decline. It is important to note that there was no association between baseline white matter integrity and decline in working memory, suggesting that either baseline integrity is not a strong predictor of pathophysiological changes associated with working memory decline or that measures lack the sensitivity to detect these associations (Charlton, Schiavone, Barrick, Morris & Markus, 2010).

One other study has examined longitudinal associations with DTI. Lovden and colleagues (2010) implemented a training programme with 20 younger and 12 older adults practising three working memory, three episodic memory and six perceptual speed tasks over approximately six months (total 100 hours training). MD and FA values were measured before and after training in five segments of the corpus callosum. Training increased white matter integrity (both MD and FA) in the genu but no other region of the corpus callosum for both older and younger adults, whereas no changes were observed in the control group. Although performance on all three cognitive domains improved over training, no significant associations were observed between change on the cognitive measures and change on the DTI measures in the genu (Lovden et al., 2010). While this is an interesting finding, it is unclear which aspect of intervention 'cause' white matter integrity change, especially given the lack of associations between brain and cognitive changes.

White matter tracts

In addition to large and small ROI analyses, studies using DTI can also utilise tractography in order to examine specific pathways between cortical regions. Using this method, white matter tracts were extracted in a small sample of 12 older and 12 younger participants (Zahr et al., 2009). Examining the whole sample (n = 24), a composite working memory score including both verbal and visuo-spatial tasks correlated with the integrity of the genu of the corpus callosum and the fornix (Zahr et al., 2009). No significant associations were observed in the splenium of the corpus callosum, the cingulum, or the uncinate or inferior longitudinal fascicule. Given that working memory is known to rely on functional connections in frontal, temporal and parietal regions, it is surprising that the uncinate or cingulum are not associated with working memory function, although this may be explained by the small sample size including both older and younger adults.

Similar tracts were extracted in a separate sample of older adults (n = 20; mean age: 68.89 yrs; SD: 5.3 yrs). Davis et al. (2009) investigated associations between tract integrity and visuo-spatial working memory, where integrity of the uncinate fasciculus was associated with performance (see Table 5.2) (Davis et al., 2009). No significant associations were observed with the genu and splenium of the corpus callosum, the cingulum or the inferior longitudinal fascicule. This was a different pattern of associations than in episodic memory, where the cingulum and the inferior longitudinal fasciculus were associated with performance. The lack of overlap between the tracts that correlate with working memory and episodic memory performance may suggest that these abilities are supported by independent white matter networks, although it is more likely that higher-order cognitive abilities are supported by multiple areas of white matter and associations are under-powered in this sample.

Table 5.2 Correlations between white matter tracts and working and episodic memory

		FA	RD	AD
Spatial Working Memory	Right Uncinate Fasciculus	r=.57**	r=−.37	r=.18
Spatial Working Memory Strategy	Right Uncinate Fasciculus	r=.52**	r=−.40*	r=.03
Visual Paired Associate Learning	Left Cingulum Bundle	r=.47*	r=−.45*	r=−.06
	Left Inferior Longitudinal Fasciculus	r=.43*	r=−.42*	r=−.32
Pattern Recognition Memory	Left Cingulum Bundle	r=.38*	r=−.37*	r=.23
	Splenium	r=.44*	r=−.53**	r=−.46*

Source: From Davis et al. (2009).

Key: * p <.05; ** p <.01.

Using a different method to examine cortico-cortical connections, a further study from the GENIE sample used voxel-based statistics to identify clusters of white matter where integrity was associated with working memory performance (Charlton, Barrick, Lawes, Markus & Morris, 2010). Ten significant clusters were identified in bilateral temporal and frontal white matter, the right thalamus and the cingulum. Tractography was performed to identify the tracts that passed through those clusters, identifying the superior parietal lobule pathway, the medial temporo-frontal pathway, the uncinate fasciculus, the fronto-parietal fasciculus and the cingulum (see Figure 5.5) (Charlton, Barrick, Lawes, Markus & Morris, 2010). Post-hoc analyses correlated the integrity of the white matter tracts with working memory performance and as a control variable fluid intelligence. FA values correlated significantly with working memory performance across temporo-parietal, temporo-frontal and fronto-parietal pathways, but no significant correlations were observed with fluid intelligence. These results are consistent with the functional MRI literature where working memory activates diffuse brain regions which can be shown to be formed into a network by these diverse neural connections (Cappell, Gmeindl & Reuter-Lorenz, 2010; Cook et al., 2007; Owen et al., 1998). The suggestion is that tracts may not be *specific* to working memory function, but this ability relies on the coordinated activity of a wide network, incorporating cortical regions known to be involved in working memory.

One other recent study has used structural equation modelling to examine associations between cognition and integrity of five bilateral white matter tracts and five projections within the corpus callosum (Voineskos et al., 2012). In a sample of 48 adults (aged 22–81) no significant associations were observed with working memory, although the splenium of the corpus callosum was associated with both executive function and episodic memory. There is a notable lack of

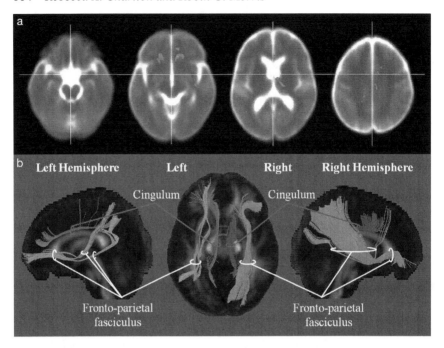

Figure 5.5 a.) Significant voxel clusters identified by linear regression for working memory and MD; b.) Fronto-parietal white matter pathways passing through significant MD clusters. White matter pathways are illustrated that pass between the frontal and parietal lobes in the left and right cerebral hemispheres

Source: Reprinted from Charlton, Barrick, Lawes, Markus & Morris (2010) with permission from Elsevier.

expected associations in this study – one would predict associations between tracts with frontal connections for working memory and executive function and that temporal connections be correlated with episodic memory. The lack of expected findings may be partly explained by low power in the structural equation modelling, with approximately 26 paths being represented and a sample of 48 subjects.

It is clear from this section, however, that tractography studies exploring age-working memory associations do not yet show any consistency. Differences may represent differences in MRI acquisition and processing, study populations, statistical methods and/or limitations of the existing techniques. Whatever the reason, results from tractography studies are less consistent than those DTI studies using a ROI approach. Despite this the appeal of tractography, both in terms of the information available and the visual representation of that data, remains.

Magnetisation transfer and working memory

Few studies have investigated the relationship between MTR and cognition. We are only aware of two such studies, one a follow-up to the Scottish Mental Health Survey, the other from our GENIE cohort.

Within the same sample of 40 subjects described in the DTI section on p. 108, MTR was examined in small ROI in the centrum semiovale and periventricular white matter (Deary et al., 2006). Across a number of cognitive measures the only significant correlation was between MTR around the posterior horns of the lateral ventricles and Letter-Number Sequencing (p = .04), although this results did not withstand corrections for multiple comparisons (Deary et al., 2006). Again, this study involves only participants of the same age and so specific ageing effects could not be studied.

Utilising whole brain white matter histograms, the GENIE study demonstrated a similar pattern, with weak associations between MTR and working memory performance in ageing (Schiavone et al., 2009). In a sample of 64 individuals aged 54–91, median MTR histogram values correlated significantly with executive function, information processing speed and episodic memory, but not with working memory performance. Correlations between MTR data and cognitive variables were weaker than with either MD or FA DTI whole brain histogram values, furthermore MD and FA *did* correlate significantly with working memory performance. MTR data were more powerful than WMH in explaining the variance in cognitive domains, but not as powerful as metrics from DTI data (Schiavone et al., 2009). While MTR offers additional sensitivity when compared to measures such as volumetrics and WMH, it lacks both the sensitivity of DTI and its potential to extract specific white matter tracts. Thus when examining integrity of white matter, DTI seems to be the method of choice over MTR.

Modelling white matter and working memory associations

In summary, there is much evidence that working memory decline associated with ageing is linked to white matter deterioration and tractography studies have identified the likely neuronal networks that are implicated. A further aspect to be considered is the degree to which there is a direct linear causal relationship starting with ageing, followed by white matter damage and consequently memory decline, or whether there are other mediating factors. This can be considered at two levels, first, by considering the essential pathophysiological effects of loss of white matter integrity in relation to specific cognitive functions and second, by more complex analyses that attempt to model interactive networks of entities. Finally, additional neurobiological factors are considered in this section, specifically genetic influences.

Representational transfer versus Dynamic Connectivity

In white matter disease, such as that associated with small vessel disease, effects are generally more subtle and produce radically different outcomes than those associated with the classical disconnection syndromes. These syndromes, introduced in the 19th Century by Wernicke, Lichtheim, Liepman and Dejerine and reintroduced in the late 20th Century by Geschwind (1965), were used to explain conditions such as forms of aphasia, apraxia, agnosia, pure alexia and amnesia (Catani & Mesulam, 2008). In humans the effect of neurosurgical lesions to particular tracts could be studied, for example in split brain patients (Sperry, 1962) and animal models that explored tract function through ablations (Gaffan & Wilson, 2008). Such syndromes have in common that they all involve symbolic representation, for example perceptual or motor information transfer. To produce their effects the white matter tract lesions are large, and the theories concerning deficit encompass complete removal of connections, halting on a gross scale the linear flow of frequently modality-specific information within a network. Furthermore, this type of information transfer has inbuilt *Shannonian* redundancy such that subtle damage, producing reductions in efficiency of information transfer, may not be readily observed in terms of behavioural outcome.

The classical disconnection syndromes contrast with those caused by more subtle pervasive damage as in white matter disease or multiple sclerosis where specific tracts may remain more or less intact and several neurocognitive systems can be involved. Here, conversely, the prediction is that the damage will affect a different type of cognitive function with the following characteristics:

1   Diffuse connectivity between modular systems in which different network connections are made. The damage to the function occurs through multiple tract involvement resulting in a mass action effect, with distributed capacity.
2   The information transmitted is related to control, coordination mechanisms, synchrony and parsing mental processes.
3   Dynamic reiterative processes in which information is continuously transferred throughout the network, not necessarily in a uni-linear fashion. Here the prediction is that inefficient information transfer will be rapidly amplified, such that subtle effects on the overall network will produce more noticeable effects on cognitive function.
4   The system will nevertheless have graceful degradation properties such that damage will not tend to produce step-like decline and the system will deteriorate gradually as more neuronal pathways are destroyed.

These characteristics, which we here termed *Dynamic Connectivity*, are found in higher order processes, including the *control processes* associated with executive functioning and working memory, and are associated with generalised properties of brain function such as *processing speed*. In relation to working memory, computational modelling approaches focusing on control mechanism have stressed the presence of patterns of activation across units within a working memory network (Durstewitz, Seamns & Sejnowski, 2000; O'Reilly, Braver & Cohen, 1999; Moutoussis, Orrell & Morris, 2004). In particular, working memory systems, whilst involving anatomically distinct processing units, also require integrated coordination or control mechanisms that produce synchronous dynamic activity (Charlton et al., 2008). So, for example, verbal working memory may be supported by the action of rehearsal-based articulatory type mechanisms and phonological storage. The coordination of such a system envisaged in the Working Memory Model (Baddeley, 2012) is via a Central Executive System (CES). The discrete neurocognitive modules associated with storage or rehearsal mechanisms are more focal, but the coordinating network has a more highly distributed capacity.

Whereas it has been speculated that working memory control mechanisms such as the CES might have a particular brain focus, evidence from ageing studies supports the notion of distributed capacity involving a widespread frontal, temporal and parietal network. This is also in accord with mathematical modelling of working memory mechanisms by Moutoussis, Orrell and Morris (2004) who have shown how such a mechanism might degrade when simulated information transfer between the specific processing units is gradually reduced. They produced modelling of coordination between oscillatory neuroactivity of reciprocally connected neuronal units as a mathematical model of working memory coordination. During simulation of more complex cognitive operations in working memory, degrading the connections between functional units showed how a breakdown in oscillatory coordination could mimic clinical data associated with working memory decline.

In relation to tractography, investigation of age-related working memory decline in this type of model is supported by the nature of tract involvement. Specifically, in our own tractography studies (Charlton, Barrick, Lawes, Markus & Morris, 2010), the tracts associated with working memory involve diverse pathways, for example, the medial temporo-frontal pathway, the uncinate fasciculus, the fronto-parietal fasciculus and the cingulum, allowing transfer of information across major regions of temporal, frontal and parietal lobes.

Interactions with other cognitive processes

Another type of theoretical modelling has been used by our group to determine the potential interaction between working memory and other aspects of cognitive functioning. This leads to consideration of the extent to which the relationship between age-related decline in white matter and other cognitive functions could be mediated by working memory decline. The GENIE study attempted to model these associations, taking into account key aspects of age-related cognitive change, namely other types of executive function and processing speed. Central to this modelling is the extent to which psychometric approaches to cognition can structure cognitive processes and their relative contributions to each other. For example, using this approach, there is evidence that multiple executive processes can be identified, such as working memory updating, set shifting and response inhibition (Miyake et al., 2000; Miyake & Friedman, 2012), and the relative contribution of these processes to intelligence can be explored (Miyake et al., 2001; Colom & Jung, 2007). Whereas the details of such models may vary between studies, a consensus has emerged that, for example, different executive functions contribute to decline of fluid intelligence. Furthermore, whereas models of age-related cognitive decline stress particular features, such as the frontal executive hypothesis (Dempster, 1993; West, 1996) and the information processing speed hypothesis (Salthouse, 1996), it is likely that an interaction between these features will provide a more complete picture.

Accordingly, our modelling incorporated the notion of a network of characteristics that mediate intellectual decline, including working memory, information processing speed and flexibility (Charlton et al., 2008). In addition, within this network white matter integrity (measured by DTI) was hypothesised to be mediated by age, and in turn to affect cognitive abilities. To test the model we used structural equation modelling in which the different features are connected via paths, signifying associative links between them and exploring the validity of these links, taking the total network into account. Within the initial model, the statistical significance of each pathway was tested. In a stepwise process, non-significant paths were removed from the model until all paths were statistically significant and the model fitted the data, thereby producing a final model. Although the hypothesised associations between the cognitive variables remained significant in the final model, there were no direct effects of age on working memory. Rather, the age-working memory association was mediated by white matter integrity, with working memory being the only cognitive variable associated with white matter (Figure 5.6). This analysis demonstrated that 'competing' hypotheses

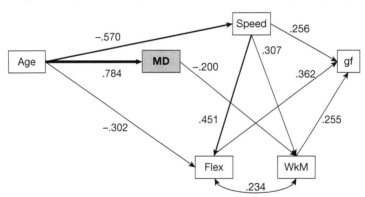

Figure 5.6 Structural Equation Model of the relationships between DTI measured white matter integrity, cognition (including working memory) and intelligence

Source: Reprinted from Charlton, Landau, Schiavone, Barrick, Clark, Markus & Morris (2010) with permission from Elsevier.

Key: Arrows reflect relationships between variables. Line thickness represents strength of association. Standardized regression coefficients are shown next to each path. Abbreviations: MD = mean diffusivity; speed = information processing speed; flex = flexibility; WkM = working memory; gf = fluid intelligence.

concerning key elements of cognitive age-related change are not mutually exclusive, and in combination may provide a more complete explanation for age-related changes (see also Penke & Deary, 2010; and Charlton et al., 2010 for a further discussion of our modelling approach).

Genetic influences

This data modelling highlights the notion that decline in specific processes might mediate the overall effects of white matter change in terms of cognition. In addition to cognitive and brain measures, Bender and colleagues have incorporated information about vascular risk into their recent model (see p. 104) (Bender & Raz, 2012). This study demonstrates different patterns of associations between working memory and brain volume in APOE-ε4 carriers compared to APOE-ε3 homozygotes. Thus the presence of high blood pressure (a significant risk factor for vascular damage) was associated with poorer working memory performance only in those individuals who carried the APOE-ε4 allele. Structural equation modelling is a valuable tool in examining the complex associations between ageing and cognition. Such modelling is a powerful method for examining the possibly cumulative effects of different risk factors as well as the effects of such risk factors across groups.

The future of white matter imaging

In this chapter we have described established white matter imaging methods, but both image acquisition and analysis methods continue to develop. Novel techniques aim to more accurately identify aspects of white matter such as myelin to resolve issues with areas where white matter fibres cross in the brain, to describe the complexity of the tissue or to describe the brain networks in terms of efficiency. At the level of image acquisition and analysis many techniques are attempting to deal with issues of fibre crossings that occur in DTI data. Fibre crossings occur where two or more white matter tracts meet in the same voxel, but have a different orientation. At such points, traditional DTI cannot accurately determine the orientation of the tracts and/or separate the tracts from one another. Being able to distinguish between crossing fibres in the brain will allow more detailed description of brain connectivity and methods are in development to acquire this level of detail within a clinically acceptable time-period (Douaud et al., 2011; Staempfli et al., 2006; for review see Tournier, Mori & Leemans, 2011).

Novel methods such as diffusional kurtosis imaging and anomalous diffusion imaging are using the diffusion signal to better characterise tissue architecture (Bar-Shir, Duncan & Cohen, 2009; Hall & Barrick, 2008; Raab et al., 2010; Zhou et al., 2010). The aim of these methods is to increase our ability to detect changes in tissue and thus monitor disease progression by better characterising the components of complex tissue (see De Santis et al., 2011 for a review of these methods). Although the sensitivity of these methods for detecting subtle age-related changes is not yet established, one can see their potential application in longitudinal studies.

On page 101 we discussed using the DTI signal to extract information about demyelination (radial diffusivity) and axonal damage (axonal diffusivity), as well as raising important concerns with regard to these metrics. The mcDESPOT sequence has been developed to quantify myelination and has been applied to both development and Multiple Sclerosis (Deoni et al., 2011; Kolind et al., 2012). Given that myelination allows rapid synchronized communication across neural networks and is hypothesised to decline in ageing (Bastin et al., 2009; Irvine & Blakemore, 2006), better quantification of myelination may clarify the role of vascular risk factors in age-related cognitive decline. With regards to examination of axons, recent method developments enable estimation of axonal diameter and density *in vivo* (Alexander et al., 2010; Assaf et al., 2008; Avram et al., 2013). It is known that axonal diameter differs across the brain with large axons allowing fast transfer of information, i.e. in the body of the corpus callosum and the corticospinal tracts, whereas smaller diameter axons are tightly packed within the genu of the corpus callosum allowing a large *quantity* of information transfer. With continued reduction in acquisition time, these methods may provide important information on the development and decline of white matter neuroanatomy and how it relates to function.

In terms of statistical methods, graph theory analysis, common in computer science, has recently been applied to examining brain networks (Bullmore & Sporns, 2009; Rubinov & Sporns, 2010). Graph theory can be applied to a range of MRI acquisitions and has been utilised with (T1-weighted) grey matter volume and DTI scans. Graph theory generates a number of metrics that describe the efficiency of the whole brain network and how efficiently local regions communicate with the rest of the network. Initial studies have demonstrated age-effects although there are some inconsistencies (Gong et al., 2009; Wu et al., 2012; Zhu et al., 2010) and regional associations with cognition are not always in keeping with the literature (Wen et al., 2011). It is important to note with graph theory analysis that effective networks will be formed by a complex combination of efficiency and strength of connections both between and within brain regions; too many connections may be just as detrimental to a network as too few. A better understanding of the 'optimal' network may be necessary before we can fully integrate the results that are being produced by graph theory.

These novel methods have not yet been applied to ageing-working memory associations, but such analyses are probable in the future (see Tournier, Mori & Leemans, 2011, for a further discussion of developments in diffusion tensor imaging). The purpose of this section is not to provide a comprehensive overview of novel methods, but rather to make the reader aware of developments that are likely to be applied to brain-cognition associations in the future.

Conclusions

We have demonstrated that working memory performance is strongly associated with the integrity of white matter in typical ageing, measured using a range of techniques. We hypothesise that working memory may be particularly sensitive to the subtle damage that occurs during ageing, as it not only relies on a widespread network but also requires reiterative communication between parts of the network. For this reason, fairly small amounts of damage as observed in healthy ageing may have a disproportionate effect on working memory when compared to other higher order cognitive abilities. Continued development of novel image acquisition and analysis methods may help to clarify the role of white matter and indeed different components of white matter, such as myelination, in cognitive ageing. Incorporating information on individual differences into future studies – whether from other cognitive abilities, brain/cognitive reserve, risk factors or comorbid conditions – will help to further clarify the importance of working memory changes in ageing.

References

Abe, O., Aoki, S., Hayashi, N., Yamada, H., Kunimatsu, A., Mori, H., Ohtomo, K. et al. (2002). Normal aging in the central nervous system: Quantitative MR diffusion-tensor analysis. *Neurobiology of Aging, 23*, 433–441.

Alexander, D. C., Hubbard, P. L., Hall, M. G., Moore, E. A., Ptito, M., Parker, G. J. M. et al. (2010). Orientationally invariant indices of axon diameter and density from diffusion MRI. *Neuroimage, 52*, 1374–1389.

Ashburner, J. & Friston, K. (2000). Voxel-Based Morphometry – The Methods. *Neuroimage, 11*, 805–821.

Assaf, Y., Blumenfeld-Katzir, T., Yovel, Y. & Basser, P. J. (2008). AxCaliber: A method for measuring axon diameter distribution from diffusion MRI. *Magnetic Resonance in Medicine, 59*, 1347–1354.

Avram, A. V., Ozarslan, E., Sarlls, J. E. & Basser, P. J. (2013). In vivo detection of microscopic anisotropy using quadruple pulsed-field gradient (qPFG) diffusion MRI on a clinical scanner. *Neuroimage, 64*, 229–239.

Baddeley, A. (2012). Working memory: Theories, models and controversies. *Annual Review of Psychology, 63*, 1–29.

Barrick, T. R., Charlton, R. A., Clark, C. A. & Markus, H. S. (2010). White matter structural decline in normal ageing; A prospective longitudinal study using tract based spatial statistics. *Neuroimage, 51*, 565–577.

Bar-Shir, A., Duncan, I. D. & Cohen, Y. (2009). QSI and DTI of excised brains of the myelin-deficient rat. *Neuroimage, 48*, 109–116.

Bastin, M. E., Clayden, J. D., Pattie, A., Gerrish, I. F., Wardlaw, J. M. & Deary, I. J. (2009). Diffusion tensor and magnetization transfer MRI measurements of periventricular white matter hyperintensities in old age. *Neurobiology of Aging, 30*, 125–136.

Bender, A. R. & Raz, N. (2012). Age-related differences in memory and executive functions in healthy APOE Ɛ4 carriers: The contribution of individual differences in prefrontal volumes and systolic blood pressure. *Neuropsychologia, 50*, 704–714.

Benedetti, B. M., Charil, A. M., Rovaris, M. M., Judica, E. M., Valsasina, P. P., Sormani, M. P. P. et al. (2006). Influence of aging on brain gray and white matter changes assessed by conventional, MT, and DT MRI. *Neurology, 66*, 535–539.

Brown, W. R. & Thore, C. R. (2011). Cerebral microvascular pathology in ageing and neurodegeneration. *Neuropathology and Applied Neurobiology, 37*, 56–74.

Budde, M. D., Xie, M., Cross, A. H. & Song, S. K. (2009). Axial diffusivity is the primary correlate of axonal injury in the experimental autoimmune encephalomyelitis spinal cord: A quantitative pixelwise analysis. *The Journal of Neuroscience, 29*, 2805–2813.

Bullmore, E. & Sporns, O. (2009). Complex brain networks: Graph theoretical analysis of structural and functional systems. *Nature Reviews Neuroscience, 10*, 312.

Burns, J. M., Church, J. A., Johnson, D. K., Xiong, C., Marcus, D., Fotenos, A. F. et al. (2005). White matter lesions are prevalent but differentially related with cognition in aging and early Alzheimer's disease. *Archives of Neurology, 62*, 1870–1876.

Cappell, K. A., Gmeindl, L. & Reuter-Lorenz, P. A. (2010). Age differences in prefontal recruitment during verbal working memory maintenance depend on memory load. *Cortex, 46*, 462–473.

Carlson, N. E., Moore, M. M., Dame, A., Howieson, D., Silbert, L. C., Quinn, J. F. et al. (2008). Trajectories of brain loss in aging and the development of cognitive impairment. *Neurology, 70*, 828–833.

Carpenter, P. A., Just, M. A. & Reichle, E. D. (2000). Working memory and executive function: Evidence from neuroimaging. *Current Opinion in Neurobiology, 10*, 195–199.

Catani, M. & Mesulam, M. (2008). The arcuate fasciculus and the disconnection theme in language and aphasia: History and current state. *Cortex, 44*, 953–961.

Charlton, R. A., Barrick, T. R., McIntyre, D. J. O., Shen, Y., O'Sullivan, M., Howe, F. A. et al. (2006). White matter damage on diffusion tensor imaging correlates with age related cognitive decline. *Neurology, 66*, 217–222.

Charlton, R. A., Landau, S., Schiavone, F., Barrick, T. R., Clark, C. A., Markus, H. S. et al. (2008). A structural equation modeling investigation of age related variance in executive function and DTI measured white matter damage. *Neurobiology of Aging, 29*, 1547–1555.

Charlton, R. A., Barrick, T. R., Lawes, I. N. C., Markus, H. S. & Morris, R. G. (2010). White matter pathways associated with working memory in normal aging. *Cortex, 46*, 474–489.

Charlton, R. A., Barrick, T. R., Markus, H. S. & Morris, R. G. (2010). The relationship between episodic long-term memory and white matter integrity in normal aging. *Neuropsychologia, 48*, 114–122.

Charlton, R. A., Landau, S., Schiavone, F., Barrick, T. R., Clark, C. A., Markus, H. S. et al. (2010). Up the garden path: A critique of Penke and Deary and further exploration concerning the Charlton et al. (2008) path analysis relating loss of white matter integrity to cognition in normal aging. *Neurobiology of Aging, 31*, 1661–1666.

Charlton, R. A., Schiavone, F., Barrick, T. R., Morris, R. G. & Markus, H. S. (2010). Diffusion Tensor Imaging detects age-related white matter change over a two-year follow-up which is associated with working memory decline. *Journal of Neurology, Neurosurgery & Psychiatry, 81*, 13–19.

Cherry, K. E. & Park, D. C. (1993). Individual difference and contextual variables influence spatial memory in younger and older adults. *Psychology and Aging, 8*, 517–526.

Colom, R. & Jung, R. E. (2007). General intelligence and memory span: Evidence for a common neuroanatomic framework. *Neuropsychology, 24*, 867–878.

Cook, I. A., Bookheimer, S. Y., Mickes, L., Leuchter, A. F. & Kumar, A. (2007). Aging and brain activation with working memory tasks: An fMRI study of connectivity. *International Journal of Geriatric Psychiatry, 22*, 332–342.

Davatzikos, C. & Resnick, S. (2002). Degenerative age changes in white matter connectivity visualized *in vivo* using magnetic resonance imaging. *Cerebral Cortex, 12*, 767–771.

Davis, S. W., Dennis, N. A., Buchler, N. G., White, L. E., Madden, D. J. & Cabeza, R. (2009). Assessing the effects of age on long white matter tracts using diffusion tensor tractography. *Neuroimage, 46,* 530–541.

Deary, I. J. P., Bastin, M. E. D., Pattie, A. B., Clayden, J. D. M., Whalley, L. J. M., Starr, J. M. M. et al. (2006). White matter integrity and cognition in childhood and old age. *Neurology, 66,* 505–512.

DeCarli, C., Fletcher, E., Ramey, V., Harvey, D. & Jagust, W. J. (2005). Anatomical mapping of white matter hyperintensities (WMH): Exploring the relationships between periventricular WMH, deep WMH, and total WMH burden. *Stroke, 36,* 50–55.

Dempster, F. N. (1993). The rise and fall of the inhibitory mechanism: Toward a unified theory of cognitive development and aging. *Developmental Review, 12,* 45–75.

Deoni, S. C. L., Mercure, E., Blasi, A., Gasston, D., Thomson, A., Johnson, M. et al. (2011). Mapping infant brain myelination with magnetic resonance imaging. *The Journal of Neuroscience, 31,* 784–791.

De Santis, S., Gabrielli, A., Palombo, M., Maraviglia, B. & Capuani, S. (2011). Non-Gaussian diffusion imaging: A brief practical review. *Magnetic Resonance Imaging, 29,* 1410–1416.

Douaud, G., Jbabdi, S., Behrens, T. E. J., Menke, R. A., Gass, A., Monsch, A. U. et al. (2011). DTI measures in crossing-fibre areas: Increased diffusion anisotropy reveals early white matter alteration in MCI and mild Alzheimer's disease. *Neuroimage, 55,* 880–890.

Duering, M., Zieren, N., Hervé, D., Jouvent, E., Reyes, S., Peters, N. et al. (2011). Strategic role of frontal white matter tracts in vascular cognitive impairment: A voxel-based lesion-symptom mapping study in CADASIL. *Brain, 134,* 2366–2375.

Duprez, D. A., De Buyzere, M. L., Van den Noortgate, N., Simoens, J., Achten, E., Clement, D. L. et al. (2001). Relationship between periventricular or deep white matter lesions and arterial elasticity indices in very old people. *Age and Ageing, 30,* 325–330.

Durstewitz, D., Seamns, J. K. & Sejnowski, J. (2000). Neurocomputational models of working memory. *Nature Neuroscience, 2S,* 1184–1191.

Enzinger, C., Fazekas, F., Matthews, P. M., Ropele, S., Schmidt, H., Smith, S. et al. (2005). Risk factors for progression of brain atrophy in aging: Six-year follow-up of normal subjects. *Neurology, 64,* 1704–1711.

Enzinger, C., Smith, S., Fazekas, F., Drevin, G., Ropele, S., Nichols, T. et al. (2006). Lesion probability maps of white matter hyperintensities in elderly individuals: Results of the Austrian stroke prevention study. *Journal of Neurology, 253,* 1064–1070.

Fazekas, F., Ropele, S., Enzinger, C., Gorani, F., Seewann, A., Petrovic, K. et al. (2005). MTI of white matter hyperintensities. *Brain, 128,* 2926–2932.

Gaffan, D. & Wilson, C. R. E. (2008). Medial temporal and prefrontal function: Recent behavioural disconnection studies in the macaque monkey. *Cortex, 44,* 928–935.

Ge, Y., Grossman, R. I., Babb, J. S., Rabin, M. L., Mannon, L. J. & Kolson, D. L. (2002a). Age-related total gray matter and white matter changes in normal adult brain. Part I: Volumetric MR imaging analysis. *American Journal of Neuroradiology, 23,* 1327–1333.

Ge, Y., Grossman, R. I., Babb, J. S., Rabin, M. L., Mannon, L. J. & Kolson, D. L. (2002b). Age-related total gray matter and white matter changes in normal adult brain. Part II: quantitative magnetization transfer ratio histogram analysis. *American Journal of Neuroradiology, 23,* 1334–1341.

Geschwind, N. (1965). Disconnexion syndromes in animals and man. *Brain, 88,* 237–194.

Gong, G., Rosa-Neto, P., Carbonell, F., Chen, Z. J., He, Y. & Evans, A. C. (2009). Age- and gender-related differences in the cortical anatomical network. *The Journal of Neuroscience, 29*, 15684–15693.

Good, C. D., Johnsrude, I. S., Ashburner, J., Henson, R. N. A., Friston, K. J. & Frackowiak, R. S. J. (2001). A voxel-based morphometric study of ageing in 465 normal adult human brains. *Neuroimage, 14*, 21–36.

Grossman, R. I., Gomori, J. M., Ramer, K. N., Lexa, F. J. & Schnall, M. D. (1994). Magnetization transfer: Theory and clinical applications in neuroradiology. *Radiographics, 14*, 279–290.

Gunning-Dixon, F. M. & Raz, N. (2003). Neuroanatomical correlates of selected executive functions in middle-aged and older adults: A prospective MRI study. *Neuropsychologia, 41*, 1929–1941.

Hall, M. G. & Barrick, T. R. (2008). From diffusion-weighted MRI to anomalous diffusion imaging. *Magnetic Resonance in Medicine, 59*, 447–455.

Hannesdottir, K. I., Nitkunan, A., Charlton, R. A., Barrick, T. R., MacGregor, G. A. & Markus, H. S. (2009). Cognitive impairment and white matter damage in hypertension: A pilot study. *Acta Neurologica Scandinavica, 119*, 261–268.

Head, D., Buckner, R. L., Shimony, J. S., Williams, L. E., Akbudak, E., Conturo, T. E. et al. (2004). Differential vulnerability of anterior white matter in nondemented aging with minimal acceleration in dementia of the Alzheimer type: Evidence from diffusion tensor imaging. *Cerebral Cortex, 14*, 410–423.

Irvine, K. A. & Blakemore, W. F. (2006). Age increases axon loss associated with primary demyelination in cuprizone-induced demyelination in C57BL/6 mice. *Journal of Neuroimmunology, 175*, 69–76.

Kennedy, K. M. & Raz, N. (2009). Aging white matter and cognition: Differential effects of regional variations in diffusion properties on memory, executive functions, and speed. *Neuropsychologia, 47*, 915–927.

Knopman, D. S., Penman, A. D., Catellier, D. J., Coker, L. H., Shibata, D. K., Sharrett, A. R. et al. (2011). Vascular risk factors and longitudinal changes on brain MRI. *Neurology, 76*, 1879–1885.

Kolind, S., Matthews, L., Johansen-Berg, H., Leite, M. I., Williams, S. C. R., Deoni, S. et al. (2012). Myelin water imaging reflects clinical variability in multiple sclerosis. *Neuroimage, 60*, 263–270.

Libon, D. J., Price, C. C., Giovannetti, T., Swenson, R., Bettcher, B. M., Heilman, K. M. et al. (2008). Linking MRI hyperintensities with patterns of neuropsychological impairment: Evidence for a threshold effect. *Stroke, 39*, 806–813.

Lovden, M., Bodammer, N. C., Kuhn, S., Kaufmann, J., Schutze, H., Tempelmann, C. et al. (2010). Experience-dependent plasticity of white-matter microstructure extends into old age. *Neuropsychologia, 48*, 3878–3883.

Madden, D. J., Bennett, I. J., Burzynska, A., Potter, G. G., Chen, N. K. & Song, A. W. (2012). Diffusion tensor imaging of cerebral white matter integrity in cognitive aging. *Biochimica et Biophysica Acta (BBA) – Molecular Basis of Disease, 1822*, 386–400.

Marquine, M. J., Attix, D. K., Goldstein, L. B., Samsa, G. P., Payne, M. E., Chelune, G. J. et al. (2010). Differential patterns of cognitive decline in anterior and posterior white matter hyperintensity progression. *Stroke, 41*, 1946–1950.

Metwalli, N. S., Benatar, M., Nair, G., Usher, S., Hu, X. & Carew, J. D. (2010). Utility of axial and radial diffusivity from diffusion tensor MRI as markers of neurodegeneration in amyotrophic lateral sclerosis. *Brain Research, 1348*, 156–164.

Miyake, A. & Friedman, N. P. (2012). The nature and organization of individual differences in executive functions: Four general conclusions. *Current Directions in Psychological Science, 21*, 8–14.

Miyake, A., Friedman, N. P., Emerson, M. J., Witzki, A. H. & Howerter, A. (2000). The unity and diversity of executive functions and their contributions to complex 'frontal lobe' tasks: A latent variable analysis. *Cognitive Psychology, 41*, 49–100.

Miyake, A., Friedman, N. P., Rettinger, D. A., Shah, P. & Hegarty, M. (2001). How are visuospatial working memory, executive functioning, and spatial abilities related? A latent-variable analysis. *Journal of Experimental Psychology: General, 130*, 621–640.

Molko, N., Pappata, S., Mangin, J. F., Poupon, F., LeBihan, D., Bousser, M. G. et al. (2002). Monitoring disease progression in CADASIL with diffusion magnetic resonance imaging: A study with whole brain histogram analysis. *Stroke, 33*, 2902–2908.

Moutoussis, M., Orrell, M. W. & Morris, R. G. (2004). Modelling discordination of cortical neuroactivity: Relevance for the executive control of attention in Alzheimer's disease. *Journal of Integrative Neuroscience, 3*, 85–104.

Nitkunan, A., Barrick, T. R., Charlton, R. A., Clark, C. A. & Markus, H. S. (2008). Multimodal MRI in cerebral small vessel disease: Its relationship with cognition and sensitivity to change over time. *Stroke, 39*, 1999–2005.

Nusbaum, A. O., Tang, C. Y., Buchsbaum, M. S., Wei, T. C. & Atlas, S. W. (2001). Regional and global changes in cerebral diffusion with normal aging. *American Journal of Neuroradiology, 22*, 136–142.

O'Brien, J. T., Wiseman, R., Burton, E. J., Barber, B., Wesnes, K., Saxby, B. et al. (2002). Cognitive associations of subcortical white matter lesions in older people. *Annals of the New York Academy of Sciences, 977*, 436–444.

Olesen, P. J., Nagy, Z., Westerberg, H. & Klingberg, T. (2003). Combined analysis of DTI and fMRI data reveals a joint maturation of white and grey matter in a fronto-parietal network. *Cognitive Brain Research, 18*, 48–57.

Oosterman, J. M., van Harten, B., Weinstein, H. C., Scheltens, P., Sergeant, J. A. & Scherder, E. J. A. (2008). White matter hyperintensities and working memory: An explorative study. *Aging, Neuropsychology, and Cognition, 15*, 384–399.

Oosterman, J. M., Vogels, R. L. C., van Harten, B., Gouw, A. A., Scheltens, P., Poggesi, A. et al. (2008). The role of white matter hyperintensities and medial temporal lobe atrophy in age-related executive dysfunctioning. *Brain and Cognition, 68*, 128–133.

O'Reilly, R. C., Braver, T. S. & Cohen, J. D. (1999). A biologically based computational model of working memory. In A. Miyake & P. Shah (Eds.), *Models of Working Memory: Mechanisms of Active Maintenance and Executive Control* (pp. 375–411). Cambridge, UK: Cambridge University Press.

O'Sullivan, M. (2008). Leukoaraiosis. *Practical Neurology, 8*, 26–38.

O'Sullivan, M., Jones, D. K., Summers, P. E., Morris, R. G., Williams, S. C. R. & Markus, H. S. (2001). Evidence for cortical 'disconnection' as a mechanism of age-related cognitive decline. *Neurology, 57*, 632–638.

O'Sullivan, M., Morris, R. G., Huckstep, B., Jones, D. K., Williams, S. C. R. & Markus, H. S. (2004). Diffusion tensor MRI correlates with executive dysfunction in patients with ischaemic leukoaraiosis. *Journal of Neurology, Neurosurgery and Psychiatry, 75*, 441–447.

O'Sullivan, M., Summers, P. E., Jones, D. K., Jarosz, J. M., Williams, S. C. & Markus, H. S. (2001). Normal-appearing white matter in ischemic leukoaraiosis: A diffusion tensor MRI study. *Neurology, 57*, 2307–2310.

Owen, A. M., Stern, C. E., Look, R. B., Tracey, I., Rosen, B. R. & Petrides, M. (1998). Functional organization of spatial and nonspatial working memory processing within the human lateral frontal cortex. *Proceedings of the National Academy of Sciences of the United States of America, 95*, 7721–7726.

Penke, L. & Deary, I. J. (2010). Some guidelines for structural equation modelling in cognitive neuroscience: The case of Charlton et al.'s study on white matter integrity and cognitive ageing. *Neurobiology of Aging, 31*(9), 1656–1660.

Pfefferbaum, A. & Sullivan, E. V. (2003). Increased brain white matter diffusivity in normal adult aging: Relationship to anisotropy and partial voluming. *Magnetic Resonance in Medicine, 49*, 953–961.

Raab, P., Hattingen, E., Franz, K., Zanella, F. E. & Lanfermann, H. (2010). Cerebral gliomas: Diffusional kurtosis imaging analysis of microstructural differences. *Radiology, 254*, 876–881.

Rabbitt, P., Scott, M., Lunn, M., Thacker, N., Lowe, C., Pendleton, N. et al. (2007). White matter lesions account for all age-related declines in speed but not in intelligence. *Neuropsychology, 21*, 363–370.

Ramirez, J., Gibson, E., Quddus, A., Lobaugh, N. J., Feinstein, A., Levine, B. et al. (2011). Lesion explorer: A comprehensive segmentation and parcellation package to obtain regional volumetrics for subcortical hyperintensities and intracranial tissue. *Neuroimage, 54*, 963–973.

Raz, N., Rodrigue, K. M. M. & Acker, J. D. M. (2003). Hypertension and the brain: Vulnerability of the prefrontal regions and executive functions. *Behavioral Neuroscience, 117*, 1169–1180.

Raz, N., Gunning, F. M., Head, D., Dupuis, J. H., McQuain, J., Briggs, S. D. et al. (1997). Selective aging of the human cerebral cortex observed *in vivo*: Differential vulnerability of the prefrontal gray matter. *Cerebral Cortex, 7*, 1047–3211.

Raz, N., Rodrigue, K. M., Kennedy, K. M. & Acker, J. D. (2007). Vascular health and longitudinal changes in brain and cognition in middle-aged and older adults. *Neuropsychology, 21*, 149–157.

Resnick, S., Goldszal, A. F., Davatzikos, C., Golski, S., Kraut, M. A., Metter, E. J. et al. (2000). One-year age changes in MRI brain volumes in older adults. *Cerebral Cortex, 10*, 464–472.

Rovaris, M., Iannucci, G., Cercignani, M., Sormani, M. P., De Stefano, N., Gerevini, S. et al. (2003). Age-related changes in conventional, magnetization transfer, and diffusion-tensor MR imaging findings: Study with whole-brain tissue histogram analysis. *Radiology, 227*, 731–738.

Rubinov, M. & Sporns, O. (2010). Complex network measures of brain connectivity: uses and interpretations. *Neuroimage, 52*, 1059–1069.

Sachdev, P., Wen, W., Chen, X. & Brodaty, H. (2007). Progression of white matter hyperintensities in elderly individuals over 3 years. *Neurology, 68*, 214–222.

Sachdev, P. S., Brodaty, H., Valenzuela, M. J., Lorentz, L., Looi, J. C., Wen, W. et al. (2004). The neuropsychological profile of vascular cognitive impairment in stroke and TIA patients. *Neurology, 62*, 912–919.

Salat, D. H., Kaye, J. A. & Janowsky, J. S. (1999). Prefrontal gray and white matter volumes in healthy aging and Alzheimer disease. *Archives of Neurology, 56*, 338–344.

Salthouse, T. A. (1996). The processing-speed theory of adult age differences in cognition. *Psychological Review, 103*, 403–428.

Salthouse, T. A., Fristoe, N., McGuthry, K. E. & Hambrick, D. Z. (1998). Relation of task switching to speed, age, and fluid intelligence. *Psychology & Aging, 13*, 445–461.

Sauseng, P., Klimesch, W., Schabus, M. & Doppelmayr, M. (2005). Fronto-parietal EEG coherence in theta and upper alpha reflect central executive functions of working memory. *International Journal of Psychophysiology, 57*, 97–103.

Scheltens, P., Barkhof, F. & Fazekas, F. (2003). White-matter changes on MRI as surrogate marker. *International Psychogeriatrics, 15*, 261–265.

Scheltens, P., Barkhof, F., Leys, D., Pruvo, J. P., Nauta, J. J., Vermersch, P. et al. (1993). A semiquantitative rating scale for the assessment of signal hyperintensities on magnetic resonance imaging. *Journal of the Neurological Sciences, 114*, 7–12.

Scheltens, P., Erkinjunti, T., Leys, D., Wahlund, L. O., Inzitari, D., del Ser, T. et al. (1998). White matter changes on CT and MRI: An overview of visual rating scales. European Task Force on Age-Related White Matter Changes. *European Neurology, 39*, 80–89.

Schiavone, F., Charlton, R. A., Barrick, T. R., Morris, R. G. & Markus, H. S. (2009). Imaging age-related cognitive decline: A comparison of diffusion tensor and magnetization transfer MRI. *Journal of Magnetic Resonance Imaging, 29*, 23–30.

Shenkin, S. D., Bastin, M. E., MacGillivray, T. J., Deary, I. J., Starr, J. M. & Wardlaw, J. M. (2003). Childhood and current cognitive function in healthy 80-year-olds: A DT-MRI study. *Neuroreport, 14*, 345–349.

Song, S. K., Sun, S. W., Ramsbottom, M. J., Chang, C., Russell, J. & Cross, A. H. (2002). Dysmyelination revealed through MRI as increased radial (but unchanged axial) diffusion of water. *Neuroimage, 17*, 1429–1436.

Song, S. K., Yoshino, J., Le, T. Q., Lin, S. J., Sun, S. W., Cross, A. H. et al. (2005). Demyelination increases radial diffusivity in corpus callosum of mouse brain. *Neuroimage, 26*, 132–140.

Sperry, R. W. (1962). Orderly function with disordered structure. In H. W. Foerster & G. W. Zopt (Eds.), *Principles of Self-Organization* (pp. 279–290). New York, USA: Pergamon Press.

Spilt, A., Goekoop, R., Westendorp, R. G. J., Blauw, G. J., de Craen, A. J. M. & van Buchem, M. A. (2006). Not all age-related white matter hyperintensities are the same: A magnetization transfer imaging study. *American Journal of Neuroradiology, 27*, 1964–1968.

Staempfli, P., Jaermann, T., Crelier, G. R., Kollias, S., Valavanis, A. & Boesiger, P. (2006). Resolving fiber crossing using advanced fast marching tractography based on diffusion tensor imaging. *Neuroimage, 30*, 110–120.

Sullivan, E. V., Rohlfing, T. & Pfefferbaum, A. (2010). Quantitative fiber tracking of lateral and interhemispheric white matter systems in normal aging: Relations to timed performance. *Neurobiology of Aging, 16*, 591–606.

Sullivan, E. V., Adalsteinsson, E., Hedehus, M., Ju, C., Moseley, M., Lim, K. O. et al. (2001). Equivalent disruption of regional white matter microstructure in ageing healthy men and women. *Neuroreport, 12*, 99–104.

Sun, S. W., Neil, J. J. & Song, S. K. (2003). Relative indices of water diffusion anisotropy are equivalent in live and formalin-fixed mouse brains. *Magnetic Resonance in Medicine, 50*, 743–748.

Taki, Y., Kinomura, S., Sato, K., Goto, R., Wu, K., Kawashima, R. et al. (2011). Correlation between gray/white matter volume and cognition in healthy elderly people. *Brain and Cognition, 75*, 170–176.

Tournier, J. D., Mori, S. & Leemans, A. (2011). Diffusion tensor imaging and beyond. *Magnetic Resonance in Medicine, 65*, 1532–1556.

van den Heuvel, D. M., ten Dam, V. H., de Craen, A. J., Admiraal-Behloul, F., Olofsen, H., Bollen, E. L. et al. (2006). Increase in periventricular white matter hyperintensities parallels decline in mental processing speed in a non-demented elderly population. *Journal of Neurology, Neurosurgery & Psychiatry, 77*, 149–153.

van der Flier, W. M., van der Vlies, A. E., Weverling-Rijnsburger, A. W. E., de Boer, N. L., Admiraal-Behloul, F., Bollen, E. L. E. et al. (2005). MRI measures and progression of cognitive decline in nondemented elderly attending a memory clinic. *International Journal of Geriatric Psychiatry, 20*, 1060–1066.

Vannorsdall, T. D., Waldstein, S. R., Kraut, M., Pearlson, G. D. & Schretlen, D. J. (2009). White matter abnormalities and cognition in a community sample. *Archives of Clinical Neuropsychology, 24*, 209–217.

Vernooij, M. W., de Groot, M., van der Lugt, A., Ikram, M. A., Krestin, G. P., Hofman, A. et al. (2008). White matter atrophy and lesion formation explain the loss of structural integrity of white matter in aging. *Neuroimage, 43*, 470–477.

Voineskos, A. N., Rajji, T. K., Lobaugh, N. J., Miranda, D., Shenton, M. E., Kennedy, J. L. et al. (2012). Age-related decline in white matter tract integrity and cognitive performance: A DTI tractography and structural equation modeling study. *Neurobiology of Aging, 33*, 21–34.

Wahlund, L.-O., Barkhof, F., Fazekas, F., Bronge, L., Augustin, M., Sjögren, M. et al. (2001). A new rating scale for age-related white matter changes applicable to MRI and CT. *Stroke, 32*, 1318–1322.

Wechsler, D., Wycherley, R. J., Benjamin, L., Callanan, M., Lavender, T., Crawford, J. R. et al. (1998). *Wechsler Memory Scale – III* (3rd edition). London, UK: The Psychological Corporation.

Wen, W. & Sachdev, P. (2004). The topography of white matter hyperintensities on brain MRI in healthy 60- to 64-year-old individuals. *Neuroimage, 22*, 144–154.

Wen, W., Zhu, W., He, Y., Kochan, N. A., Reppermund, S., Slavin, M. J. et al. (2011). Discrete neuroanatomical networks are associated with specific cognitive abilities in old age. *The Journal of Neuroscience, 31*, 1204–1212.

West, R. L. (1996). An application of prefrontal cortex function theory to cognitive aging. *Psychological Bulletin, 120*, 272–292.

Wheeler-Kingshott, C. A. & Cercignani, M. (2009). About 'axial' and 'radial' diffusivities. *Magnetic Resonance in Medicine, 61*, 1255–1260.

Wu, K., Taki, Y., Sato, K., Kinomura, S., Goto, R., Okada, K. et al. (2012). Age-related changes in topological organization of structural brain networks in healthy individuals. *Human Brain Mapping, 33*, 552–568.

Young, V. G., Halliday, G. M. & Kril, J. J. (2008). Neuropathologic correlates of white matter hyperintensities. *Neurology, 71*, 804–811.

Zahr, N. M., Rohlfing, T., Pfefferbaum, A. & Sullivan, E. V. (2009). Problem solving, working memory, and motor correlates of association and commissural fiber bundles in normal aging: A quantitative fiber tracking study. *Neuroimage, 44*, 1050–1062.

Zhang, Y., Du, A. T., Hayasaka, S., Jahng, G. h., Hlavin, J., Zhan, W., Weiner, M. W. & Schuff, N. (2010). Patterns of age-related water diffusion changes in human brain by concordance and discordance analysis. *Neurobiology of Aging, 31*(11), 1991–2001.

Zhou, X. J., Gao, Q., Abdullah, O. & Magin, R. L. (2010). Studies of anomalous diffusion in the human brain using fractional order calculus. *Magnetic Resonance in Medicine, 63*, 562–569.

Zhu, W., Wen, W., He, Y., Xia, A., Anstey, K. J. & Sachdev, P. (2010). Changing topological patterns in normal aging using large-scale structural networks. *Neurobiology of Aging, 33*, 899–913.

6 Adult age differences in working memory

Evidence from functional neuroimaging

Irene E. Nagel and Ulman Lindenberger

Introduction

The brain's neurochemistry, anatomy, and functional dynamics undergo marked age-related changes (Bäckman et al., 2006; Madden, Bennett & Song, 2009; Morgan & May, 1990; Morrison & Hof, 1997; Raz, 2004; Raz et al., 2008; Raz et al., 2005; Salat et al., 2004; Suhara et al., 1991; Tisserand & Jolles, 2003; Westleye et al., 2010). These anatomical changes are paralleled by cognitive declines, particularly with respect to fluid cognitive functions. One such function is working memory, the ability to hold information online over short periods of time (Baddeley, 2003; Jonides et al., 2008). Working memory is involved in almost any cognitive task, and is of vital importance for everyday competence. Relative to other cognitive functions, working memory is particularly compromised in old age (Babcock & Salthouse, 1990). Its decline typically starts in young or middle adulthood, and accelerates in old age, from about age 60 onwards (Bäckman et al., 1999; Craik & Salthouse, 2000; de Frias et al., 2007; Li et al., 2004; Park et al., 2002). The marked age-related decline of working memory and other higher cognitive functions like selection and monitoring is paralleled by a particularly early and strong age-related decline of a part of the brain that plays a key role within the working memory network, the prefrontal cortex (e.g. Lindenberger, Burzynska & Nagel, 2013; Raz et al., 2005; Tisserand et al., 2002; Tisserand & Jolles, 2003; West, 1996).

Brain declines are modulated by genetic differences, and, to some extent, malleable by experience. Individual differences in working memory increase rather than decrease with advancing adult age, presumably because individual differences that already exist in early adulthood are further augmented by normal aging (de Frias et al., 2007; Lindenberger et al., 2013; Lindenberger & Ghisletta, 2009; Schmiedek, Lövdén & Lindenberger, 2009; Wilson et al., 2002), and by an age-associated increase in the incidence and prevalence of cognition-related pathologies (Bäckman et al., 1999). Understanding the mechanisms underlying this heterogeneity may inform attempts at preserving working memory into advanced old age.

This chapter approaches working memory functioning in old age from the more general perspective of individual differences in brain aging. We start by summarizing general adult age trends in functional brain activation in relation to working memory. In view of the substantial heterogeneity of aging trajectories, which often amplifies the between-person differences that are present in early adulthood, we note that individual differences in brain activation patterns and performance are particularly large in old age. Based on these considerations, we advance the claim that higher levels of performance on working memory tasks in old age are associated with greater neurochemical and structural preservation and more "youth-like" task-related brain activation patterns (see also Nyberg et al., 2012). We will report the results of two recent studies that support this claim (Nagel et al., 2009, 2011), adding a few cautionary notes on the interpretation of fMRI results in the context of aging studies. We discuss four different ways to address working memory aging and end with a plea for multimodal longitudinal studies of individual brain aging trajectories that are capable of shedding light on the ways in which preserved brain structure and function may help to preserve cognitive competence in old age.

General age trends from early to late adulthood in functional brain activation during working memory performance

Over the last decade, an increasing number of cross-sectional fMRI studies on cognitive aging in general and working memory aging in particular have been conducted. Typically, age differences in functional brain activation are observed (Spreng, Wojtowicz & Grady, 2010). The pattern of findings, though, is not easily interpretable, as some studies report underactivation of task-relevant brain areas in older adults, whereas others find overactivation relative to young adults (Rajah & D'Esposito, 2005; Reuter-Lorenz et al., 2000; Reuter-Lorenz & Lustig, 2005; Rypma & D'Esposito, 2000; Rypma et al., 2001). Accordingly, age differences in the amount and patterning of functional brain activation have been explained in different ways.

Underactivation typically is interpreted as a sign of age-related structural and neuromodulatory brain changes. As we will explain later in detail, age-related changes in the hemodynamic response and other changes in neurovascular coupling are likely to contribute as well (D'Esposito et al., 1999; Gazzaley & D'Esposito, 2003; Hock et al., 1997; Reuter-Lorenz, 2002). Overactivation has been reported in the form of larger activation in older compared to younger adults either in the same regions that are active among younger adults, or in additional regions. Particularly the latter has been suggested to serve a compensatory function. According to that interpretation, old-age-specific overactivation points to successful compensation if performance is high and to attempted compensation if performance is low (Cabeza, 2002; Cabeza et al., 2002; Cabeza et al., 1997; Grady et al., 1994; Rajah & D'Esposito, 2005; Reuter-Lorenz et al., 2000). Overactivation, however, may also be dysfunctional (Logan et al., 2002). It may reflect inefficient neuromodulation and inhibition resulting in noisier and less distinct patterns of brain activation (Li, Lindenberger & Sikström, 2001; Li & Sikström, 2002; Park et al., 2002; Reuter-Lorenz et al., 2000). More specifically, declines in dopaminergic neuromodulation lower the signal-to-noise ratio of neural information processing, which, in turn, increases processing noise, resulting in less distinctive brain activation patterns (Braver & Barch, 2002; Li, Lindenberger & Sikström, 2001; Li & Sikström, 2002) and impaired cognitive performance (Bäckman et al., 2000; Bäckman et al., 2006; Erixon-Lindroth et al., 2005; Li, Naveh-Benjamin & Lindenberger, 2005; Volkow et al., 1998).

The concepts of compensation and dysfunction are not necessarily mutually exclusive. Instead, reductions in processing efficiency might lead to compensatory reactions (Buckner, 2004; Park & Reuter-Lorenz, 2009; cf. Bäckman & Dixon, 1992). Presumably compensatory overactivation occurs in response to deficient processing that is particularly pronounced in frontal regions (Reuter-Lorenz & Mikels, 2006; Reuter-Lorenz & Sylvester, 2005). Thus, activation of additional regions may function as an aid or scaffold to preserve working memory and other cognitive functions (Park & Reuter-Lorenz, 2009) in the presence of age-related losses in structure and function. Given their pivotal function for the organization of behavior (e.g. Miller & Cohen, 2001; Stuss, 2006), prefrontal regions carry the promise to attenuate the adverse effects of brain aging (Cappell, Gmeidl & Reuter-Lorenz, 2010; Grady, McIntosh & Craik, 2005). Hence, older adults are exposed to the quandary that prefrontal cortex is increasingly needed but at the same time decreasingly capable of counteracting the adverse consequences of senescence (Lindenberger, Marsiske & Baltes, 2000; Nagel et al., 2007; for review, see Seidler et al., 2010). Furthermore, it should be noted that the dynamic re-allocation of resources to compensate for brain declines might have its drawbacks. Over-recruitment of prefrontal or other working memory regions may be beneficial in simple tasks, but when task difficulty increases, activation may already be at its maximum and thus cannot be further increased (Reuter-Lorenz & Mikels, 2006).

Relative to young adults, functional imaging studies often report overactivation at low task difficulty (e.g. low working memory load) among older adults (e.g. Reuter-Lorenz & Lustig, 2005). As task difficulty increases, however, older adults tend to show a more constrained BOLD response than younger adults, particularly at high load (Nyberg et al., 2008; Mattay et al., 2006). Mattay and colleagues (2006), for example, found that activation patterns in left DLPFC increased with higher load in younger adults. In contrast, activation patterns in left DLPFC peaked at the lowest load in older adults, showing no further increase with higher loads. It has been suggested that the point of maximum activation may be a neural indicator of a working memory capacity limit (Todd & Marois, 2005; Callicott et al., 1999). Accordingly, Mattay and colleagues interpret their results to suggest that older adults reached their capacity limit already at the lowest load condition (see also Nyberg et al., 2008). These findings are in accordance with the Compensation-Related Utilization of Neural Circuits Hypothesis (CRUNCH), according to which older adults show overactivation at low load, presumably as a compensatory response to neurobiological decline. At higher load, activation cannot be further increased, leading to a compromised BOLD response (Cappell et al., 2010; Reuter-Lorenz & Cappell, 2008). Thus, older adults' possible range of brain activation seems to be diminished (Spreng, Wojtowicz & Grady, 2010).

Available evidence suggests that, generally, older adults tend to show overactivation in frontal regions rather than posterior regions compared to younger adults (Cabeza et al., 2004; Cappell et al., 2010; Grady, Yu & Alain, 2008; Rajah & D'Esposito, 2005; Reuter-Lorenz et al., 2000). The evidence also allows for various interpretations of the findings, including no age differences, dedifferentiation, or compensation. Furthermore, hemispheric differences seem to exist with left-lateralized overactivation in older adults being related to higher performance in older adults and right-lateralized overactivation being related to lower performance in older adults (Rajah & D'Esposito, 2005; Spreng, Wojtowicz & Grady, 2010).

As can be seen from the above description of interpretations of overactivation, the term compensation is often used in the context of fMRI studies on cognitive aging to describe situations in which overactivation in older adults is beneficial for task performance. It is, however, important to note that such a "compensatory response" is not necessarily a sign of successful aging, as is sometimes implied. Instead, it rather seems to be the case that such compensatory overactivation is the neural equivalent of increased effort, caused by age-related neurobiological declines, whereas even more successful aging would be marked by an absence or decreased need to show such overactivation in the first place. We will come back to this point when describing our fMRI studies on individual differences in working memory aging.

Normal aging not only affects functional brain activation locally, but also alters the coupling between different brain regions (Bennett et al., 2001; Cabeza et al., 1997; Cook et al., 2007; Grady, McIntosh & Craik, 2003). Given that working memory is based on a large-scale network spanning across a variety of brain regions (D'Esposito, 2007), it is conceivable that the coordination of processing across regions is of pivotal importance for efficient working memory performance. According to the Disconnection Hypothesis, age differences in cognitive ability are in part due to a disconnection of task-relevant brain regions caused by white matter changes. An increasing amount of studies confirm that white matter integrity declines with increasing adult age (Burzynska et al., 2010; Sullivan, Rohlfing & Pfefferbaum, 2010; Pfefferbaum et al., 2000; see also Charlton & Morris, Chapter 5 in this volume). Such declines in white matter integrity have been related to age differences in functional and effective connectivity of brain activation and to cognitive performance (Bennet et al., 2001). However, most of the work on this topic investigates resting state connectivity, episodic memory or age-changes in relation to mild cognitive impairment (e.g. Damaoiseaux, 2012; Schwindt et al., 2013; Hafkemeijer et al., 2012; Yi et al., 2012; Shu et al., 2012; Jones et al., 2011) rather than working memory in healthy older adults. Bennett and colleagues (2001) showed that the connections among brain regions activated during episodic memory differed between younger and older adults. Given that older and younger adults did not differ in performance levels, it is conceivable that the connections unique to older adults developed as a compensatory response to age-associated neurobiological declines. Andrews-Hanna and colleagues (2007) showed that the functional couplings between regions differed between age groups such that older adults had decreased coupling between frontal and posterior regions, a finding that is in accordance with the disconnection hypothesis (see also Arnsten et al., 2010; Cook et al., 2007; Grady, McIntosh & Craik, 2003; Li et al., 2009). Although in some cases, particularly in low load conditions (Bennett et al., 2001), new connections might be established in older adults' brains, the more typical finding is one of decreased connectivity in older adults. Such a decline in task-related connectivity of functional activation is in accordance with findings of compromised white matter integrity in older adults (Gunning-Dixon & Raz, 2000; Sullivan, Rohlfing & Pfefferbaum, 2010; Pfefferbaum et al., 2000).

In summary, findings of over- and underactivation of the working memory network among older relative to younger adults are common. We discussed how findings of underactivation are typically explained by neurobiological brain declines, whereas findings of overactivation are either interpreted as dedifferentiation due to impaired neurotransmitter function or as compensatory activation. Three points are of note here. First, as summarized in the CRUNCH hypothesis, recruitment of additional compensatory regions may aid task performance at low load but may come with the cost that further recruitment at higher levels of task difficulty is no longer possible. Second, we pointed to the quandary that the very same – prefrontal – regions that are thought to aid older adults' processing are also the regions that are particularly vulnerable to age-related neurobiological declines. Third, we noted that compensatory activation, even if beneficial for task performance, is not a sign of entirely successful aging but instead points to neurobiological brain changes that need to be compensated for. Instead, we propose that older individuals who do not show a need for altered brain activation patterns to achieve high levels of working memory performance should be considered as more convincing instantiations of successful cognitive aging.

Generally, due to age differences in neurovascular coupling, a point we will come back to in a later section, it is advisable to compare younger and older adults in their relative differences in activation between, for example, different task load levels rather than comparing activation patterns contrasted with a fixation baseline. Furthermore, with regard to the interpretation of the age differences in functional brain activation related to working memory, it should be noted that meaningful interpretations can only be made if brain activation patterns are related to task performance (i.e. overactivation can only be interpreted as compensatory if performance is higher in individuals showing the additional activation). Some of the apparent inconsistencies in the fMRI literature on adult age differences in working memory aging reflect methodological problems of this sort (cf. Spreng, Wojtowicz & Grady, 2010). In particular, Schneider-Garces and colleagues (2010) convincingly demonstrated that load-related changes in BOLD activation are linked to load-dependent changes in memory span. Thus, it is important to consider task difficulty in fMRI studies on working memory aging.

Experimental investigations of age differences in functional brain activation during working memory such as the ones reported above generally examine group effects, with the aim of finding patterns that can be generalized to the population.

Hence, performance is commonly averaged across individuals and between-person variation is neglected (Conway, Jarrold, Kane, Miyake & Towse, 2008; Hertzog, 1996). Studies taking this approach have yielded important results about the pronounced working memory decline on the population level. However, findings from differential and developmental psychology show that individual differences in working memory are reliable and substantial at all age periods (Miyake, 2001). As pointed out above, these differences increase with advancing adult age because aging individuals differ in the onset and the severity of age-related cognitive declines (Bäckman et al., 1999; Craik & Salthouse, 2000; de Frias et al., 2007; Lindenberger, Burzynska & Nagel, 2013; Lindenberger & Baltes, 1997; Nesselroade & Salthouse, 2004). It therefore seems warranted to consider individual differences in cognitive aging research (cf. Baltes, Reese & Nesselroade, 1977; Hertzog, 1985, 1996). Thus, considering individual differences in task performance and corresponding brain activation patterns is likely to yield valuable new insights into the heterogeneity of working memory in old age. To illustrate this point, we now turn to two studies from our own lab that investigate individual differences in working memory aging.

Empirical illustrations of an individual differences approach to the investigation of working memory aging and related brain activation

Performance level modulates adult age differences in brain activation during spatial working memory

Nagel et al. (2009) examined individual differences in brain activation during spatial working memory performance in younger and older adults with the aim to address the increased heterogeneity in older adults' performance and processing. Spatial working memory, which refers to the online retention of spatial memory contents, appears to be more affected in aging than verbal working memory (Jenkins et al., 2000; Park et al., 2002). The neural network typically activated during spatial working memory tasks involves lateral PFC, premotor cortex (PMC), posterior parietal cortex (PPC), and temporal brain regions (D'Esposito et al., 1998). FMRI studies averaging across age groups reveal that decreased working memory performance in older adults is accompanied by age-related changes in functional brain activation patterns (Jonides et al., 2000; Gazzaley & Esposito, 2007; Rypma & Esposito, 2000; Reuter-Lorenz et al., 2000).

As described before, memory load is known to affect the degree and pattern of activation of the working memory network in younger adults (Braver et al., 1997; Callicott et al., 1999; Jansma et al., 2000). The load-dependent increase of the BOLD signal can be characterized as a dose-response function (Schneider-Garces et al., 2010). Some researchers have reported monotonically increasing functions that are either linear (Braver et al., 1997) or nonlinear (Smith & Jonides, 1998; Cohen et al., 1997). Others have found inverted U-shaped functions (Callicott et al., 1999), where activation in dorsolateral PFC increases with load up to a certain difficulty level, and then decreases (Schneider-Garces et al., 2010).

Only a few studies have investigated the shape of dose-response functions in older adults (Cappell et al., 2010; Mattay et al., 2006; Nyberg et al., 2008; Petrella et al., 2005; Schneider-Garces et al., 2010). Mattay et al. (2006) reported brain activations peaking at load three in younger and at load one in older adults during a spatial n-back task, and concluded that older adults reach their capacity limits at lower levels of difficulty than younger adults. By contrast, Petrella et al. (2005) reported that activation in task-relevant regions increased with load in a delayed recognition task among older adults as well. Conceivably, these discrepancies across studies reflect the dependency of the BOLD response on performance level, which may have differed across studies, both within and across age groups. Given that individual differences in working memory performance are substantial and increase with age, and that functional activation is associated with performance in both younger and older adults, it is surprising that the modulation of age differences in memory-related brain activation patterns by performance levels has only rarely been investigated thus far. Notably, most of these studies used episodic memory tasks rather than working memory tasks (e.g. Persson et al., 2006; Duverne, Motamedinia & Rugg, 2009). As a result, performance heterogeneity, which can be expected to be particularly high in samples of older adults, is often left unanalyzed, thereby confounding differences in BOLD responses across age groups with differences in performance level within age groups (Schneider-Garces et al., 2010).

To examine age whether performance level modulates the BOLD response to a working memory challenge in younger and older adults, we tested 30 younger adults and 30 older adults with a spatial working memory delayed matching task during fMRI scanning. We expected that performance modulation may differ between age groups, such that signal change increases linearly in young high performers and follows a quadratic pattern in old low performers, with young low and old high performers showing intermediate patterns (cf. Nyberg et al., 2008). We used a spatial delayed-matching task, in which subjects saw points appearing on a screen. After a mask and a fixation delay, a probe point appeared. Participants had to indicate by a button press whether the location of the probe matched the location of one of the stimulus points they had seen in a given trial. Working memory load was manipulated by showing 1, 3, or 7 points during a trial.

As expected, older adults were less accurate and responded more slowly. Also, accuracy decreased and response times increased with task load. Interactions with age group indicated that effects of task load on accuracy and response times were stronger in older adults than in younger adults. To examine the association between performance level and brain activation patterns within the two age groups, we formed extreme groups by selecting the ten highest and ten lowest performers of each age group, based on their mean accuracy levels at loads 3 and 7.

Next, we conducted a ROI analysis, with ROIs in bilateral DLPFC, rostrodorsal PMC, and PPC, based on functional activation during spatial working memory performance. To examine the influence of age and performance group on BOLD signal changes in the spatial working memory network under varying load conditions, we extracted percent signal change from ROIs in the left and right

DLPFC, rostrodorsal PMC, and PPC for both age groups and for high and low performers in each age group. Initial analyses of the two age groups as a whole (i.e. irrespective of performance level) seemingly confirmed earlier claims that the BOLD signal is less responsive to increasing spatial working memory demands in old age. However, these average age group effects were qualified by differences between high and low performers within each of the two age groups (see Figure 6.1). In the young group, the BOLD signal of high performers increased up to load 7 in left DLPFC and bilateral RDPMC and less so in right DLPFC and bilateral PPC. However, in the sample of old low performers, there was no increase in activation from load 3 to load 7 for any of the ROI. In fact, in old low performers, activation declined reliably in most ROI after load 3. In contrast, the dose-response functions of old high performers resembled those of the young, suggesting that similarities in functional activation patterns were related not only to chronological age, but also – and even more so – to performance level. Follow-up analyses also revealed that the compromised BOLD response observed in the total sample of older adults was due to the group of low performers. At the same time, increases in activation with load among old high performers that resembled activation patterns observed in younger adults would have gone unnoticed in the whole-group analysis.

In sum, the results of this study suggest that some of the discrepant results of earlier fMRI studies on working memory in old age may reflect differences in performance level (e.g. sampling variability). Given the marked heterogeneity in neuronal and behavioral aging, it seems necessary to qualify statements about adult age differences in brain activation patterns in light of individual differences in performance within age groups. Hidden heterogeneity in activation patterns may lead to inadequate generalizations.

BOLD responsivity to load predicts verbal working memory performance in younger and older adults

In a related study, Nagel et al. (2011) investigated whether individual differences in performance also contribute to adult age differences in BOLD responsivity during verbal, rather than spatial working memory performance. Based on earlier findings (e.g. Cappell et al., 2010), we expected that load-dependent changes in BOLD responses would differ between age groups. Informed by the previous study, we also hypothesized that individual differences in responsivity of local BOLD response would be related to individual differences in working memory performance, such that greater responsivity is related to better performance in both age groups. Finally, we expected that individual differences in task-dependent functional (e.g. effective) connectivity within the working memory network would be related to individual differences in working memory performance.

We administered a verbal version of the n-back task to 30 younger and 30 older adults. Participants were instructed to watch a sequence of letters on the screen and indicate for each letter by a button press whether the letter they currently saw was the same as the one they had seen before. Working memory load was varied

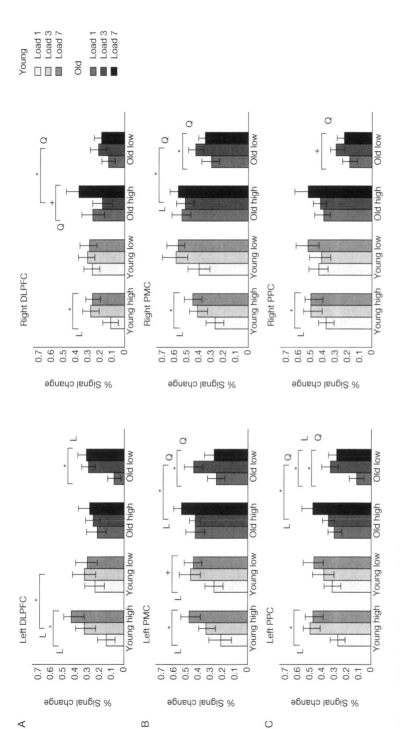

Figure 6.1 Region-of-interest analysis for extreme groups. BOLD signal changes in high- and low-performing younger and older adults across load (lower task demand is represented by lighter colors). There are marked differences in BOLD response between high and low performers within and across age groups. Source: Adapted from Nagel et al., 2009, with permission. Key: * p < .05; + = .05 < p < .10; L = linear contrast; Q = quadratic contrast.

by instructing participants to compare the current letter to the letter 1, 2, or 3 positions back in the sequence. As expected, older adults were less accurate and responded more slowly. Accuracy decreased and response times increased with task load. An interaction of load with age group indicated that effects of task load on response times were stronger in older adults than in younger adults; for accuracy, a trend in the same direction was observed.

To inspect group differences in load-dependent changes in BOLD signal in task-relevant regions, we conducted ROI analyses. Testing the age-by-load interaction revealed significant linear interaction contrasts in several ROIs, reflecting the linear increase of BOLD signal with load in younger but not older adults. In detail, interaction contrasts were reliable in left FPC, bilateral DLPFC, SMA, bilateral PPC, and at trend level in left PMC. Follow-up on analyses separately for each age group showed that activation increased linearly up to the highest load level (3-back) in all ROIs except right VLPFC in younger adults, but not in older adults.

In addition to forming subgroups based on performance level, we also created an index of responsivity, delta, by subtracting signal change in the 1-back condition from signal change in the 3-back condition. Hierarchical regression analyses using age group, delta, and their interaction term as factors were conducted to test whether delta accounted for individual differences in 3-back performance beyond age group. The corresponding R^2-change statistics were significant in left PMC, right PMC, and right PPC, and at trend level in left DLPFC and right DLPFC, showing that delta beyond age reliably predicted n-back performance. The interaction term of age group and delta was not significant for any of the ROIs, apart from a trend level significance in right PPC ($p = .09$). Figure 6.2 displays the scatterplots illustrating the associations between delta and accuracy.

Furthermore, a psycho-physiological interaction (PPI) analysis revealed that the load-dependent changes in connectivity between the left DLPFC and other brain regions differed between age groups. PPI provides a measure of effective connectivity by quantifying how the coupling of a seed region and any other voxel in the brain changes with task condition (Rogers et al., 2007; Friston et al., 1997). Younger adults showed changes in effective connectivity across load in key working memory regions including bilateral PFC, SMA, left PMC, and right PPC, whereas older adults showed load-dependent changes in coupling only in left anterior frontal cortex and temporal regions. To test whether changes in coupling predict working memory performance, we computed a hierarchical regression using age group and PPI scores as predictors and accuracy at 3-back as the dependent variable. As a trend ($p = .064$, uncorrected), load-dependent functional connectivity changes between the left DLPFC and the left PMC predicted 3-back performance beyond age group (see Figure 6.3), and the simple correlation (i.e. not controlling for age group) between connectivity changes and performance was reliable ($r = .31$, $p < .05$). Again, the interaction term did not account for significant additional amounts of variance in 3-back performance.

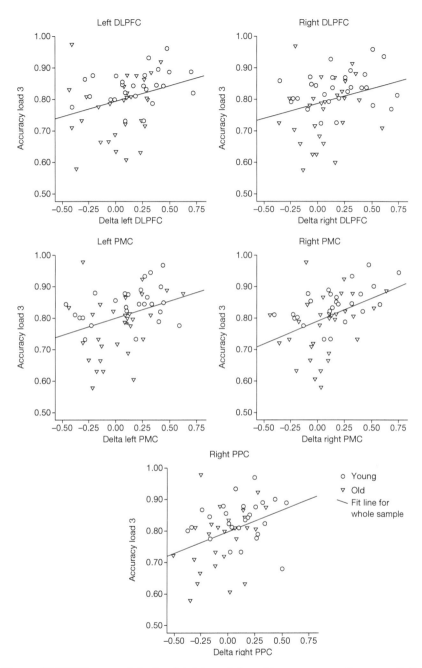

Figure 6.2 BOLD responsivity is related to verbal working memory performance. Delta (BOLD signal change 3-back minus 1-back condition, z-standardized) predicts accuracy at load 3 in bilateral PMC, right PPC and at trend level in bilateral DLPFC. The predictive relation does not differ reliably between groups of younger and older adults

Source: Adapted from Nagel et al., 2011, with permission.

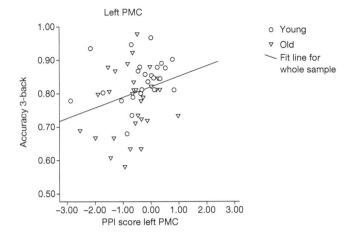

Figure 6.3 Psychophysical interaction analysis of verbal working memory performance. Task-dependent changes in coupling between left DLPFC and left PMC predict accuracy at load 3. This suggests that the coupling between left DLPFC and left PMC contributes to proficient verbal working memory in both younger and older adults

Source: Adapted from Nagel et al., 2011, with permission.

This study confirms and extends the results of the earlier study reported by Nagel et al. (2009) as well as related earlier work (e.g. Cappell et al., 2010; Mattay et al., 2006; Nyberg et al., 2008; Schneider-Garces et al., 2010). As a group, younger adults showed an increased BOLD response to a working memory challenge, whereas the corresponding response in older adults, as a group, was compromised. However, when examining individual differences in dose-response functions with the delta score, we found that local BOLD responsivity predicts working memory performance in both age groups, indicating that task-related modulation of activity in the prefrontal and parietal cortices contributes to proficient task performance.

Thus, the results of this study suggest that a substantial portion of the local and global network characteristics that permit individuals in the adult age range to adequately respond to working memory challenges is actually age-invariant (cf. Cappell et al., 2010; Nagel et al., 2009; Schneider-Garces et al., 2010). From this perspective, normal aging reduces the likelihood of an adequately responsive working memory network, due to factors that may be more or less similar to the reasons that bring about individual differences in working memory performance in age-homogeneous samples.

Summary: Functional neuroimaging investigations of age-related working memory decline

The two studies reported in detail above underscore the importance and magnitude of individual differences in working memory aging. They also serve as a demonstration that fMRI studies on cognitive aging need to take individual differences into account. In both studies, older adults with relatively high levels of working memory performance were more likely to increase brain activity in task-relevant brain regions with increasing working memory load than low-performing older adults, who tended to show flat or inverted-U shape activation profiles. This heterogeneity would have gone unnoticed if older adults had been conceived and analyzed as a homogenous group (see also Craik, Byrd & Swanson, 1987). The patterns of local and coordinated brain activity that were associated with high working memory performance looked strikingly similar across age groups.

Cautionary note: Use of fMRI in aging research

FMRI is well suited to the investigation of cognitive aging because it provides the possibility to test non-invasively how age-related regional changes in functional activation are related to age-related changes in cognitive performance (D'Esposito, Deouell & Gazzaley, 2003). However, age-comparative fMRI studies rest on the assumption that both age groups have similar cerebral blood flow and hemodynamic responses. FMRI outcomes depend on neurovascular coupling, the process by which neural activity leads to a local change in the ratio of oxygenated and deoxygenated blood by influencing the cerebral blood volume and local oxygen consumption. During performance on a cognitive task, a hemodynamic response is generated that results in increased blood flow and volume. The increased blood flow leads to locally excessive amounts of oxygenated blood, which are reflected in the BOLD response that is measured in fMRI. In quasi-experimental imaging studies investigating group differences in functional brain activation, it is commonly assumed that vascular properties do not differ reliably across groups. In the course of the transition from early to late adulthood and old age, however, vascular structures become less elastic, reactivity to chemical modulators such as oxygen is reduced, and cerebral blood flow (CBF) decreases. Furthermore, various medical conditions like minor infarctions, stroke, and diabetes also alter the BOLD signal. These changes lead to a decrease in the signal-to-noise ratio, and a decrease in the amplitude and spatial extent of the BOLD signal (D'Esposito, Deouell & Gazzaley, 2003; Rajah & D'Esposito, 2005). Therefore, aging studies can be confounded by age-related differences in the hemodynamic response and resting CBF (D'Esposito, Deouell & Gazzaley, 2003; Gazzaley & D'Esposito, 2005).

It has been suggested that one way to tackle this problem is to establish baselines that are specific for each group or subject. By having each participant perform a simple visual or sensorimotor task in the scanner, one can determine the specific signal and noise characteristics and model the BOLD response accordingly. Modeling the response in one region based on the activation in another might, however, be problematic if the hemodynamic response differs between regions to a greater degree in older adults (Buckner et al., 2000). Another way to circumvent possible confounds is to use parametric designs. In parametric designs, between-group comparisons are made only with regard to the difference in activation from one load level to the other (Rajah & D'Esposito, 2005). Finally, BOLD responses that correlate with behavior in a meaningful way are less likely to be entirely due to age differences in neurovascular coupling (Gazzaley & D'Esposito, 2005).

In the imaging studies reported above, parametric designs were used, and load-dependent differences in BOLD responses were correlated with load-dependent corresponding differences in behavior. Moreover, individuals with a self-reported history of strokes were excluded from the study. For all of these reasons, it is unlikely that age differences in the hemodynamic response account for the reported results.

Open issues and future directions

How to address cognitive aging: Compensation, preservation, restoration, and selection

When discussing common approaches to the interpretation of age differences in functional brain activation during performance of working memory tasks, we mentioned that both under- and overactivation in older adults are reported, which are both likely to reflect age-related neurobiological changes in prefrontal cortex and other regions of the working memory network. We pointed out that the prefrontal cortex is at the heart of a quandary: increasingly needed but decreasingly capable of counteracting the adverse consequences of senescence on behavior.

What are ways to confront these age-related declines and to reach high levels of performance in old age? In the following we describe four routes to face age-related declines on brain and cognition. In particular, we propose that compensatory activation might in some cases be beneficial for task performance, but, unlike "youth-like activation," may not necessarily be seen as a sign of successful aging.

Compensation

As pointed out above, high levels of cognitive functioning in old age may reflect instances of successful compensation (Cabeza, 2002; Cabeza et al., 2002; Grady, 2008; Park & Reuter-Lorenz, 2009; Reuter-Lorenz & Cappell, 2008; Stern, 2009). Compensation is hard to define conceptually and difficult to pinpoint empirically because alternative explanations (some of which we will describe in the following) are not easily ruled out. Conceptually, a general and a developmental definition can be set apart. In general terms, compensation refers to any process or mechanism in response to a change in task demands. A typical example would be an increase in brain activation with increasing task demands, where the additional recruitment of cerebral resources compensates for the increase in difficulty. Note that this increase in difficulty is defined in relation to an individual's resources. Hence, a task may become more difficult either because the task itself has increased in difficulty or because brain resources have decreased (see also Cappell, Gmeindl & Reuter-Lorenz, 2010; Schneider-Garces et al., 2010).

According to a narrower definition, compensation in the context of normal aging refers to a structural or functional reorganization of the brain that evolves *in response to aging-induced losses in brain functioning* (Bäckman & Dixon, 1992; Baltes & Baltes, 1990; Park & Reuter-Lorenz, 2009; Riediger, Li & Lindenberger, 2006). This kind of compensation was described earlier in the chapter. It does not consist of the re-establishing of the substrate or function that was lost, but in creating something new in response to a loss (see Logie, Horne & Petit, Chapter 2 in this volume). This definition of compensation is analogous to compensation in response to discrete events such as stroke or other acute insults to the brain (Buckner et al., 1996; Kopp et al., 1999). However, it is likely that positive effects of compensation on performance, if present at all, do not extend to more advanced stages of brain aging (Persson et al., 2006).

Preservation

Even though compensation might be an important aspect of older adults' cognitive functioning, the studies reported in this chapter highlight another potential scenario. In the two studies by Nagel et al. (2009, 2011), older adults with more "youth-like" brain responsivity to increasing task demands showed higher levels of working memory performance than older adults whose brain responsivity differed from younger adults.[1] A straightforward interpretation of this finding is that individuals differ in the rate and extent of senescent alterations of brain metabolism and brain structure. According to this view, the brains of individuals whose cerebral anatomy and neurochemistry is relatively well preserved are more likely to show functional brain activation patterns that resemble those of younger adults, and that are germane to proficient performance. An important implication of this view is that cognitive interventions should aim at preserving or restoring "youth-like" brain structure and functions. Thus, only when preservation of working memory and related processing is no longer possible may compensatory processes need to come into play.

Restoration

Given that postponing and reducing brain aging is arguably the best way to avoid its negative effects on cognition, *preservation* is probably a generally accepted intervention goal. Similarly, restoration makes use of the remaining potential for plastic change (Lövdén et al., 2010a), and refers to attempts to re-install properties of the brain that were lost in the course of aging, with the hope that recovery of function and behavior will ensue. A recent study by Lövdén et al. (2010b) suggests that restoration through behavioral intervention may be a viable strategy. Lövdén et al. (2010b) used cognitive training (see Neely & Nyberg, Chapter 4 in this volume), DTI, and structural MRI to investigate the plasticity of white matter tracts that connect the left and right hemisphere of the frontal lobes. Over a period of about 180 days, 20 younger adults and 12 older adults trained for a total of 101 1-hour sessions on a set of three working memory, three episodic memory, and six perceptual speed tasks. Control groups were assessed at pre- and post-test. Training affected several DTI metrics and increased the area of the anterior part of the corpus callosum. These results show that experience-dependent plasticity of white matter microstructure extends into old age. Moreover, they suggest that age-related disruptions of structural interhemispheric connectivity of the frontal lobes, which are common and pronounced in normal aging, can be restored through experience, at least to some extent. It should be noted that restoration differs from compensation in that it refers to re-installing properties that were lost rather than relying on the aid of additional regions that might then not be available when needed for their initial function.

Selection

Brain-behavior relations are often many-to-one in the sense that younger adults' brains can execute a given task in more than one way (cf. Edelman, 1987). Evidence supporting this proposition comes from studies using transcranial magnetic stimulation to implement temporary functional lesions in specific areas of the brain (Pascual-Leone et al., 2005). These studies have shown that younger adults can adapt to some of these functional lesions instantaneously by recruiting different brain areas (e.g. Lee et al., 2003). It is likely that different brain implementations of a given behavior are differentially vulnerable to aging. Some brain areas or activation patterns may be more resilient to normal aging than others. Thus, inclusion of these regions in certain functions was present as an option in younger adults' repertoire, and came to the fore under the selection pressures of normal aging. The increasing role of some regions with advancing age may thus in some cases signal selective survival rather than the compensatory development of new functional activation patterns.

The three cross-sectional, age-comparative studies reported above are generally consistent with the hypothesis that older adults who maintain higher white matter integrity or more "youth-like" brain activation patterns also show higher levels of working memory performance. The described four possible routes to confront working memory aging are not mutually exclusive, and their importance, feasibility, and reciprocal relations remain to be determined. Clearly, methodological advances are of importance here and are needed to better discriminate among preservation, restoration, selection, and compensation.

A Plea for an individual-differences-focused, multimodal and longitudinal investigation of working-memory aging

What differentiates older adults with shallower decline and higher levels of performance from those with steeper decline and lower levels of performance? Do high- and low-functioning individuals differ primarily in the burden of primary neurobiological aging changes, or rather in the way their brains adapt to these changes? And what are the factors contributing to either of these differences? The substantial heterogeneity in working memory aging and related functional brain activation was the dominant theme of this chapter. Aging of the prefrontal cortex and other core regions of the working memory network is embedded in a web of grey matter changes, white matter changes, and neurochemical changes, but the timing and interrelations of these changes have not been examined in full. Therefore, currently, little is known about the mechanisms contributing to interindividual differences in aging trajectories (Hertzog et al., 2009; Nyberg et al., 2010). Accordingly, methodological advances in terms of a focus on individual differences, and multimodal and longitudinal designs are needed.

Individual differences

The studies reported in detail in this chapter provide important examples as to how an individual difference approach in research on working memory aging can help deepen the understanding of working memory aging. The prevailing focus on comparing group averages comes at a double cost. This focus hides the heterogeneity of working memory response patterns within the samples that are being contrasted, such as groups of younger and older adults. At the same time, the focus on average group differences also hides the notable degree of invariance in the brain characteristics that promote proficient working memory performance across age groups. To the degree that variations around the mean are governed by similar mechanisms as the mechanisms causing mean decline, the focus on individual differences bears the promise to help identify mechanisms that contribute to both the invariant and the malleable aspects of normal cognitive aging.

Multimodal approach

In this context, it is noteworthy that adult changes in neuroanatomy, neuro-chemistry, neural activation, and behavior have rarely been investigated in concert. Hence, little is known about the ways in which age-related changes at one level (e.g. brain structure) map onto changes at other levels (e.g. brain function), and how mechanisms observed at each of these levels generate both the invariant and the variable properties of normal cognitive aging (cf. Li & Lindenberger, 2002; Lindenberger, Li & Bäckman, 2006). Future studies need to further strengthen the links between structural, neurochemical, and functional properties of the brain, and their interacting and recursive links to behavior (Lindenberger, Li & Bäckman, 2006). To address structure-function-behavior relations in aging populations, the corresponding measures need to be assessed in samples that are sufficiently large to permit multivariate modeling of individual differences.

Longitudinal study design

Longitudinal studies comprising PET, SPECT, MRI, fMRI, and behavioral data (e.g. Beason-Held, Kraut & Resnick, 2008a, 2008b; Nyberg et al., 2010) along with assessment of vascular risk factors are needed to trace the evolution of neurochemical, grey matter, white matter, functional, and working memory performance changes in greater detail. It will be of particular importance for the understanding of working memory aging to examine how far the rates of decline in frontal and striatal dopamine differ across individuals, relate to other aspects of brain aging, and are influenced by genetic factors. The early onset of dopamine decline may trigger or accentuate the effects of other physiological changes in the aging brain, such as grey matter loss, in part by compromising the functional integrity of subcortical-cortical connections. Longitudinal data on individual differences in age-related brain changes continue to be sparse. With respect to volume, reliable individual differences in shrinkage have been found, but similar data about individual differences in neurochemical changes and changes in white matter integrity are lacking (see Charlton & Morris, Chapter 5 in this volume). Given the volumetric and behavioral findings, it is likely that age trends in other dimensions of brain aging also show considerable variation across individuals. Longitudinal studies combining MR-based measures of regional volumes and structural connectivity with PET-based measures of transmitter availability would help researchers to study the temporal relation between changes in transmitter systems and anatomical alterations of the aging brain.

Such studies are needed to identify the antecedents and correlates of successfully preserved working memory functioning in old age. They will help to delineate the neural mechanisms underlying maintenance, restoration, selection, and compensation. To the extent that the relevant mechanisms can be manipulated, the resulting findings may inform interventions that foster successful working memory aging.

In this chapter we described and discussed common findings on age-related differences in functional brain activation during working memory. We reported two studies that used a quasi-experimental design to take a closer look at individual differences in working memory. A high degree of heterogeneity was noted among older individuals, with older adults performing at high levels showing youth-like activation patterns. Working memory functioning may be both more heterogeneous (e.g. within groups) and more invariant (e.g. across groups) than commonly assumed. Documenting this heterogeneity in neural processing in relation to performance opens a window to delineating mechanisms that promote positive cognitive outcomes.

Acknowledgments

The authors thank Lars Bäckman, Aga Burzynska, Hauke Heekeren, Shu-Chen Li, Lars Nyberg, and Claudia Preuschhof for their contributions to the empirical studies that are reported in detail in this chapter (Nagel et al., 2009, 2011).

Note

1 In the domain of episodic memory, studies by Rugg and colleagues have yielded a similar pattern of results (e.g. Duverne, Motamedinia & Rugg, 2009).

References

Andrews-Hanna, J. R., Snyder, A. Z., Vincent, J. L., Lustig, C., Head, D., Raichle, M. E. et al. (2007). Disruption of large-scale brain systems in advanced aging. *Neuron, 56,* 924–935.

Arnsten, A. F. T., Paspalas, C. D., Gamo, N. J., Yang, Y. & Wang, M. (2010). Dynamic network connectivity: A new form of neuroplasticity. *Trends, 14,* 365–375.

Babcock, R. L. & Salthouse, T. A. (1990). Effects of increased processing demands on age differences in working memory. *Psychology and Aging, 5,* 421–428.

Bäckman, L. & Dixon, R. A. (1992). Psychological compensation: A theoretical framework. *Psychological Bulletin, 112,* 259–283.

Bäckman, L., Ginovart, N., Dixon, R. A., Wahlin, T. B., Wahlin, A., Halldin, C. et al. (2000). Age-related cognitive deficits mediated by changes in the striatal dopamine system. *American Journal of Psychiatry, 157,* 635–637.

Bäckman, L., Nyberg, L., Lindenberger, U., Li, S.-C. & Farde, L. (2006). The correlative triad among aging, dopamine, and cognition: Current status and future prospects. *Neuroscience and Biobehavioral Reviews, 30,* 791–807.

Bäckman, L., Small, B. J., Wahlin, A. & Larsson, A. (1999). Cognitive functioning in very old age. In F. I. Craik & T. Salthouse (Eds.), *Handbook of aging and cognition* (Vol. 2, pp. 499–558). Mahwah, NY: Erlbaum.

Baddeley, A. (2003). Working memory: Looking back and looking forward. *Nature Reviews Neuroscience, 4,* 829–839.

Baltes, P. B. & Baltes, M. M. (1990). Psychological perspectives on successful aging: The model of selective optimization with compensation. In P. B. Baltes & M. M. Baltes (Eds.), *Succcessful aging: Perspectives from the behavioral sciences* (pp. 1–34). New York: Cambridge University Press.

Baltes, P. B., Reese, H. W. & Nesselroade, J. R. (1977). *Life-span developmental psychology: Introduction to research methods.* Monterey, CA: Brooks-Cole Publishing.

Beason-Held, L.-L., Kraut, M. A. & Resnick, S. M. (2008a). I. Longitudinal changes in aging brain function. *Neurobiology of Aging, 29,* 483–496.

Beason-Held, L.-L., Kraut, M. A. & Resnick, S. M. (2008b). II. Temporal patterns of longitudinal change in aging brain function. *Neurobiology of Aging, 29,* 497–513.

Bennett, P. J., Sekuler, A. B., McIntosh, A. R. & Della-Maggiore, V. (2001). The effects of aging on visual memory: Evidence for functional reorganization of cortical networks. *Acta Psychologia, 107,* 249–273.

Braver, T. S., Cohen, J. D., Nystrom, L. E., Jonides, J., Smith, E. E. & Noll, D. C. (1997). A parametric study of prefrontal cortex involvement in human working memory. *Neuroimage, 5,* 49–62.

Braver, T. S. & Barch, D. M. (2002). A theory of cognitive control, aging cognition, and neuromodulation. *Neuroscience & Biobehavioral Reviews, 26,* 809–817.

Buckner, R. L. (1996). Beyond HERA: contributions of specific prefrontal brain areas to long-term memory retrieval. *Psychonomic Bulletin & Reviews, 3,* 149–158.

Buckner, R. L. (2004). Memory and executive function in aging and AD: Multiple factors that cause decline and reserve factors that compensate. *Neuron, 44,* 195–208.

Buckner, R. L., Snyder, A. Z., Sanders, A. L., Raichle, M. E. & Morris, J. C. (2000). Functional brain imaging of young, nondemented, and demented older adults. *Journal of Cognitive Neuroscience, 12,* 24–34.

Burzynska, A. Z., Preuschhof, C., Bäckman, L., Nyberg, L., Li, S.-C., Lindenberger, U. et al. (2010). Age-related differences in white matter microstructure: Region-specific patterns of diffusivity. *Neuroimage, 49*, 2104–2112.

Cabeza, R. (2002). Hemispheric asymmetry reduction in older adults: The HAROLD model. *Psychology and Aging, 17*, 85–100.

Cabeza, R., Anderson, N. D., Locantore, J. K. & McIntosh, A. R. (2002). Aging gracefully: Compensatory brain activity in high-performing older adults. *Neuroimage, 17*, 1394–1402.

Cabeza, R., Daselaar, S. M., Dolcos, F., Prince, S. E., Budde, M. & Nyberg, L. (2004). Task-independent and task-specific age effects on brain activity during working memory, visual attention and episodic retrieval. *Cerebral Cortex, 14*(4), 364–375.

Cabeza, R., McIntosh, A. R., Tulving, E., Nyberg, L. & Grady, C. L. (1997). Age-related differences in effective neural connectivity during encoding and recall. *NeuroReport, 8*, 3479–3483.

Callicott, J. H., Mattay, V. S., Bertolino, A., Finn, K., Coppola, R., Frank, J. A. et al. (1999). Physiological characteristics of capacity constraints in working memory as revealed by functional MRI. *Cerebral Cortex, 9*, 20–26.

Cappell, K. A., Gmeindl, L. & Reuter-Lorenz, P. A. (2010). Age differences in prefontal recruitment during verbal working memory maintenance depend on memory load. *Cortex, 46*, 462–473.

Cohen, J. D., Perlstein, W. M., Braver, T. S., Nystrom, L. E., Noll, D. C., Jonides, J. et al. (1997). Temporal dynamics of brain activation during a working memory task. *Nature, 386*, 604–608.

Conway, A. R. A., Jarrold, C., Kane, M. J., Miyake, A. & Towse, J. N. (2008). *Variation in working memory*. New York: Oxford University Press.

Cook, I. A., Bookheimer, S. Y., Mickes, L., Leuchter, A. F. & Kumar, A. (2007). Aging and brain activation with working memory tasks: An fMRI study of connectivity. *International Journal of Geriatric Psychiatry, 22*, 332–342.

Craik, F. I. M. & Salthouse, T. A. (Eds.) (2000). *The handbook of aging and cognition* (2nd ed.). Mahwah, NY: Erlbaum.

Craik, F. I. M., Byrd, M. & Swanson, J. M. (1987). Patterns of memory loss in three elderly samples. *Psychology and Aging, 2*, 79–86.

Damoiseaux, J. S. (2012). Resting-state fMRI as a biomarker for Alzheimer's disease? *Alzheimer's Res. Ther., 4*(2), 8.

D'Esposito, M. (2007). From cognitive to neural models of working memory. *Philosophical Transactions of the Royal Society of London, 362*, 761–772.

D'Esposito, M., Deouell, L. Y. & Gazzaley, A. (2003). Alterations in the BOLD fMRI signal with ageing and disease: A challenge for neuroimaging. *Nature Reviews Neuroscience, 4*, 863–872.

D'Esposito, M., Aguirre, G. K., Zarahn, E., Ballard, D., Shin, R. K. & Lease, J. (1998). Functional MRI studies of spatial and nonspatial working memory. *Cognitive Brain Research, 7*(1), 1–13.

D'Esposito, M., Zarahn, E., Aguirre, G. K. & Rypma, B. (1999). The effect of normal aging on the coupling of neural activity to the bold hemodynamic response. *Neuroimage, 10*, 6–14.

de Frias, C. M., Lövdén, M., Lindenberger, U. & Nilsson, L.-G. (2007). Revisiting the dedifferentiation hypothesis with longitudinal multi-cohort data. *Intelligence, 35*, 381–392.

Duverne, S., Motamedinia, S. & Rugg, M. D. (2009). The relationship between aging, performance, and the neural correlates of successful memory encoding. *Cerebral Cortex, 19*, 733–744.

Edelman, G. M. (1987). *Neural Darwinism. The theory of neuronal group selection.* New York: Basic Books.

Erixon-Lindroth, N., Farde, L., Robins Wahlin, T. B., Sovago, J., Halldin, C. & Bäckman, L. (2005). The role of the striatal dopamine transporter in cognitive aging. *Psychiatry Research: Neuroimaging, 138*, 1–12.

Friston, K. J., Buechel, C., Fink, G. R., Morris, J., Rolls, E. & Dolan, R. J. (1997). Psychophysiological and modulatory interactions in neuroimaging. *Neuroimage, 6*, 218–229.

Gazzaley, A. & D'Esposito, M. (2003). The contribution of functional brain imaging to our understanding of cognitive aging. *Science of Aging Knowledge Environment*, 2003(4), PE2.

Gazzaley, A., & D'Esposito, M. (2005). BOLD functional MRI and cognitive aging. In R. Cabeza, L. Nyberg & D. Park (Eds.), *Cognitive neuroscience of aging: Linking cognitive and cerebral aging* (pp. 107–131). New York: Oxford University Press.

Gazzaley, A. & D'Esposito, M. (2007). Top-down modulation and normal aging. *Annals of the New York Academy of Science, 1097*, 67–83.

Grady, C. L. (2008). Cognitive neuroscience of aging. *Annals of the New York Academy of Science, 1124*, 127–144

Grady, C. L., Yu, H. & Alain, C. (2008). Age-related differences in brain activity underlying working memory for spatial and nonspatial auditory information. *Cerebral Cortex, 18*(1), 189–199.

Grady, C. L., McIntosh, A. R. & Craik, F. I. (2003). Age-related differences in the functional connectivity of the hippocampus during memory encoding. *Hippocampus, 13*, 572–586.

Grady, C. L., McIntosh, A. R. & Craik, F. I. M. (2005). Task-related activity in prefrontal cortex and its relation to recognition memory performance in young and old adults. *Neuropsychologia, 43*, 1466–1481.

Grady, C. L., Maisog, J. M., Horwitz, B., Ungerleider, L. G., Mentis, M. J., Salerno, J. A. et al. (1994). Age-related changes in cortical blood flow activation during visual processing of faces and location. *The Journal of Neuroscience, 14*, 1450–1462.

Gunning-Dixon, F. M. & Raz, N. (2000). The cognitive correlates of white matter abnormalities in normal aging: A quantitative review. *Neuropsychology, 14*, 224–232.

Hafkemeijer, A., van der Grond, J. & Rombouts, S. A. (2012). Imaging the default mode network in aging and dementia. *Biochimica et Biophysica Acta, 1822(3)*, 431–441.

Hertzog, C. (1985). An individual differences perspective: implications for cognitive research in gerontology. *Research on Aging, 7*, 7–45.

Hertzog, C. (1996). Research design in studies of aging and cognition. In J. E. Birren & K. W. Schaie (Eds.), *Handbook of the psychology of aging* (pp. 24–37), San Diego, CA: Academic Press.

Hertzog, C., Kramer, A. F., Wilson, R. S. & Lindenberger, U. (2009). Enrichment effects on adult cognitive development: Can the functional capacity of older adults be preserved and enhanced? *Psychology in the Public Interest, 9*(1), 1–65.

Hock, C., Villringer, K., Muller-Spahn, F., Wenzel, R., Heekeren, H., Schuh-Hofer, S. et al. (1997). Decrease in parietal cerebral hemoglobin oxygenation during performance of a verbal fluency task in patients with Alzheimer's disease monitored by means of near-infrared spectroscopy (NIRS): Correlation with simultaneous rCBF-PET measurements. *Brain Research, 755,* 293–303.

Jansma, J. M., Ramsey, N. F., Coppola, R. & Kahn, R. S. (2000). Specific versus nonspecific brain activity in a parametric N-back task. *Neuroimage, 12,* 688–697.

Jenkins, L., Myerson, J., Joerding, J. A. & Hale, S. (2000). Converging evidence that visuospatial cognition is more age-sensitive than verbal cognition. *Psychology and Aging, 15,* 157–175.

Jones, D. T., Machulda, M. M., Vemuri, P., McDade, E. M., Zeng, G., Senjem, M. L. et al. (2011). Age-related changes in the default mode network are more advanced in Alzheimer disease. *Neurology, 77(16),* 1524–1531.

Jonides, J., Lewis, R. L., Nee, D. E., Lustig, C. A., Berman, M. G. & Moore, K. S. (2008). The mind and brain of short-term memory. *Annual Review of Psychology, 59,* 193–224.

Jonides, J., Marshuetz, C., Smith, E. E., Reuter-Lorenz, P. A., Koeppe, R. A. & Hartley, A. (2000). Age differences in behavior and PET activation reveal differences in interference resolution in verbal working memory. *Journal of Cognitive Neuroscience, 12,* 188–196.

Jonides, J., Schumacher, E. H., Smith, E. E., Lauber, E. J., Awh, E., Minoshima, S. et al. (1997). Verbal working memory load affects regional brain activation as measured by PET. *Journal of Cognitive Neuroscience, 9,* 462–475.

Kopp, B., Kunkel, A., Mühlnickel, W., Villringer, K., Taub, E. & Flor, H. (1999). Plasticity in the motor system related to therapy-induced improvement of movement after stroke. *NeuroReport, 10,* 807–810.

Lee, L., Siebner, H. R., Rowe, J. B., Rizzo, V., Rothwell, J. C. et al. (2003). Acute remapping within the motor system induced by low frequency repetitive transcranial magnetic stimulation. *Journal of Neuroscience, 23,* 5308–5318.

Li, S.-C. & Sikström, S. (2002). Integrative neurocomputational perspectives on cognitive aging, neuromodulation, and representation. *Neuroscience & Biobehavioral Reviews, 26,* 795–808.

Li, S.-C., Lindenberger, U. & Sikström, S. (2001). Aging cognition: From neuromodulation to representation to cognition. *Trends in Cognitive Sciences, 5,* 479–486.

Li, S.-C., Naveh-Benjamin, M. & Lindenberger, U. (2005). Aging neuromodulation impairs associative binding: A neurocomputational account. *Psychological Science, 16,* 445–450.

Li, S.-C., Lindenberger, U., Hommel, B., Aschersleben, G., Prinz, W. & Baltes, P. B. (2004). Transformations in the couplings among intellectual abilities and constituent cognitive processes across the life span. *Psychological Science, 15,* 155–163.

Li, S.-C., Lindenberger, U., Nyberg, L., Heekeren, H. R. & Bäckman, L. (2009). Dopaminergic modulation of cognition in human aging. In W. Jagust & M. D'Esposito (Eds.), *Imaging the aging brain* (pp. 71–91). Oxford: Oxford University Press.

Li, K. Z. & Lindenberger, U. (2002). Relations between aging sensory/sensorimotor and cognitive functions. *Neuroscience and Biobehavioral Reviews, 26(7),* 777–783.

Lindenberger, U. & Baltes, P. B. (1997). Intellectual functioning in old and very old age: Cross-sectional results from the Berlin Aging Study. *Psychology and Aging, 12,* 410–432.

Lindenberger, U., Burzynska, A. Z. & Nagel, I. E. (2013). Heterogeneity in frontal lobe aging. In D. T. Stuss & R. T. Knight (Eds.), *Principles of frontal lobe function* (2nd. ed., pp. 609–627). New York: Oxford University Press.

Lindenberger, U. & Ghisletta, P. (2009). Cognitive and sensory declines in old age: Gauging the evidence for a common cause. *Psychology and Aging, 24(1),* 1–16.

Lindenberger, U., Li, S.-C. & Bäckman, L. (2006). Delineating brain-behavior mappings across the lifespan: Substantive and methodological advances in developmental neuroscience. *Neuroscience & Biobehavioral Reviews, 30*, 713–717.

Lindenberger, U., Marsiske, M. & Baltes, P. B. (2000). Memorizing while walking: Increase in dual-task costs from young adulthood to old age. *Psychology and Aging, 15*, 417–436.

Logan, J. M., Sanders, A. L., Snyder, A. Z., Morris, J. C. & Buckner, R. L. (2002). Under-recruitment and nonselective recruitment: Dissociable neural mechanisms associated with aging. *Neuron, 33*, 827–840.

Lövdén, M., Bäckman, L., Lindenberger, U., Schaefer, S. & Schmiedek, F. (2010a). A theoretical framework for the study of adult cognitive plasticity. *Psychological Bulletin, 136*, 659–676.

Lövdén, M., Bodammer, N. C., Kühn, S., Kaufmann, J., Schütze, H., Tempelmann, C. et al. (2010b). Experience-dependent plasticity of white-matter microstructure extends into old age. *Neuropsychologia, 48*, 3878–3883.

Madden, D. J., Bennett, I. L. & Song, A. W. (2009). Cerebral white matter integrity and cognitive aging: Contributions from diffusion tensor imaging. *Neuropsychology Review, 19*, 415–435.

Mattay, V. S., Fera, F., Tessitore, A., Hariri, A. R., Berman, K. F., Das, S. et al. (2006). Neurophysiological correlates of age-related changes in working memory capacity. *Neuroscience Letters, 392*, 32–37.

Miller, E. K. & Cohen, J. D. (2001). An integrative theory of prefontal cortex function. *Annual Review of Neuroscience, 24*, 167–202.

Miyake, A. (2001). Individual differences in working memory: Introduction to the special section. *Journal of Experimental Psychology: General, 130*, 163–168.

Morgan, D. G. & May, P. C. (1990). Age-related changes in synaptic neurochemistry. In Schneider and Row (Eds.), *Handbook of the biology of aging* (pp. 219–250). New York: Academic Press.

Morrison, J. H. & Hof, P. R. (1997). Life and death of neurons in the aging brain. *Science, 278*, 412–419.

Nagel, I. E., Preuschhof, C., Li, S.-C., Nyberg, L., Bäckman, L., Lindenberger, U. & Heekeren, H. R. (2009). Performance level modulates adult age differences in brain activation during spatial working memory. *Proceedings of the National Academy of Sciences of the United States of America, 106*, 22552–22557.

Nagel, I. E., Preuschhof, C., Li, S.-C., Nyberg, L., Bäckman, L., Lindenberger, U. & Heekeren, H. R. (2011). Load modulation of BOLD response and connectivity predict working memory performance in younger and older adults. *Journal of Cognitive Neuroscience, 23*, 2030–2045.

Nagel, I. E., Werkle-Bergner, M., Li, S.-C. & Lindenberger, U. (2007). Perception. In J. E. Birren (Ed.), *Encyclopedia of gerontology* (2nd ed., pp. 334–342). Oxford: Elsevier.

Nesselroade, J. R. & Salthouse, T. A. (2004). Methodological and theoretical implications of intraindividual variability in perceptual-motor performance. *The Journals of Gerontology. Psychological Sciences and Social Sciences, 59*, P49–P55.

Nyberg, L., Dahlin, E., Stigsdotter, N. A. & Bäckman, L. (2008). Neural correlates of variable working memory load across adult age and skill: Dissociative patterns within the fronto-parietal network. *Scandinavian Journal of Psychology, 50*, 41–46.

Nyberg, L., Lövdén, M., Riklund, K., Lindenberger, U. & Bäckman, L. (2012). Memory aging and brain maintenance. *Trends in Cognitive Sciences, 16*, 292–305.

Nyberg, L., Salami, A., Andersson, M., Eriksson, J., Kalpouzos, G., Kauppi, K. et al. (2010). Longitudinal evidence for diminished frontal cortex function in aging. *Proceedings of the National Academy of Sciences of the United States of America, 107*(52), 22682–22686.

Park, D. C. & Reuter-Lorenz, P. (2009). The adaptive brain: Aging and neurocognitive scaffolding. *The Annual Review of Psychology, 60*, 173–196.

Park, D. C., Lautenschlager, G., Hedden, T., Davidson, N.S., Smith, A. D. & Smith, P. K. (2002). Models of visuospatial and verbal memory across the adult life span. *Psychology and Aging, 17*, 299–320.

Pascual-Leone, A., Amedi, A., Fregni, F. & Merabet, L. B. (2005). The plastic human brain cortex. *Annual Review of Neuroscience, 28*, 377–401.

Persson, J., Nyberg, L., Lind, J., Larsson, A., Nilsson, L. G., Ingvar, M. et al. (2006). Structure-function correlates of cognitive decline in aging. *Cerebral Cortex, 16*, 907–915.

Petrella, J. R., Townsend, B. A., Jha, A. P., Ziajko, L. A., Slavin, M. J., Lustig, C. (2005). Increasing memory load modulates regional brain activity in older adults as measured by fMRI. *Journal of Neuropsychiatry and Clinical Neuroscience, 17*, 75–83.

Pfefferbaum, A., Sullivan, E. V., Hedehus, M., Lim, K. O., Adalsteinsson, E. & Moseley, M. (2000). Age-related decline in brain white matter anisotropy measured with spatially corrected echo-planar diffusion tensor imaging. *Magnetic Resonance Medicine, 44*, 259–268.

Rajah, M. N. & D'Esposito, M. (2005). Region-specific changes in prefrontal function with age: A review of PET and fMRI studies on working and episodic memory. *Brain, 128*, 1964–1983.

Raz, N. (2004). The aging brain observed in vivo: Differential changes and their modifiers. In R. Cabeza, L. Nyberg & D. C. Park (Eds.), *Cognitive neuroscience of aging: Linking cognitive and cerebral aging* (pp. 17–55). New York: Oxford University Press.

Raz, N., Lindenberger, U., Ghisletta, P., Rodrigue, K. M., Kennedy, K. M. & Acker, J. D. (2008). Neuroanatomical correlates of fluid intelligence in healthy adults and persons with vascular risk factors. *Cerebral Cortex, 18*, 718–726.

Raz, N., Lindenberger, U., Rodrigue, K. M., Kennedy, K. M., Head, D., Williamson, A. et al. (2005). Regional brain changes in aging healthy adults: General trends, individual differences, and modifiers. *Cerebral Cortex, 15*, 1676–1689.

Reuter-Lorenz, P. A. (2002). New visions of the aging mind and brain. *Trends in Cognitive Sciences, 6*, 394–400.

Reuter-Lorenz, P. A. & Cappell, K. (2008). Neurocognitive aging and the compensation hypothesis. *Current Directions in Psychological Science, 18*, 177–182.

Reuter-Lorenz, P. A. & Lustig, C. (2005). Brain aging: Reorganizing discoveries about the aging mind. *Current Opinion in Neurobiology, 15*, 245–251.

Reuter-Lorenz, P. A. & Mikels, J. A. (2006). The aging mind and brain: Implications of enduring plasticity for behavioral and cultural change. In P. B. Baltes, P. A. Reuter-Lorenz & F. Rösler (Eds.), *Lifespan development and the brain* (pp. 255–276). New York: Cambridge University Press.

Reuter-Lorenz, P. A. & Sylvester, C.-Y. C. (2005). The cognitive neuroscience of working memory and aging. In R. Cabeza, L. Nyberg & D. C. Park (Eds.), *Cognitive neuroscience of aging: Linking cognitive and cerebral aging* (pp. 186–217). New York: Oxford University Press.

Reuter-Lorenz, P. A. et al. (2000). Age differences in the frontal lateralization of verbal and spatial working memory revealed by PET. *Journal of Cognitive Neuroscience, 12*, 174–187.

Riediger, M., Li, S.-C. & Lindenberger, U. (2006). Selection, optimization, and compensation as developmental mechanisms of adaptive resource allocation: Review and preview. In J. E. Birren & K. W. Schaie (Eds.), *The handbooks of aging: Vol. 2. Handbook of the psychology of aging* (6th ed., pp. 289–313). Amsterdam: Elsevier.

Rogers, B. P., Morgan, V. L., Newton, A. T. & Gore, J. C. (2007). Assessing functional connectivity in the human brain by fMRI. *Magnetic Resonance Imaging, 23*, 1347–1357.

Rypma, B. & D'Esposito, M. (2000). Isolating the neural mechanisms of age-related changes in human working memory. *Nature Neuroscience, 3*, 509–515.

Rypma, B., Prabhakaran, V., Desmond, J. E. & Gabrieli, J. D. (2001). Age differences in prefrontal cortical activity in working memory. *Psychology and Aging, 16*, 371–384.

Salat, D. H., Buckner, R. L., Snyder, A. Z., Greve, D. N., Desikan, R. S., Busa, E. et al. (2004). Thinning of the cerebral cortex in aging. *Cerebral Cortex, 14*, 721–730.

Schmiedek, F., Lövdén, M. & Lindenberger, U. (2009). On the relation of mean reaction time and intraindividual reaction time variability. *Psychology and Aging, 24*, 841–857.

Schmiedek, F., Lövdén, M. & Lindenberger, U. (2010). Hundred days of cognitive training enhance broad cognitive abilities in adulthood: Findings from the COGITO study. *Frontiers in Aging Neuroscience, 2*, 27.

Schneider-Garces, N. J., Gordon, B. A., Brumback-Peltz, C. R., Shin, E., Lee, Y., Sutton, B. P. et al. (2010). Span, CRUNCH, and beyond: Working memory capacity and the aging brain. *Journal of Cognitive Neuroscience, 22*, 655–669.

Schwindt, G. C., Chaudhary, S., Crane, D., Ganda, A., Masellis, M., Grady, C. L. et al. (2013). Modulation of the default-mode network between rest and task in Alzheimer's Disease. *Cerebral Cortex, 23(7)*, 1685–1694.

Seidler, R. D., Bernard, J. A., Burutolu, T. B., Fling, B. W., Gordon, M. T., Gwin, J. T. et al. (2010). Motor control and aging: Links to age-related brain structural, functional, and biochemical effects. *Neuroscience and Biobehavioral Reviews, 34*, 721–733.

Shu, N., Liang, Y., Li, H., Zhang, J., Li, X., Wang, L. et al. (2012). Disrupted topological organization in white matter structural networks in amnestic mild cognitive impairment: relationship to subtype. *Radiology, 265(2)*, 518–527.

Smith, E. E. & Jonides, J. (1998). Neuroimaging analyses of human working memory. *Proceedings of the National Academy of Sciences of the United States of America, 95*, 12061–12068.

Spreng, R. N., Wojtowicz, M. & Grady, C. L. (2010). Reliable differences in brain activity between young and old adults: A quantitative meta-analysis across multiple cognitive domains. *Neuroscience and Biobehavioral Reviews, 34*(8), 1178–1194.

Stern, Y. (2009). Cognitive reserve. *Neuropsychologia, 47*, 2015–2028.

Stuss, D. E. (2006). Frontal lobes and attention: Processes and networks, fractionation and integration. *Journal of the International Neuropsychological Society, 12*, 261–271.

Suhara, T., Fukudopamine, H., Inoue, O., Itoh, T., Suzuki, K., Yamasaki, T. et al. (1991). Age-related changes in human D1 dopamine receptors measured by positron emission tomography. *Psychopharmacology, 103*, 41–45.

Sullivan, E. V., Rohlfing, T. & Pfefferbaum, A. (2010). Longitudinal study of callosal microstructure in the normal adult aging brain using quantitative DTI fiber tracking. *Developmental Neuropsychology, 35*, 233–256.

Tisserand, D. J. & Jolles, J. (2003). On the involvement of prefrontal networks in cognitive ageing. *Cortex, 39*(4–5), 1107–1128.

Tisserand, D. J., Pruessner, J. C., Sanz Arigita, E. J., van Boxtel, M. P., Evans, A. C., Jolles, J. et al. (2002). Regional frontal cortical volumes decrease differentially in aging: An MRI study to compare volumetric approaches and voxel-based morphometry. *Neuroimage, 17*(2), 657–669.

Todd, J. J. & Marois, R. (2005). Posterior parietal cortex activity predicts individual differences in visual short-term memory capacity. *Cognitive, Affective, and Behavioral Neuroscience, 5*, 144–155.

Volkow, N. D., Gur, R. C., Wang, G. J., Fowler, J. S., Moberg, P. J., Ding, Y. S. et al. (1998). Association between decline in brain dopamine activity with age and cognitive and motor impairment in healthy individuals. *American Journal of Psychiatry, 157*, 344–349.

West, R. L. (1996). An application of prefrontal cortex function theory to cognitive aging. *Psychological Bulletin, 120*, 272–292.

Westlye, L. T., Walhovd, K. B., Dale, A. M., Bjørnerud, A., Due-Tønnessen, P., Engvig, A., Grydeland, H., Tamnes, C. K., Østby, Y. & Fjell, A. M. (2010). Life-span changes of the human brain white matter: Diffusion tensor imaging (DTI) and volumetry. *Cerebral Cortex, 20*, 2055–2068.

Wilson, R. S., Beckett, L. A., Barnes, L. L., Schneider, J. A., Bach, J., Evans, D. A. et al. (2002). Individual differences in rates of change in cognitive abilities in older persons. *Psychology and Aging, 17*, 179–193.

Yi, L., Wang, J., Jia, L., Zhao, Z., Lu, J., Li, K. et al. (2012). Structural and functional changes in subcortical vascular mild cognitive impairment: a combined voxel-based morphometry and resting-state fMRI study. *PLoS One, 7(9)*, e44758.

Index

Colom 12, 118
compensatory mechanisms 67–8, 110,
    130–3, 142–4
complex span 4–12, 24, 83–7, 103–5
complexity effects 2
confidence 4
context 3, 12–14, 49–52
Conway 134
Cook 113, 132–3
Cowan 29, 53, 68, 70–3
Craik 35, 48–53, 55–9, 61–4, 66–7, 72–3,
    88, 129, 131–4, 141
cross sectional studies 8, 11–13, 23, 32,
    98, 101, 105, 107–11, 130–44

Dahlin 84–6, 89, 91–2
Damaoiseaux 132
Daneman 6, 73, 86
Davatzikos 98
Davis 67, 112–13
Deary 22, 37, 108, 110, 115, 119
DeCarli 100, 106
de Frias 10, 129, 134
Della Sala 24, 32, 33, 35, 61, 70
Dempster 118
Deoni 120
De Santis 119
D'Esposito 130, 132, 134, 141–2
differential decline 24, 28
diffusion tensor imaging 98, 101–2,
    107–14, 118–20, 144
divided attention 48, 55–60, 66, 71:
    encoding 49–50, 62–3; retrieval 50–2,
    62–5; working memory 67–71
dopamine system 90, 131, 146
Douaud 119
dual tasking: adult ageing 28–34, 55,
    68–9; processing speed 34–7, 55;
    training 81–3; visual inspection
    time 37–9
Duering 106
dull hypothesis 21, 22, 39
Duprez 97
Durstewitz 90, 117
Duverne 135, 143
dynamic connectivity 97, 116

Edelman 144
Edmonds 37
Engle 6, 80, 86, 88
environmental support 50–2
Enzinger 99
Erixon-Lindroth 131

executive functions 24, 28, 82, 84–6, 89,
    97, 104, 106, 108, 110, 113, 116–17

false memory 49–50
Fazekas 99, 103
Fernandes 56–7, 60–1, 63–5, 67, 72
fluid intelligence Gf 11–15, 23, 79, 81,
    83–6, 103, 108, 110, 113, 118
Forstmann 37
Fox 40
Framingham 105
Friedman 83, 118
Friston 102, 138
fronto-parietal networks 88–90, 103, 112,
    117, 133–4, 140

Gabrieli 80
Gaffan 116
Gazzaley 130, 134, 141–2
Ge 98, 103
genetics 104, 119
GENIE project 98, 101, 107–8, 111, 113,
    115, 117
Geschwind 116
Gick 73
Giovanello 53, 54–7, 72
Gong 120
Good 98
Göthe 36
Grady 60–1, 63–5, 130–3, 142
grey matter volume 103–4, 146
Grossman 103
Gunning-Dixon 106, 133

Hafkemeijer 132
Hale 10
Hall 119
Han 132
Hannesdottir 107
HAROLD model 67
Hartley 36, 39
Hasher 48, 80
Hawthorne effects 81
He 132
Head 101
Hertzog 79, 134, 145
Hess 66
Hillman 90
Hitch 41, 80–2
Hock 130

intercorrelations: within tasks 8–11;
    between tasks 6–8, 11–17

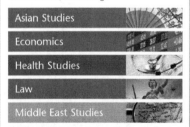